Growing up with
Audrey Hepburn

MANCHESTER
UNIVERSITY PRESS

Inside Popular Film

General editors Mark Jancovich and Eric Schaefer

Inside Popular Film is a forum for writers who are working to develop new ways of analysing popular film. Each book offers a critical introduction to existing debates while also exploring new approaches. In general, the books give historically informed accounts of popular film, which present this area as altogether more complex than is commonly suggested by established film theories.

Developments over the past decade have led to a broader understanding of film, which moves beyond the traditional oppositions between high and low culture, popular and avant-garde. The analysis of film has also moved beyond a concentration on the textual forms of films, to include an analysis of both the social situations within which films are consumed by audiences, and the relationship between film and other popular forms. The series therefore addresses issues such as the complex intertextual systems that link film, literature, art and music, as well as the production and consumption of film through a variety of hybrid media, including video, cable and satellite.

The authors take interdisciplinary approaches, which bring together a variety of theoretical and critical debates that have developed in film, media and cultural studies. They neither embrace nor condemn popular film, but explore specific forms and genres within the contexts of their production and consumption.

Already published:

Thomas Austin *Hollywood, hype and audiences*
Harry M. Benshoff *Monsters in the closet: homosexuality and the horror film*
Julia Hallam and Margaret Marshment *Realism and popular cinema*
Joanne Hollows and Mark Jancovich (eds) *Approaches to popular film*
Nicole Matthews *Gender in Hollywood: comedy after the new right*
Jacinda Read *The new avengers: feminism, femininity and the rape-revenge cycle*
Aylish Wood *Technoscience in contemporary film: beyond science fiction*

Growing up with Audrey Hepburn

Text, audience, resonance

Rachel Moseley

Manchester University Press

Manchester and New York

distributed exclusively in the USA by Palgrave

Published by Manchester University Press
Oxford Road, Manchester M13 9NR, UK
and Room 400, 175 Fifth Avenue, New York, NY 10010, USA
www.manchesteruniversitypress.co.uk

Distributed exclusively in the USA by
Palgrave, 175 Fifth Avenue, New York,
NY 10010, USA

Distributed exclusively in Canada by
UBC Press, University of British Columbia, 2029 West Mall,
Vancouver, BC, Canada V6T 1Z2

British Library Cataloguing-in-Publication Data
A catalogue record for this book is available from the British Library

Library of Congress Cataloging-in-Publication Data applied for

ISBN 0 7190 6310 8 *hardback*
      0 7190 6311 6 *paperback*

First published 2002

10 09 08 07 06 05 04 03 02   10 9 8 7 6 5 4 3 2 1

Typeset in Sabon with Frutiger
by Northern Phototypesetting Co. Ltd, Bolton

Printed in Great Britain
by Bell & Bain Ltd, Glasgow

For my family

Contents

List of figures

Every effort has been made to obtain permission to reproduce copyright images in this book. If any proper acknowledgement has not been made, copyright-holders are invited to contact the publisher.

Acknowledgements

The research presented in this book was funded by the Arts and Humanities Research Board of the British Academy.

I would like to thank all of the women who contributed to this research by sharing their memories, stories and time with me, both those who wished to remain anonymous, and those who wanted to be named: Margaret Brice, Sylvia Brown, Debra Budd, Yvonne Docker, R. Freeman, Elaine Gamble, Ann Gray, Jacqueline Hallum, Alice Macdonald, Valerie Orpen, Louise Plester, Nicola Rasores, Lara Ratnaraja, Myrna Richmond, Kath Stanford, Margaret Taylor, Marie Turner. Special thanks go to the correspondent and her mother who so kindly supplied me with their collection of Audrey-style paper patterns.

I am particularly grateful to Pam Cook, who supervised the early stages of this research at the University of East Anglia, Norwich in 1996, and to my PhD supervisor at Warwick, Charlotte Brunsdon, for her unfailing support, encouragement and advice throughout. Thanks must also go to colleagues and students at Warwick, and to all at Manchester University Press. The book would not have been written without the valued friendship and intellectual companionship of Jacinda Read, the support of my parents, or without John's calming influence and steady supply of cups of tea. Finally Mum – thanks for introducing me to Audrey.

Introduction

In *Only You* (Norman Jewison, 1994), Faith (Marisa Tomei) travels to Rome in search of the man she has believed she is destined to marry since the age of eleven. 'Damon Bradley' is the name of this man, conjured up by a Ouija board, a fortune teller and her brother, and a reference to Joe Bradley – the character played by Gregory Peck in *Roman Holiday* (William Wyler, 1953). *Only You* continually invokes this, Audrey Hepburn's first Hollywood film, revisiting key locations and moments ('the mouth of truth', the Trevi fountain, the couple's first encounter – she passes out in his arms), but also Hepburn's star persona. In the casting and costuming of Marisa Tomei, whose elfin features and short dark hair recall 'the Hepburn look'; in its repeated conjuring of the fairy tale in general and the Cinderella story in particular (the magic helpers, the lost slipper which 'fits like a glove', the flight down the stairs to the chime of the clock, 'the pumpkin moment'); in its concern with ideas of romantic love and idealised heterosexual romance and in its generic identity, the film suggests the lasting resonance and cultural power of the star, the fairy-tale femininity she embodied, and the genre of romantic comedy with which she was primarily associated.

The success of more recent films such as *She's All That* (Robert Iscove, 1999), an 'updated' version of *My Fair Lady* (George Cukor, 1964) addressing the teen market, suggests the continuing appeal of the combination of the Pygmalion transformation narrative and fairy-tale romance with which Hepburn was primarily associated. However, like the young women whose stories I draw upon in Chapter 6, in *Only You* Faith and her girlfriends watch an old black and white romantic musical on TV and proclaim that 'life's not like it is in the movies'. In Rome, Faith and Peter self-consciously replay the 'mouth of truth' moment from *Roman Holiday* in which Joe

Bradley pretends to the princess (Audrey Hepburn) that his hand has been bitten off by the stone mouth. In Audrey-lore this moment is held precious, for it is reported that the star was unaware that Peck would withdraw his hand into his sleeve, and thus that her reaction as captured on film is entirely genuine. While the 1990s film celebrates and depends upon such moments for its charm, nevertheless it seems to be continually in negotiation with its romantic heritage – simultaneously reinforcing and dismantling the fairy tale it invokes.

In general, the 1990s witnessed a renewed interest in Audrey Hepburn which continues at the moment of writing with a new print of *Breakfast at Tiffany's*, box sets of videos and DVDs, newspaper and magazine features and an exhibition of photographs of Hepburn by Bob Willoughby at the Proud Camden Moss Gallery, London in 2002. This most recent visibility has seen the repeated circulation of the image of Hepburn as Holly Golightly, the 'kooky' but high-class call girl from *Breakfast at Tiffany's* (Blake Edwards, 1961), in a black Givenchy evening dress, a diamond tiara and pearls. In June 1996 a version of this image was featured on the cover of *Harpers and Queen* (figure I.1), one of a number of quality women's glossies to run features and polls on 'the world's most alluring women', in which Hepburn almost exclusively came out top, with a feature on the return of the tiara and the 'princess' look.

These features coincided with the launch of Chanel's new fragrance, its first in many years, 'Allure'. The campaign for Elizabeth Arden's new fragrance '5th Avenue' featured a woman in an outfit clearly recalling that worn by Hepburn in *Breakfast at Tiffany's*. The 'timeless' appeal of the Audrey Hepburn image, a star the height of whose career was in the mid-1950s, began to be repeatedly mobilised during the summer of 1996 as the epitome of feminine elegance and sophistication. At the same moment, *Vanity Fair* (July 1996) ran a short piece by John Brodie entitled 'Cocktail nation: how we're becoming 1990s hepcats' which discussed the contemporary revival of easy listening, lounge music and cocktail culture which was going on at that moment in clubs and bars in Britain and the United States. This contemporary scene was marked by a retro-mood both nostalgic and ironic, delighting in a period of music and style perceived to be the height of sophistication, and, for instance, by night clubs where you could order board games, from backgammon to buckaroo, with your 'manhattan'. The re-emergence of Hepburn as an ideal of femininity in this contemporary stylistic climate appears to produce her as a depthless, timeless

I.1 Cover, *Harpers and Queen* (June 1996)

image, obscuring the socially and historically specific ways in which that image can be understood. Was this sudden new mobilisation of the Hepburn image simply the result of her death, the celebratory rhetoric which often surrounds the passing of a major Hollywood star, or was there something more at work?

The sites of the recirculation of this image have been largely associated with feminine culture, in for instance endless features on the popularity of and how to achieve the 'Audrey look' in newspapers and in magazines for young women (see figure I.2, Craik 1999 and Lowthorpe 2002) and on make-over shows such as *Style Challenge*.

She has been repeatedly cited as the favourite star of young British female celebrities such as Darcey Bussell, Jayne Middlemiss and Martine McCutcheon, who offered the insight that Hepburn as Holly Golightly in *Breakfast at Tiffany's* was 'a girl from a not very rich family who wanted to be someone' (Threlfall 1997: 6). She remains at the top of lists of 'women we admire'. Even Daria, subversive animated heroine of the MTV series of the same name, is featured as Audrey in *Breakfast at Tiffany's* in the credits to the show (figure I.3).

Her image has adorned club flyers and greetings cards, and was used to publicise an exhibition at London's National Portrait

I.2 'Steal the Style' – how to get the 'Hepburn look', in *Shine* (April 1999), p. 107

I.3 MTV's Daria as Holly Golightly

Gallery: 'The pursuit of beauty: five centuries of body adornment in Britain' in 1997. *Breakfast at Tiffany's* is regularly screened to mark Valentine's Day at regional film theatres, described as a 'classy' film, full of 'timeless and sophisticated charm' (National Film Theatre programme, February 1997). Hepburn has featured in pop songs such as 'Breakfast at Tiffany's' by Deep Blue Something and, via a soundbite from the same film, in a track used in a television advertisement for Pantene shampoo. Up-market clothing retailers Racing Green have named trousers, amongst other items, after her, to signal not only a style associated with her ('Audrey trousers' – fitted Capri pants with a small split at the hem) but also a certain level of quality. Similarly, 1990s advertisements for Gordon's gin have used her image to suggest authenticity and originality. In August 1997 the National Film Theatre, in conjunction with *New Musical Express*, screened *Breakfast at Tiffany's*, and, in keeping with the current vogue for lounge culture, the film was introduced by Neil Hannon, new age crooning front man with band The Divine Comedy. In an appropriately ironic tone, Hannon placed the film and its soundtrack squarely in the context of this contemporary climate as the epitome of 'cool'. While on one hand this might, in a spirit of pastiche, simply produce Hepburn, as Holly Golightly, as a commodified and sophisticated retro image, on the other the screening was attended by a number of young women dressed up, with perfect attention to detail, Audrey Hepburn-style.

Here, then, is the formative context for this research. Why did Audrey Hepburn, amongst the proliferation of femininities on offer, still have such purchase for young British women in the 1990s? What did this image mean to these women, and what did it mean to young women growing up in the 1950s and 1960s? Why have women invested in Audrey Hepburn as a star and in 'the Hepburn look' as a model of fashionable style, and how are those investments articulated in everyday practices? Have understandings of this image shifted considerably over the past forty-five years, or has it retained its currency through the same meanings? What might be the 'temporary congruences of taste' (Thumim 1995: 163) which have determined Hepburn's popularity at historical moments forty years apart?

The research presented in this book can be understood in a number of ways. First, it represents a situated critical study of the construction, circulation and reception of a star who has so far not been considered in any extended way, which attempts to answer questions about the enduring appeal of this star for British women. Secondly, this is an interdisciplinary project which addresses the boundaries of film studies, cultural studies and, in a limited way, social history, in relation to femininity. In this respect, the project suggests a useful approach to doing film history, in which three methodological approaches are woven together: film textual analysis, archival research in women's and film fan magazines, and interviews with women who have admired Hepburn both in the initial period of her stardom – the mid-1950s to mid-1960s – and in the 1990s. In this way the book attempts to sketch socially, nationally and historically specific discursive contexts within which to understand the appeal of Audrey Hepburn for young women in both of these periods.

This study should also be understood, in two senses, as a postfeminist project. It is concerned to engage with the exclusions of second-wave feminism and the fragmentation of the category gender (Brooks 1997). Theories of postmodernism describe the fragmented, dispersed and non-unitary subject and the loss of faith in 'grand narratives' and overarching explanatory structures as characteristic of the late modern, or postmodern, age. It becomes difficult to retain ideas of 'women' and 'social class' as meaningful categories of analysis in this contemporary theoretical climate. Nancy Fraser and Linda Nicholson discuss Jean-François Lyotard's call for precisely *local* social criticism and his notion of the social field as heterogeneous and non-totalisable (Fraser and Nicholson 1990: 25). This would rule out social theory which uses categories like gender, race and class, and they argue that

> if postmodern feminist critique must remain theoretical, not just any kind of theory will do. Rather, theory here would be explicitly historical,

attuned to the cultural specificity of different societies and periods. Thus the categories of postmodern-feminist theory would be inflected by temporality . . . [and] would replace unitary notions of woman and feminine gender identity with plural and complexly constituted conceptions of social identity, treating gender as one relevant strand among others, attending also to class, race, ethnicity, age and sexual orientation.

(Fraser and Nicholson 1990: 34–35)

This study attempts in particular to reinstate the significance of class in understanding the specificity of investments made by women in relation to gender. The study engages less with questions of race, largely because of the 'whiteness' of my interview sample. Nevertheless, as I discuss in Chapter 1, the significance of the 'whiteness' of this project, and of the star around whom it is focused, should not be underestimated. It is also 'postfeminist' in the more popular understanding of the term, in the sense that it addresses conventionally feminine concerns of clothes and beauty culture, and is centrally occupied with questions of femininity. I am interested throughout this study in the constitution, appeal and production of what are often very conventional modes of femininity for and by women in relation to a star who represents a hegemonic feminine ideal.

As the project has progressed, other methodological and theoretical questions have developed, namely, the task, in a study which is concerned to investigate the relationship between audiences and cultural forms, of integrating textual analysis with audience accounts. What I hope to have achieved in writing up this research is an approach which attends to both text and audience without privileging either, and indeed without denying the relationship between them. It is this problematic which has literally shaped the book, determining the organisation and structuring of the material. What began as a 'broken-backed' project, the first half devoted to the 'text' Audrey Hepburn and the second to 'audience' – interviewees' understandings of the star – has gradually become more integrated, with textual analysis interwoven with audience accounts. I intend this strategy to avoid the production of implicit assumptions about the location of meaning, the temptation to 'check' audience accounts against my own textual reading as a critic, and to facilitate a more discursive approach. As a result, the study understands 'Audrey Hepburn' as discursively produced, through critical and popular writing, films, my own reading of these, and audience accounts. I have tried to work with a notion of meaning as produced

in the coming together of textuality and subjectivity, both of which
are understood to be discursively constituted. Consequently, meaning is not seen to reside *either* in the text *or* in the reader; this
approach accommodates both my reading and the understandings of
Hepburn generated in the interviews, without privileging either one.
As a result of this different way of thinking about relationships
between 'text' and 'audience', and the nature of the material produced in the interviews, I have come to the notion of 'resonance and
recognition' as a way of thinking about spectatorship outside of the
psychoanalytic paradigm (cf. Mulvey 1975; Doane 1982; Stacey
1994). I will argue that it is in its combination of structure, harmony
and imprecision – and in its suggestion of a perpetual 'back and
forth' – that the usefulness of the term 'resonance' resides.

Janet Thumim has argued that looking at the relationship between
a female audience and 'the cultural object' raises insurmountable
methodological and theoretical problems, for instance in producing
a widely dispersed audience as a homogenous and coherent group in
a move which does not pay attention to the specific constitution of
individual women in both psychic and social terms (Thumim 1995:
160). I would suggest not only that here this 'dispersed audience' is
in some ways centrally organised through a common appreciation of
a star and by the discourses through which she is produced, but also
that an attention to methodology and the building of an appropriate
theoretical framework through which to approach interview material can produce an invaluable understanding of the ways in which
hegemonic media images mean for differently constituted women. It
is essential to understand, for instance, that although I am investigating two reasonably defined contexts of understanding a particular image (1950s/1960s and 1990s), recent mobilisations of the
Hepburn image can inform the memories of the first group of
women as well as the experiences of the second, in the same way that
pre-existing meanings of this image have clearly informed the more
recent manifestations. Furthermore, it is essential to acknowledge
the way in which the experience of conducting and transcribing
interviews whilst working on the films and doing archival research
significantly inflected my own reading of the text 'Audrey Hepburn'.

Chapter 1 includes a short account of a pilot study I conducted at
the beginning of the research, designed to investigate a specific non-
verbal practice through which women have related to female stars –
dressmaking – and to check the validity and potential of my area of

study. Audrey Hepburn was the most significant figure to emerge from this research, and the study demonstrated the need to develop a theoretical framework which could be sensitive to the key intersection of class and gender which had emerged, in preparation for the main body of interviews. While initially I had turned away from the notion of the 'textually constructed spectator' of film studies and towards a more cultural studies approach to the audience, the material in the pilot interviews suggested the possibility of a gendered gaze produced through socially and culturally acquired competencies and practices. This made me return to the text to ask whether indeed there might be a specifically female gaze inscribed in it – not simply in the operation of the filmic system or in a particular economy of looks – but rather a look produced through a discursive address across an image-text incorporating films, publicity and magazine articles. I discuss this notion of the gendered address of Audrey Hepburn in Chapter 2.

While the 'dressmaking' focus of the first interviews had been informed by theorisations of an 'active' and even 'resisting' spectator, the findings demonstrated how important it would be to account for the ways in which women may not in fact 'resist' but are nevertheless not simply 'passive' consumers of media images. The material surveyed in Chapter 1 reflects this, and asks how film studies might consider the question of subjectivity in spectatorship, outside a psychoanalytically informed paradigm. A primary concern of this research, then, in theoretical terms, is to rethink 'the female spectator' through an attention to both text and audience which takes account of the way concretely situated subjects have made use of a prevailing media image of femininity. Chapter 2 offers a reading of the 'star-text' Audrey Hepburn and its address to a gendered spectator, utilising textual analysis and archival research, and Chapter 3 functions as an introduction to audience accounts of Hepburn, but also begins the attempt to understand the relationship between the 'text' and those accounts. Chapters 4 and 5 continue this, focusing on discussions of Hepburn by women growing up in the 1950s and 1960s. The former looks at the way the address suggested in Chapter 2 is taken up in practice, through a consideration of stories of doing 'the Hepburn look', and the latter considers the Cinderella motif structuring both the Hepburn text and audience accounts. Chapter 6 is concerned with the interest in Audrey Hepburn among young women growing up in the 1980s and 1990s.

In the course of the research, my original questions about the enduring appeal of Audrey Hepburn have given rise to other kinds of questions – methodological and theoretical as well as empirical. While the book has turned out to be about those questions in quite significant ways, nevertheless it has retained its focus on the original impetus: to find out how and why the appeal of Audrey Hepburn for British women has endured from the 1950s into the twenty-first century.

Chapter 1

On the subject of film studies: class, gender and the female spectator

> If gender is a representation subject to social and ideological coding, there can be no simple one-to-one relationship between the image of woman inscribed in a film and its female spectator. On the contrary, the spectator's reading of the film (including interpretive and affective responses, cognitive and emotional strategies) is mediated by her existence in, and experience of, a particular universe of social discourses and practices in daily life.
>
> (de Lauretis 1987: 96)

This call from the field of feminist film theory and criticism for a more situated account of the relationship between text and spectator is indicative of a more general concern within the study of culture to investigate the 'situatedness' of the consumption of media texts. This question has to an extent been addressed by ethnographic work within the discipline of cultural studies, particularly through work on romance-novel readers and the television audience which attends to the context of viewing (e.g. Morley and Brunsdon 1999; Gillespie 1995; Morley 1986, 1992; Radway 1991; Press 1991).[1] However, the division between the textually inscribed spectator which has been debated within feminist film theory since the publication of Laura Mulvey's polemical article 'Visual pleasure and narrative cinema' (Mulvey 1975), psychoanalytically informed theories of identification, and the 'audience' considered in cultural studies, for the most part remains.[2] Valerie Walkerdine, amongst others, has argued that a film cannot in itself produce a reading that 'fixes the subject' because the viewer is always already caught up in and constituted by particular practices which come into play in the act of viewing and determine the kinds of readings made. This approach, she argues, 'should make it possible to deal with the issue of specific readings, and the location of readers/viewers, without collapsing into essentialism' (Walkerdine 1990: 193).

Walkerdine has also argued of audience research that the question of 'the subject' has received little attention (1997: 108); this omission might be seen as a further symptom of the split between the spectator of film studies and the 'social audience' of cultural studies. It is this critical gap between what is seen as the monolithic subject textually produced by classical narrative cinema, so far accounted for almost exclusively in psychosexual terms, and the social audience devoid, in Walkerdine's judgement, of 'any understanding of subjectivity', which has yet to be adequately theorised and accounted for. This space to be negotiated between 'subjects' and 'viewers' has been identified by Judith Mayne as 'the horizon of film spectatorship' (Mayne 1993: 9), and with the exception of Walkerdine's own work on video watching (Walkerdine 1986) and a few notable works which I discuss below, this shift with regard to the subject in the audience has remained almost exclusively at the level of hypothetical, theoretical debate.

The research presented in this book is intended in part to address this division between film and cultural studies and the resulting void in scholarship on the subject of film studies. The aim of this chapter, then, is twofold. While it serves in part as the customary 'review of literature in the field', exploring existing scholarship relevant to this area of study and situating my own research in relation to that field, it also addresses key methodological issues.

I began this research by attempting to collect data through: (i) a letter published in the magazine *Sewing with Butterick* (spring 1997) asking women to write to me about film-star fashions and their own dressmaking practices; (ii) questionnaires completed by those women who eventually responded; and (iii) a pilot study of six interviews, conducted over the winter of 1996 and the spring of 1997, which were formative in situating the project theoretically and which produced the very specific body of literature considered here. The study produced rich data on star styles and home dressmaking in the 1950s and 1960s, and stands as a research project in its own right.[3] The data discussed in the main part of the book is drawn from fourteen interviews. A number of these are with women who offered themselves as interested in talking about Audrey when they heard about the project, either from friends or from me. Those women then introduced me to relatives, friends and colleagues they thought would be willing to be interviewed, and so the sample snowballed in a conventional manner. Seven of the interviews are with women who grew up with Hepburn in the 1950s and 1960s (Caroline, Liz, Barbara, Janet, Bernie, Pat and Rosie); seven are with younger women who have come to Hepburn in quite a different way in the 1980s and 1990s (Lucy, Chloë, Anna, Cally, Jayne, Mel and Verity).[4] Although only one woman took up my offer of anonymity, in the process of transcribing and working on the interviews I have decided to protect the identities of the women who took part in this study through the bestowal of pseudonyms. As Penny Summerfield, who adopts the same approach in her book *Reconstructing Women's Wartime Lives*, points out:

> Anonymity screens interviewees from the ultimate manifestation of the power imbalance in the oral history relationship, the historian's inter- pretation and reconstruction in the public form of print of intimate aspects of their lives. (Summerfield 1998: 26)

Class, gender and 'resistance'

The purpose of a pilot study for a qualitative project such as this is to enable the researcher to refine the focus of the research and spec- ify the most useful questions to ask, both of the subjects taking part in the research and of the data. While my pilot interviews, which were designed around the practice of dressmaking in the relation- ship of women to their favourite female film stars, certainly pro- vided this, they also enabled me to produce a kind of 'grounded theory' (Hermes 1993) for approaching the main body of the research. First, Audrey Hepburn was the most significant figure to emerge from those interviews – she was the star whose 'look' the women mainly wanted to talk about. Furthermore, the flexibility of her star image in relation to class and generation was apparent, and these disparate yet linked accounts clearly illustrated the ways in which star images can be filtered and adapted, certain elements retained, others discarded, to suit the individual, in much the same way that the women I interviewed used their paper patterns: 'I'll take that top and that skirt and that sleeve – basically, you can get them to fit' (Shirley).

Second, the study suggested the importance of paying attention to the role played by the conjunction of class, gender, education and generation in relation to national identity, in understanding the complex relationship which was being articulated between the star, Audrey Hepburn, and the women who talked about admiring her style. The non-verbal practices through which they articulated that admiration – shopping, dressmaking, hair, make-up – suggested the social embeddedness of that relationship. The pilot interviews, then, assured me of the validity and potential of my research, narrowed the focus of the project as a whole, and demonstrated the necessity of constructing a theoretical and methodological framework which could be sensitive to the intersection particularly between class, gender, generation and national identity as social positionings. This study has little to say on the matter of race – all but one of the women I interviewed were white. That is not to suggest, however, that questions of race and ethnicity are irrelevant to the project – the 'whiteness' of this study is in itself significant. It is essential to recognise that the whiteness of 'Audrey Hepburn' is key to the hegemonic status of her femininity.[5] Dyer notes 'the special purity of whiteness', commenting that 'to be a lady is to be as white as it gets' (1997: 57). In this respect, the comments of one of the women who took part in the pilot interviews are revealing. Talking about her admiration for Doris Day, she commented on that star's preference for white clothes, and that 'from the very first film she wore gloves' (also true of Hepburn). She explained 'wearing gloves' as a style she shared with the star through her upbringing:

> I was taught when I was a child that you weren't dressed unless you wore gloves, summer and winter. And of course, you don't wear gloves in summer anymore, unfortunately . . . When I was a teenager, I wouldn't go out without gloves on, if I was going out dressed up . . . I used to wear lacy gloves, in the summer, because as far as I was concerned, I wasn't dressed – because that was the thing then; it was like cleaning your shoes, I mean, we weren't allowed to go out without polishing our shoes.
>
> (Shirley)

Clearly, a class and gender-related notion of respectability is at work in this emphasis on being 'properly dressed', clean and tidy. Furthermore, the wearing of gloves by women in the summer preserved a white skin, in differentiation from those of lower social classes who worked outside, and thus acquired sun-tanned skin. Such an emphasis on 'whiteness' clearly also carries racial significance. Dyer also points to the wedding, and the whiteness of its iconography as 'the privileged moment of heterosexuality, that is (racial) reproduction' (1997: 124). As I discuss in later chapters, 'Audrey Hepburn-style' was frequently discussed by women in relation to their own choice of wedding dress. Hepburn was repeatedly referred to throughout this study as 'a lady' and 'not sexy', and if, as Beverley Skeggs argues, femininity has been coded historically as middle-class and white, with working-class and black women coded as sexual and deviant (and thus not feminine), then I would argue that the repeated production of Hepburn's femininity through association with the wedding dress (whiteness, purity – absence of sex) is inextricably tied to the star's identity in terms of both race and class. Ruth Frankenberg (1993) describes whiteness as an unmarked, unnamed agent of structural dominance. Hepburn's whiteness is unmarked in the same way that the middle-classness of her 'look' remains unmarked and appears as 'classic', and although the question of race is not addressed directly in the rest of the book, the whiteness of 'Audrey Hepburn' should be understood throughout as central to the star-text/discursive formulation at the heart of the research.

Carolyn Steedman in her autobiographical work *Landscape for a Good Woman* contends that 'class and gender, and their articulations, are the bits and pieces from which psychological selfhood is made' (Steedman 1986: 121). Steedman's comment is a concretely situated call for a mode of enquiry which pays attention to the meeting of (primarily) class and gender amongst other social positionings in the production of subjectivity; it is also, as Elspeth Probyn notes, 'a call for a project that may recognize the conjunctural exigencies of self even as it refuses to celebrate that self as "resistant", or even very special' (Probyn 1993: 109).

This comment reflects a recent shift in cultural studies work which positions itself against the 'resistance' paradigm characteristic of much of the scholarship in this field associated with the Centre for Contemporary Cultural Studies at the University of Birmingham in the mid to late 1970s and its inheritors. Broadly (and this is necessarily reductive), work on this model has as its project the constitution of audiences as 'active' consumers and producers of culture as opposed to 'passive dupes', and the equation of this with pleasure and/or resistance to dominant ideological meanings.

So far, there is a relatively small body of work which critically discusses or positions itself against this paradigm (see Roman *et al.* 1988; Morris 1990; Stacey 1994: 47); again, much of this remains at the level of theory. However, there are two recent works which offer useful positions from which to investigate and argue against this model, through ethnographic and autobiographical investigations of the social and psychic situatedness of the relationship between women and popular representations. At the same time, they argue for the retention of a notion of 'the subject', although one which can be mobilised against the universalising tendency of film studies theorisations of the spectator of classical narrative cinema which draw on psychoanalytically informed analysis. Beverley Skeggs's research in *Formations of Class and Gender: Becoming Respectable* (1997) and Valerie Walkerdine's (1997) *Daddy's Girl: Young Girls and Popular Culture* both offer potential for significantly extending and refining the terms of the debate about the situated nature of cultural consumption, and particularly for rethinking the elusive subject at the centre, and yet paradoxically in the margins of, this ongoing debate.

Discourse and subjectivity

> It is not individuals who have experience, but subjects who are constituted through experience.
>
> (Scott 1992: 25)

Before I go on to a more extended discussion of the possibilities offered by Skeggs and Walkerdine, I want to position these texts in relation to a body of work which draws on the notion of 'discourse' to address the relationship between representation and subjectivity, often directly in opposition to the universal model of spectatorship offered by the Freudian-Lacanian paradigm which has been common to much work within feminist film theory and criticism.

In her essay 'Femininity as discourse' Dorothy Smith (1988) elaborates her understanding of femininity as a 'socially given form of subjectivity' which can be examined through attention to actual practices and activities which are concretely situated in particular social, cultural and historical moments. This, she suggests, allows femininity to be seen as 'a distinctly textual phenomenon' (38) embedded in specific practices. Furthermore, Smith places emphasis on women's 'active' part in social organisation, although not simply as a result of patriarchal oppression. Rather her contention is that

> [w]omen aren't just the passive products of socialization; they are active; they create themselves. At the same time, their self-creation, their work, the uses of their skills, are co-ordinated with the market for clothes, make-up, shoes, accessories, etc., through print, film, etc. This dialectic between the active and creative subject and the organization

of her activity in and by texts co-ordinating it with the market is captured here using the concept of a textually-mediated discourse.

(Smith 1988: 39)

Smith sees her appropriation of Foucault's concept of 'discourse' to provide an account of femininity as 'textually-mediated' as an approach which, while maintaining a concern with the subject, displaces Foucault's original emphasis on texts to reveal 'the social relations in which texts are embedded and which they organize' (40). At the same time, Smith manages to account for women's expressly *local* and *historical* activity in producing themselves in relation to textual discourses, and an understanding of how gendered knowledge and experience comes into play in the interpretation of texts, without positing that activity as necessarily 'resisting' dominant ideology (45).

In a similar way, Teresa de Lauretis has introduced the term 'technologies of gender', drawn from Foucault's theory of sexuality as 'a technology of sex', to describe the way in which gender 'both as representation and as self-representation, is the product of various social technologies, such as cinema, as well as institutional discourses, epistemologies, and critical practices, as well as practices of daily life' (de Lauretis 1987: 2). De Lauretis discusses the way in which the understanding of cinema as a social technology – the theory of 'the cinematic apparatus' – has been taken up by feminist film theory and used to develop a notion of gendered spectatorship which explains the mechanism by which the individual spectator is addressed by the film system, thus addressing the question of gender in a way that Foucault does not (13). Referring to post-structuralist notions of subjectivity which understand the subject as non-unified and constituted in and through discourse, she turns to Wendy Hollway's essay 'Gender difference and the production of subjectivity' (1984) which discusses the notion of individual 'investments' in particular discursive positions, suggesting that

> power is what motivates (and not necessarily in a conscious or rational manner) individuals' 'investments' in discursive positions. If at any one time there are several competing, even contradictory, discourses on sexuality – rather than a single, all-encompassing or monolithic, ideology – then what makes one take up a position in a certain discourse rather than another is an 'investment' . . . something between an emotional commitment and a vested interest, in the relative power (satisfaction, reward, payoff) which that position promises (but does not necessarily fulfil).

(de Lauretis 1987: 16)

De Lauretis argues that this can perhaps explain why historically, individuals have made particular investments, allowing for the suggestion that other dimensions of social positioning such as 'class, race and age intersect with gender to favor or disfavor certain positions' (Hollway 1984: 239, in de Lauretis 1987: 16).

Similarly, Sean Nixon (1996), in his attempt to retain an idea of identification outside a psychoanalytically informed framework, investigates visual representations of 'new man' imagery in the 1980s and uses Foucault to think through the relationship between subjectivity and discourse. He introduces the term 'lived masculinity' to describe the way in which discursive subject positions meet an historical individual on the ground.

While such scholarship suggests a considerable challenge to existing ways of thinking about the subject in film studies, at the same time, it has remained largely in the abstract realm of the theoretical.[6] The concept of 'discourse' as a key tool through which to view identity and identification as outlined in these investigations certainly suggests a move towards an approach which could account for the ways in which certain kinds of representations might be understood to hold particular appeal for specifically situated individuals. While Nixon's formulation does not offer an account of the reasons why particular discursive positions might be taken up by particular individuals, Hollway's notion of 'investment' does offer a way of addressing this question. It does not, however, quite explain how and in what circumstances such investments might be made.

I will argue that more recent work by Skeggs and Walkerdine represents a significant shift in these debates. Not only does it move the question of the subject into the realm of the concrete, socially, culturally and historically specific through ethnographic approaches, but the arguments they present offer vital ways to refine and extend the theoretical questions raised in the work surveyed above, particularly with regard to the question of the nature of the relationship between text and audience.

In *Formations of Class and Gender: Becoming Respectable*, Beverley Skeggs mobilises a notion of subjectivity as constituted in and through discourse, and argues that class remains a key category for understanding the formation of identity, despite its relative absence from contemporary feminist analysis. Skeggs uses the metaphors of capital offered in the work of Pierre Bourdieu to suggest a way of understanding 'the intersections of class and gender in subjective production' (Skeggs 1997: 7).

Skeggs discusses the relationship between cultural capital (which according to Bourdieu may be embodied, objectified or institutionalised in the form of lasting dispositions of mind and body, cultural goods, and, for instance, educational qualifications) and symbolic capital (whereby cultural capital becomes powerful through legitimation). She suggests, following an argument made by Toril Moi (1991) that femininity (and masculinity) as a discourse can become embodied and thereby used as a cultural resource (Skeggs 1997: 8). However, she also notes that this kind of cultural capital can only become powerful in particular contexts:

> [i]f one's cultural capital is delegitimated then it cannot be traded as an asset; it cannot be capitalized upon (although it may retain significance and meaning to the individual) and its power is limited. Femininity, for example, can be seen as a form of cultural capital. It is the discursive position available through gender relations that women are encouraged to inhabit and use. Its use will be informed by the network of social positions of class, gender, sexuality, region, age and race which ensure that it will be taken up (and resisted) in different ways . . . the ability to capitalize on femininity is restricted. It provides only restricted access to potential forms of power.
>
> (Skeggs 1997: 10)

Through an examination of the historical meanings of respectability, femininity (which she argues is always '(middle)-classed' (98)), heterosexuality, and their conjunction with race and the social position 'working class', Skeggs argues that historically '[a] respectable body is white, desexualised, hetero-feminine and usually middle-class' (82). Respectability is seen here as a middle-class hegemony, a discursive position differentially available relative to particular conjunctions of social positions (87).

Through a detailed ethnographic study carried out over a period of eleven years with a group of white, working-class women who were training to be professional carers, Skeggs explores the concrete implications of the contradictions of being white, female and working-class. Heterosexuality, which, she suggests, should 'normalise' working-class women, in fact does not, because historically this group has been associated, along with black women and lesbians, with dangerous and even perverse sexuality (118). Being 'respectable' emerges as a key way of 'passing' for middle-class, through appearance and conduct, which while producing great anxiety (87), enables relative access to certain kinds of power otherwise unavailable to working-class women. Working-class women have, she argues, embodied the distance between femininity and sexuality, and Skeggs offers the notion of 'glamour', which while difficult to achieve, she argues is perhaps the only way of holding together femininity and sexuality with respectability for working-class women (110). In her discussion of the roles played by class and gender in producing subjectivity, Skeggs's analysis suggests a useful framework through which to account for the appeal of certain widely disseminated representations of gender (e.g. 'Audrey Hepburn') to particularly constituted subjectivities, shedding light on the notion of 'investment'. Referring to Smith's article 'Femininity as discourse' (1988), she argues '[i]f subjectivity is produced through experience we can see how becoming respectable proceeds through the experience of textually mediated femininity' (Skeggs 1997: 98). I will suggest that this new scholarship, in conjunction with the work by Walkerdine discussed below, represents an important development for rethinking the problematic question of identification in the relationship between female star and female audience member. Skeggs also argues for the understanding of 'recognition' to play a critical role in identification. While in her study, refusal to recognise was the key way in which the women she worked with *dis*identified themselves from the social position 'working-class' (164), Valerie Walkerdine (1997) suggests the central importance of this concept in making representations and fictions meaningful.

In *Daddy's Girl: Young Girls and Popular Culture*, Walkerdine argues forcefully against the 'resistance' paradigm common to much cultural studies work addressing working-class identities, and rather for an understanding of the strategies for 'coping and surviving' mobilised by 'ordinary working people'. Further, she examines the role 'of the popular in the making of feminine subjectivity' and the place of dominant fictions and practices in constituting the working-class person as subject (Walkerdine 1997: 3, 23, 35).

In what is in some senses a continuation of 'Dreams from an ordinary childhood' (Walkerdine 1990), Walkerdine gives an autobiographical account of class mobility and aspiration, of growing up working-class and becoming educated, which reveals the centrality of class and gender in the production of subjectivity, arguing that 'we cannot . . . separate something called "working-class experiences" from the fictions and fantasies in which those lives are produced and read'(35). Writing an exploratory account of the production of her own subjectivity into the analysis, she suggests the ways in which particular representations appeal to specifically constituted subjects (Walkerdine 1997: 25).

A theoretical position against the notion of 'resistance' is implicit in Skeggs's work. While she notes the importance for the women in her study of refusing to recognise themselves either *as* working-class or *in* representations of working-class femininity, she nevertheless argues for class as a 'structuring absence' and for the importance of understanding the hegemony of middle-class notions of respectable and appropriate femininity to which the women with whom she worked aspired (74). Walkerdine, however, argues explicitly against the 'resistance' paradigm in *Daddy's Girl*, through a discussion of her own experience of being an educated working-class woman. Recalling having joined the Left intellectual scene in the 1970s, she declares:

> I came from the class which these people were supposed to be interested in, but there was nothing exotic about my former life. Indeed, I felt that none of the markers of anything interesting were present at all. I dreamt of glamour, read comics, listened to pop music, worked hard at school and my father died early. I couldn't find in my history any of the exotic subcultural resistance that cultural studies wanted to find.
>
> (Walkerdine 1997: 19)

Walkerdine criticises cultural studies for its exclusive concern with 'the conscious working class, those that have subcultures and can demonstrate resistance' (20) and for what she sees as a complete lack of concern with ordinary, non-politicised working people (22). For instance, in a comment which sheds interesting light on some of the specific material on practices of shopping, dressmaking and colour which emerged from my pilot study (Moseley 2001), she recalls:

> When I had no money for clothes as a teenager I derived great pleasure from going to Derby market to buy cheap pieces of material with which to make my own. Indeed, I was proud of the way that I could sew in ways that wealthier girls could not and that my clothes often were more spirited and dramatic than theirs. (I was always a great fan of *shocking* pink!) I think that it makes a travesty of what was a culturally and psychically complex act to call this resistance.
>
> (Walkerdine 1997: 52)

Noting what she perceives as the lack of interest in 'the subject' of much ethnographic work (108), she argues for holding onto an idea of the psychological or psychic, playing with and then discarding the theories of fantasy offered by Laplanche and Pontalis. She argues that this work might offer a way of historicising the activation of unconscious structures, but in the final analysis it cannot engage with the questions she has raised about a psychology of survival because of the normalising and universalising character of such models (177–179). Centrally, she argues for the possibility of being able to talk about 'coping' and 'surviving', of the ways in which ordinary people are formed as subjects through complex everyday practices (21), demonstrated, for instance, in her desire to defend young working-class girls whose femininities and fantasies might be perceived as 'not radical' enough by feminism (154).

Much of the existing scholarship on the gendered consumption of popular forms retains a relationship to this notion of resistance which Walkerdine here argues so passionately against. Mary Ellen Brown, for instance, in *Soap Opera and Women's Talk: The Pleasure of Resistance* (1994) typifies this tendency which also equates pleasure with resistance, arguing that 'feminine discourse' is a 'particularly resistive form in our culture' (1), and identifying the gaps opened up by the 'leaky' character of hegemony as those to which women relate (5). I think Brown perhaps here mistakes 'feminine discourse' for a particularly gendered mode of address which may appeal to those who occupy certain subject positions. As Walkerdine's argument suggests, this approach leaves little if any room for the woman who might not identify with the 'gaps' in ideology, but who rather invests in the dominant discourse. What is needed here is a more flexible concept of hegemony, in which consent is secured through representations which might be dominant and appealing because they offer a particular power to those who do not possess it, even while this power may be seriously circumscribed. The research presented in this book is precisely about the notion of 'investment', and is offered in the hope of providing a concretely situated understanding of how such hegemonic representations work, outside simple notions of resistance or complicity.

Janice Radway's final suggestion in *Reading the Romance* was that through the activity of romance reading, the women of her study were able to find significant 'interstices' in this dominant popular form which enabled them to imagine 'a more perfect social state as a way of countering despair' (Radway 1991: 222). Radway's rereading of her extremely influential ethnographic study of romance reading in the new introduction to the 1991 edition explicitly positions this work and its attempt to discover an active, creative reader, with that of the 'Birmingham School' of cultural studies. This study, as she argues, is particularly of its time, being first published in 1984, but more recent work still adheres to this paradigm. Janet Thumim's 1992 study *Celluloid Sisters*, while hoping to examine how 'female audience members make use of film texts' (Thumim 1992: 2), offers thematic and discursive readings of key texts in a sample of the most popular films in Britain between 1945 and 1965, refuting the possibility of investigating the audience (34). She refers throughout the study to the important role played by star personae and publicity in determining the meanings made by audience members, but this kind of investigation is outside of her methodological remit and thus the complex questions she wants to ask about the audience cannot be answered other than in theory. Indeed, Thumim's reluctance to address the audience perhaps limits her interpretation of Teresa de Lauretis's use of the term 'technology of gender' to describe popular cinema. Reading this as characterising cinema as a means by which the patriarchal order constantly renews itself (3), she concludes her analysis with the hope that the representations of women she has discussed 'may be used by some women in the audience to enable their recognition of the inequities of the patriarchal order and thence to strengthen their resolve to resist' (212). In her refusal to engage with the question of the audience in anything but hypothetical terms, seemingly because this kind of data raises complex methodological problems (34), she reduces the insights that de Lauretis's term potentially offers for the examination of the operations of hegemony through popular representations to a model which presumes that ideology is entirely successful in its interpellation of the subject. Consequently, Thumim turns to a hope for potential 'resistance' which is impossible within the model of ideology that she has constructed in speculation, inspite of her original hope to provide some insight into 'how . . . female audience members "read" the images they were offered' and her acknowledgement of 'the discrete social experience of individual readers' (157).

In contrast, Andrea Press's work on American women watching television attends to gender, class and generation and attempts to understand 'how women in our time use the images and ideas our culture makes available to them as they construct their own identities in the world' (Press 1991: 3). Press concludes that neither a concept of resistance nor a concept of accommodation can adequately account for the processes involved in women's reception of television. Her study is carefully contextualised, both historically, culturally and theoretically and, like Beverley Skeggs, she discovers 'middle-class hegemony' to play an important role in the way working-class women construct their identities in relation to the images of femininity offered to them on television (Press 1991: 102). This work is particularly significant in its attempt to address the importance of social class in the process of media consumption.[7] Similarly, Jacqueline Bobo's 1995 study of black women's responses to Terry McMillan's novel *Waiting to Exhale*, and the films *Daughters of the Dust* (Julie Dash, 1991) and *The Color Purple* (Steven Spielberg, 1985), is an important challenge to theoretical work on gendered film spectatorship, providing a concrete account of ethnicity as an element of subjectivity that determines the ways in which readings of films might be made. While Bobo's study draws heavily on the notions of 'resistance' and 'reading against the grain', the political agenda of her project allies this approach to the original impetus for studying the possibility of resistance in working-class cultures in British cultural studies in the 1970s. In *Black Women as Cultural Readers*, Bobo makes visible a previously unrepresented group of film spectators, and in so doing significantly advances the field of film spectatorship.

Beverley Skeggs refines the argument presented by Mary Ann Doane (1982) which suggests that 'masquerade' enables women to achieve a distance from the image of femininity. Skeggs suggests that working-class women are always already at a distance from femininity through their social and historical positioning as nonrespectable (Skeggs 1997: 105). This offers an even more situated account of an argument about the 'impossibility of femininity' made by Jackie Stacey in her book *Star Gazing: Hollywood Cinema and Female Spectatorship* (Stacey 1994: 213), which is the most extended scholarship so far to attempt to put 'spectators back into theories of spectatorship' (Stacey 1994: 76). *Star Gazing* presents research on the relationship between female spectators and female Hollywood stars in the wartime and post-war periods in Britain, gathered from hundreds of questionnaires and letters received by the author. Stacey thus locates her study very precisely in social, cultural and historical terms, and offers an invaluable account of the multiple processes of identification, both 'cinematic' (taking place in front of the filmic image) and 'extra-cinematic' (taking place outside the cinematic experience itself), thereby demonstrating the way in which identifications take place as much in the realm of 'cultural activity' (171) or practices as through the workings of universal unconscious psychosexual structures. She argues that, in social and historical terms, the modes of femininity offered to women through Hollywood cinema were 'impossible' for British women in the context of post-war austerity. Skeggs's analysis in *Formations of Class and Gender* could perhaps be used to refine this point, through the suggestion that for particular groups of women, 'femininity' as a subject position might always be an impossibility, as a result of the historical production of its meaning (105). At the same time, such a move is problematic, as Skeggs's research in some ways produces working-class femininity as a singular and clearly delineated identity, which it is not. The comparison, however, perhaps highlights social class as an absence in Stacey's study, despite the section in her research questionnaire designed to produce this information. While she contends that her sample was 'a relatively homogenous group' of respondents shifting across middle class and working class (Stacey 1994: 61), in contrast Walkerdine states from her own research that 'there are massive differences at many levels between the young women and families designated middle-class and working-class' (Walkerdine 1997: 34).

While Stacey critically addresses the psychoanalytically informed paradigms upon which theories of spectatorship are for the large part predicated, she nevertheless returns to this paradigm to discuss identification. Amongst others, Stacey employs Jessica Benjamin's concept of 'identificatory and ideal love' (Benjamin 1990) which uses object relations theory and the concept of recognition to account for the relationship between self and external other. The idea that 'recognition' might play a part in the relationships between audiences and cultural forms is noted by Stacey, but she rejects Ien Ang's use of Bourdieu's understanding of 'recognition' in her study of *Dallas* viewers (Stacey 1994: 173) and returns to a psychoanalytic framework to refine an argument about stars as 'good and bad others' (228) which she has previously convincingly framed in socially and historically grounded terms (205). While Stacey acknowledges the problems in this move back to the unconscious, she is committed to an analysis which examines psychic processes and the use of a psychoanalytic model. In this respect then, Stacey's work, while remaining a critical intervention in the study of the female spectator and her relationship to Hollywood stars, is significantly positioned at a moment which indicates the shifts underway in feminist film studies. While *Star Gazing* clearly put the spectator back into spectatorship, in its emphasis on the male gaze and adherence to the psychoanalytic paradigm it remains very much of a moment before the appearance of such scholarship as that by Skeggs and Walkerdine discussed here. My aim in this research is to try to think about the nature of that relationship between female star and female spectator outside hegemonic conceptualisations of identification in film theory, whilst recognising that unconscious processes play a part in constructing that relationship. As I discuss in Chapter 3, I mobilise ideas of resonance and recognition as a way of understanding that relationship.

In relation to the body of scholarship discussed here, the shift represented in this research and the approach towards it I take in this book is usefully illustrated by the metaphor of putting Stacey's study under a magnifying glass. In attending to both text and audience, I move one step closer, looking at one star, and conducting detailed work with a smaller group of women. At the same time, from the vantage point of my particular historical and theoretical position as discussed here, I hope to bring to the investigation of how and why Audrey Hepburn has appealed to particular women some insight into the role played by subjectivity in determining the meanings women make of media texts. In her book *Reconstructing Women's Wartime Lives*, Penny Summerfield suggests that

> [p]ersonal narratives draw on the generalised subject available in discourse to construct the particular personal subject. It is thus necessary to encompass within oral history analysis and interpretation, not only the voice that speaks for itself, but also the voices that speak to it, the discursive formulations from which understandings are selected and with which accounts are made.
>
> (Summerfield 1998: 15)

I begin, in the next chapter, with an analysis of one such discursive formulation: Audrey Hepburn.

Notes

1 See Janice Radway's rereading of her own work in the introduction to *Reading the Romance* (1991) for an account which points to the kinds of shifts I am interested in here, and Geraghty (1998) for a broad historical overview of work on the audience.

2 In Chapter 2 of *Star Gazing*, Jackie Stacey (1994) offers an extremely full account of the debates within both of these fields, so that ground will not be covered here.

3 See Moseley (2001) for a detailed account of this study.

4 See Appendix I for brief biographical notes on the main interviewees and interview questions, along with details of conventions I have used in transcribing the interviews. This sample is small, but as Tulloch (1999: 112) has argued, the value of small-scale qualitative research is that it can contribute to an understanding of the overall identity of a culture, or of a practice, rather than speaking for the collective.

5 In Chapter 2, I discuss the ways in which Hepburn's hegemonic femininity 'manages' difference.

6 While Hollway's research is based on interviews, her article still remains within a specifically psychoanalytic paradigm outside of which the work I am concerned with here attempts to think.

7 Ang and Hermes (1991) offer an important contribution to the question of the use of class and gender as interpretive categories in the analysis of media consumption.

Chapter 2

Audrey Hepburn: a woman's star

Oh, you can talk about your Howard Hawkses and George Stevenses, your Billy Wilders and Sam Peckinpahs, your auteur theories. But when I get to dreaming about movies – especially those I've seen dozens of times, like *Gentlemen Prefer Blondes*, *Swing Time*, and *Sabrina* – I pause less and less at the directorial achievements and more and more at the clothes that encourage me to identify with the heroines. Yeah, yeah, I know Hawks is the genius behind *Gentlemen Prefer Blondes*, but it isn't his invisible editing that makes it endlessly watchable. Rather, it's Travilla's idea of playclothes: that is, Jane Russell's black halter *bustier* and clinging pedal pushers pulled over spiked, ankle-strapped heels.

(Carrie Rickey 1982: 57)

The aims of this chapter are twofold. First, I offer a discursive, historically situated exploration of the construction and circulation of Audrey Hepburn as a star in the initial period of her celebrity, roughly equivalent to the duration of her main Hollywood screen career: 1953–68. As I suggest in the introduction, the life of Hepburn as image-text – a term I discuss below – extends well beyond these fifteen years. The material presented here offers an introductory context for the following chapters in which I conduct an extended analysis of interviews with fans of Hepburn who were young women in the late 1950s, early 1960s and 1990s. The data in these chapters is interwoven with a more detailed consideration of aspects of the image-text 'Audrey Hepburn' which emerged as particularly significant in those discussions.

To produce the account in this chapter, I have looked to the key films of Hepburn's career and to press, publicity, interviews, stills and so on, but I have also drawn on wider sources, those which could be considered 'ephemera' such as British film fan magazines like *Photoplay* and *Picture Show*. Publications of this kind often had a women's page concerned with film-star fashion and social conduct; these, and women's magazines 'proper' of the time, have proved an invaluable resource for building up an understanding of historically and nationally specific discourses of femininity circulating during this initial period of Hepburn's stardom in the 1950s and early 1960s in Britain. Particularly interesting is the way in which what were in effect modern versions of the 'conduct book' dealt with the modes of femininity offered through the Hollywood and Continental European cinemas and their female stars in the advice they offered to their young female readers.[1] An understanding of Hepburn's relation to such discourses, and through them to other femininities on offer in the form of stars such as Brigitte Bardot, Leslie Caron and Sandra Dee, is essential to an understanding of her importance for young women in this period and today. I pick out these stars not just because they featured frequently in the sources I refer to above, but also because, along with Marilyn Monroe and Katharine Hepburn, they recurred in the interviews which form the main body of this research, as well as the letters and questionnaires I received in the pilot study. In an important way, Audrey Hepburn is constructed through accounts of them by these women who admired her in this period. Consequently, for methodological reasons to which I drew attention in the introduction, some of this archival material is offered in the chapters which consider those accounts. I include some such material here, however, in order to sketch a nationally and historically specific discursive context within which to begin to grasp the significance of Audrey Hepburn for young women at that moment.

Second, I argue that Hepburn should be understood as a star who addressed her audience as feminine through the constitution and circulation of her image within discourses and in sites conventionally associated with feminine culture. As I discuss in Chapter 5, as image-text, 'Audrey Hepburn' is marked by the 'Cinderella' motif – a trope which extends beyond its significance as the narrative structure of the major films of her career into the wider extra-filmic discourse around her as a star – for instance in Hepburn's relationship with *couturier* Hubert de Givenchy who dressed her, with notable exceptions, on screen and off for most of her career. This motif of transformation, and the discourses of fashion and beauty – often, consequently, in the form of the make-over – which are central to Hepburn as a text play a key role in producing this address. In displacing 'respectable' academic approaches to the cinema such as the auteur theory in favour of the pleasures of looking at clothes in the movies, in the epigraph to this chapter from her piece 'The couture theory' Carrie Rickey suggests another agenda, and a different gaze privileging other kinds of detail. I will argue in relation to Audrey Hepburn that such detail is indeed often privileged by the text itself, and is instrumental in producing its particular address to its audience as feminine.

In relation to this feminine address, I consider a small but significant body of work around Hepburn which has played a significant role in the construction and consolidation of her image. There have been a number of short articles and sections on Hepburn in longer works, written by feminist critics and women in the media which have been produced at three historical/theoretical moments: early 'images of women' feminist film criticism in the 1970s (Haskell (1973); Rosen (1973)); female autobiographical/constitution of subjectivity work (Hulanicki (1983); Fell (1985); Walkerdine (1997) respectively)); and celebratory work produced around Hepburn's death in the early 1990s (Haskell (1991); Francke (1993); Wilson (1993)). This work shares not only a significant autobiographical slant, but also an understanding of Hepburn as having offered young women a particular mode of femininity and subjectivity which is perceived to have been oppositional or alternative to dominant forms in the late 1950s and early 1960s. This understanding of Audrey Hepburn has become widely accepted and in this respect should be unpacked, but in attending to this material I am also concerned that although it represents a different kind of 'evidence' (while often in the 'confessional' mode these are also the accounts of professional writers) it be seen also alongside the accounts I have gathered through conversational interviews with other women fans of Audrey Hepburn.

I have used the broad term 'image-text' for a number of reasons. Clearly, it relates to Richard Dyer's notion of the 'total star text' – the star as read across all her different media manifestations (1982: 17). At the same time, the work I present on Hepburn is a reading amongst the other readings engaged with here, and therefore should be considered as becoming, alongside those readings, part of the image-text. I also see this more general definition as retaining Dyer's notion that a star image can be seen as constructed from the sum of all the information available on the figure. This would include not only film roles, gossip and literature including criticism and biography, press and publicity and the way the image is used in other contexts, but also those aspects of a star's personal life which are made available for public consumption (Dyer 1986: 2–3). In using the term 'image-text', I intend then to indicate the indebtedness of this study to Dyer's work on stars and his concepts of star image and total star text, but in combining them to produce 'image-text', signal the centrality of the visual, the image, the 'look' in relation to this particular star.

While there have been a number of studies attempting to revise Dyer's initial theory of stardom (1979; 1991), for instance King (1991), Dyer's notions of star image and character remain adequate tools, and in relation to Hepburn his piece 'Four films of Lana Turner' (Dyer 1991) is particularly illuminating. Considering the high degree of interpenetration between Turner's publicly available private life and her films, he argues that 'the star phenomenon depends upon collapsing the distinction between star-as-person and the star-as-performer' (1991: 216). As I discuss below, there is an extremely close identification between what is widely known of Hepburn's private life, her star image and characters, resulting in the way in which she always appears simply to 'be herself', a quality I describe as the transparency of her image. In the same piece, Dyer also proposes that a major form of the relationship between a star and their social context is the reconciliation of contradiction: 'stars frequently speak to dominant contradictions in social life – experienced as conflicting demands, contrary expectations, irreconcilable but equally held values – in such a way as to appear to reconcile them' (1991: 225).

In Chapters 4, 5 and 6, which consider the material emerging from the interviews, the ways in which Hepburn can be understood to reconcile such key contradictions for young women both in the 1950s and 1960s and in the 1990s becomes apparent, and is revealed as a significant aspect of her appeal. Barry King's argument is partly with the distinction drawn in *Stars* between star image and character (Dyer 1979: 99). However, this distinction enabled Dyer to introduce the notion of degrees of 'fit' between image and character. It is essential to bear in mind the way in which a star image is in part constituted by screen roles, which cumulatively contribute to or inflect the range of meanings carried by a star image. The notion of 'fit' is essential to a precise understanding of how this works. In Hepburn's case, for instance, her roles as Giraudoux's water sprite in *Ondine* on Broadway in the early 1950s and Rima the 'bird-girl' in *Green Mansions* (Mel Ferrer, 1959) were figures of wild, natural innocence. In her role as Rachel in *The Unforgiven* (John Huston, 1959), a Native American girl adopted by white settlers who remains unaware of her origins, Hepburn's 'difference' and wildness were consolidated through a not unproblematic discourse around race. In *Breakfast at Tiffany's* (1961), Holly's reflection on her character that Doc Golightly was 'always lugging home wild things' and trying to tame them fitted then, despite the fact that Hepburn's transformation from Lulamae to sophisticated urbanite Holly has taken place before the film opens, and indeed despite Truman Capote's insistence that 'she was just wrong for that part' (Truman Capote, quoted in Paris 1998: 168). In some respects, Hepburn's casting in this part was a prime example of a perfect fit between star image and the character of Holly as drawn in the novella. Visually she fits the bill – she is 'skinny' with a 'flat little bottom' (14); this is Capote's initial description of Holly – a representation within a photograph: 'an odd wood sculpture, an elongated carving of a head, a girl's, her hair sleek and short as a young man's, her smooth wood eyes too large and tilted in the tapering face, her mouth wide, overdrawn, not unlike clown lips' (Capote 1961: 12). Holly's was 'a face beyond childhood, yet this side of belonging to a woman. [He] thought her anywhere between sixteen and thirty' (17); 'she was always well groomed, there was a consequential good taste in the plainness of her clothes, the blues and grays and lack of lustre, that made her, herself, shine so' (19). The physical and stylistic similarities are obvious, and it will become apparent as I go on to explore the way Hepburn has been constructed in greater detail that Holly was drawn by Capote through discourses remarkably similar to those through which the star who went on to play her is understood. The production of Holly as a photographic image and also as 'art' at the beginning of the novella (above) in conjunction with a sense of her energy and restlessness – 'Miss Holiday Golightly, travelling' – is typical of a dominant discourse in the celebratory literature around Hepburn and in the accounts discussed in Chapter 4, as is the positioning of her between girl and womanhood, and in between in terms of class.[2]

Furthermore, Joe Bell's admission in the novella of *Breakfast at Tiffany's*, 'Sure I loved her. But it wasn't that I wanted to touch her'(14),[3] suggests the sense of distance and untouchability which has largely surrounded Hepburn since the beginning of her career, producing volume after volume of biographical, celebratory, 'coffee table' picture books and since her death commemorative writing but no extended critical work. The sense of familiarity with Hepburn resulting from the transparency of her persona – the way in which she just 'is' – ironically produces in many critics an inability to pin her down, to say anything concrete about her. As Joe Bell says, she's 'a stranger who's a friend'.

Transparency and authenticity

She's a phoney, but she's a real phoney.[4]

Simon Brett pointed out at the height of Hepburn's career that 'the chief characteristic of her skill is its apparent absence. The distinction between Hepburn and the character she is playing is almost impossible to draw, so closely does she identify with her' (Brett 1964: 9). Hepburn's roles throughout her career were in this sense prime examples of what Dyer would term a 'perfect fit' with her star image (Dyer 1979: 145), and later self-consciously referred to and played upon key aspects of it, particularly in *Funny Face* (Stanley Donen, 1956). However, as I note above, the relationship between a star image and character is more complex perhaps than this one-directional model allows. Particularly interesting is the extent to which Hepburn's image is, or appears to be, as one with the details of her 'real' off-screen life (for example, her romances with older, controlling men). In the case of Audrey Hepburn, Dyer's notion of the collapse of person with performer intensifies the fit between image and character to a significant degree.

Hepburn embodied aristocratic European femininity, as established through her debut Hollywood role as Princess Ann in *Roman Holiday* and consolidated by the series of successful transformation scenarios which reversed this story of a princess who became 'ordinary' for a day: the Cinderella motif which marks Hepburn as a star. This narrative trope forms the basis of the key films of her career: *Sabrina* (Billy Wilder, 1954), *Funny Face*, *Breakfast at Tiffany's* and of course *My Fair Lady*. The 'princess' element of Hepburn's screen image was supported by the fact that her maternal ancestry was aristocratic, as Ian Woodward (1984) demonstrates. Hepburn also trained with the Ballet Rambert; ballerinas, princesses and models are traditional ideal fairy-tale femininities, the embodiment of delicacy, poise, grace and refinement. Hepburn had an early career modelling for glossy magazines and was associated with French *couturier* Hubert de Givenchy who designed collections and even a fragrance, 'L'interdit', around her. The central role played by either Paris or France in almost every transformation narrative (but also in other films), the high status accorded to them in relation to women's fashion, and Hepburn's origins have meant that she is strongly associated with Europe. This first role as a princess who becomes an ordinary modern girl for a day firmly established Hepburn as representative of pared-down, modern femininity – both ordinary and special in Dyer's terms (1979: 49) – and, in conjunction with the 'authenticity' or transparency of this in relation to her image (she is both an 'aristocrat' and shown in 'un-posed' publicity shots to be natural and ultra-modern in terms of personal style) secured the success of her subsequent Cinderella narratives, while at the same time naturalising them. In a way, these transformations simply reveal what is already known. At the same time this trope, central to her image, repeatedly produces comments like 'She was very special, but she was also very ordinary' from those who admire her: 'She seemed gifted yet kept her "ordinariness"' (*Sewing with Butterick* respondent); 'Audrey Hepburn looks like every girl and like no girl' (quoted in Paris 1998: 1).

The transparency of Hepburn's image means that we have a strong sense of familiarity with her which has been key to her appeal. As Dyer has argued, outside 'camp' appreciation, 'authenticity' is necessary to secure star status generally, and also to be a guarantee of other qualities a star might embody. This 'authenticating authenticity', in turn, he argues, produces charisma (Dyer 1982: 133), and in many ways this is Hepburn's defining characteristic. This transparency of her image is also at times consolidated in specifically filmic ways. *Roman Holiday* is exemplary in providing a textual reinforcement of this sense of intimacy which Hepburn inspires. At the beginning of the film, the spectator is introduced to the princess through the inscription of a public, international gaze established through a newsreel film of her tour of Europe. During the following scene at a ball held for her reception in Rome, our access to the princess's interiority is achieved through a shot beneath her skirt which shows her rubbing her tired feet and attempting to retrieve her lost shoe without compromising her external serenity. This sudden separation of the spectator from the emphatically public gaze so far inscribed is accompanied by the temporary dropping out of sound from the ballroom and allows us a glimpse of the private beneath the public. This moment, in conjunction with our repeated access to the character's point of view optically and psychologically, begins the lasting sense, not only in this film but throughout Hepburn's screen career, that this is someone with whom we are familiar, to whom we are *close*. This touch continues throughout *Roman Holiday* as we follow her on her stolen day off from her public duties. We will be privy to 'the private and secret longings of a princess, her innermost thoughts as revealed to your Rome correspondent in a personal, exclusive interview' complete with 'love angle and pictures', as Joe Bradley later describes his 'scoop' – which, aside from the princess and her companions, only the viewer shares. We are allowed a sense of a privileged and intimate relationship with both character and, through the transparency of Hepburn's image, star.

This sense of familiarity with the star, the difficulty of drawing a distinction between Hepburn and her screen roles, appears to have produced a critical paralysis which has been in place from the beginning of her Hollywood career. She is 'so close to our grasp and yet lost to us, and of another world' (Muller 1954). In *Breakfast at Tiffany's* 'the quality she engenders defeats description' (Barker 1961). 'She is . . . she is so many things that after having spoken about her so much I feel that I have still said nothing.'[5] At the same time, for this interviewer and others, she seems like a friend: 'she takes you in but holds you off' (Baskette 1954). It is perhaps significant then that 'L'interdit', the name of the perfume created for Hepburn by Givenchy, can be translated both as 'the forbidden' and 'dumbfounded'. From the beginning, Hepburn has been discussed in terms of 'that indefinable something'[6] which cannot be articulated and seems to be, in her case, more than the charisma usually accorded film stars – it has become her defining, if indefinable, feature.[7]

In one of the few pieces of critical writing on Hepburn, Roland Barthes proclaimed that 'The face of Garbo is an Idea, that of Hepburn an Event' (Barthes 1972: 57), an unusual attribution of depth to the face of a female star. The passivity suggested in this emphasis on appearance is not simple. Her face is an *event*. This potential contradiction (simultaneous activity and passivity) in Hepburn's persona is frequently expressed through a discourse which figures her as at once creator and created, artist and model, active and passive.[8] As accounts of Hepburn's appeal for women like Haskell (1991) above illustrate, her combination of independence and beauty is a central way in which consent has been secured around her image. Cecil Beaton, discussing the quality of Hepburn's beauty and her style of make-up, described her thus, as both model or work of art (passive, created) and artist (active and creative):

> She is like a portrait by Modigliani where the various distortions are not only interesting but make a completely satisfying composite . . . Like the natural artist she is, Audrey Hepburn is bold and sure in her effects.
> (Cecil Beaton in *Vogue* (NY) (1 November 1954), p. 129)

The same discourse operates in the novella *Breakfast at Tiffany's*, in Capote's description of Holly Golightly in terms of a carving in a photograph, her occupation: 'travelling'. Similarly, Richard Avedon summed up these complexities around Hepburn when he described the 'perfect moment' in which he saw her walking her dog through the Tuileries: 'I cannot lift her to greater heights. She is already there. I can only record, I cannot interpret her. There is no going further than who she is. She paralyzes me. She has achieved in herself her ultimate portrait' (Avedon 1990: 94). Here, again, she is figured as both art and artist. There is a need to maintain distance from her as an image; she has aura. At the same time, she is simply as she looks: she is transparent – there is nothing to interpret, to understand – she just *is*.

'Once upon a time . . .': fairy tales, fashion and femininity

Hepburn's association with ideal, fairy-tale femininities both on screen and in her earlier off-screen careers produced her as princess, model and ballerina rolled into one. This, in conjunction with the narrative of transformation which marks so many of her screen roles, locates her persona within discourses familiar from what is tradition-ally considered feminine culture. The narrative of transformation is a staple of women's culture: the fairy-tale 'Cinderella' is traditional reading matter for little girls, and the 'rags to riches' scenario which it articulates is endlessly repeated in girls' story books and magazines for young women in narratives of aspiration and achievement.[9] With the exception of *My Fair Lady*, the 'Once upon a time . . .' premise of the Cinderella story surrounding Hepburn is not 'long, long ago', but is up-to-date and very much of the fashionable moment. This basic cultural trope feeds into feminine culture in endless ways. The 'before and after' make-over in terms of fashion and beauty is typical of women's magazines, and endures today on daytime television, a realm which has also been associated with the feminine, in infinite varieties extending to face, body, home and garden.[10] The narrative of fashionable transformation has been a popular basis for 'women's films' from *Now, Voyager* (Irving Rapper, 1942) to *Pretty in Pink* (Howard Deutch, 1986) and *Pretty Woman* (Garry Marshall, 1990) – which inscribes Hepburn as a significant 'woman's star' in this sense by having Julia Roberts watch *Charade* (Stanley Donen 1963) – and Hepburn's career is marked by such successful transformations throughout the 1950s and 1960s. This is not only true of her screen roles, for even her first meeting with *couturier* Hubert de Givenchy is narrated in this way; as she tried on his designs, he remembers, 'the change from the little girl who arrived that morning was unbeliev-able' (Collins 1995: 173). Hepburn's screen career is filled with balls, dances and parties. In transformation narratives, the dance is a sig-nificant moment of 'coming out', both in terms of fashion and in terms of 'growing up'. Indeed, in Givenchy's narrative, it is fashion which facilitates the shift from little girl to young woman. The ball or dance is of course a moment of increased visibility which, as I discuss in Chapter 5, is not simply about beauty and elegance but can also be intimately tied to social class. Often, the dance is the scene of a very specific desire which precedes and sometimes motivates the transformation, and furthermore, even where the dance is not tied to a transformation, it often functions as a moment of discovery or investigation in Hepburn's films, as for instance in *Roman Holiday*.

Givenchy's comment suggests another key aspect of Hepburn's image: she is perceived as perpetually caught at the moment of 'becoming a woman'. The familiar image of Hepburn as Holly Golightly from *Breakfast at Tiffany's* which has accompanied her renewed popularity captures her precisely here: an article in *Photo-play* (November 1961) was entitled 'How does a girl become a woman?' and featured stills from the film accompanied by similar dresses available at department-store prices (Perez Prichard 1981). It is interesting to note furthermore that the 'kitten' heel has been described in the following terms: 'The purchase of a girl's first high heels is often a signal of puberty and the onset of sexual maturity. The "kitten" stiletto of the early 1960s was devised for this purpose; the one inch heel was the first step towards graduation' (Wright 1989: 16). Hepburn's continued association with this style of shoe fixes her precisely and perpetually at this point of transition between girl and woman. Even in a role such as that of Joanna in *Two for the Road* (Stanley Donen, 1966), opposite Albert Finney, the non-chronological structure of the narrative which follows Joanna from teenager to mature woman and mother means that Hepburn remains in flux between the two.

Roman Holiday, Sabrina, Funny Face, Breakfast at Tiffany's and *My Fair Lady* all have as their central premise and attraction the transformation of Hepburn into an ideal femininity in which a fashion and beauty make-over is instrumental, even when, as in the case of *Breakfast at Tiffany's*, this has taken place before the film opens. Hepburn's early modelling career for quality fashion journals and her ongoing association with Paris *haute couture* through Givenchy not only strongly inform these narratives but are central to her persona throughout her career. Elizabeth Wilson (1985: 158) notes a significant shift which occurs with the development of snapshot photography in the late 1940s and early 1950s. A 'candid camera' snapshot style became the most desirable aesthetic in fashion photojournalism; and as Yann Tobin points out in relation to the modernity of Hepburn's image at the height of her career, at this moment 'the creative avant-garde was working itself out on the pages of *Vogue*' (Tobin 1991: 101). Despite being clearly calculated, this aesthetic approach was considered more 'realist', with models caught unaware, off guard or in the process of completing an action – often resulting in 'accidents' which meant that the spontaneity of the moment was captured on film. Throughout *Roman Holiday*, the princess is followed on her 'day off' by a reporter and photographer who secretly capture her image at key moments: her first cigarette, her dance with the barber who cut her hair, and so on. The princess remains unaware she is being photographed and the result is a series of captioned photographs which bear a clear relation to contemporary fashion photojournalism.

The influence of Hepburn's earlier modelling career on her image is equally discernible in typical posed publicity shots in this period. The photograph of Hepburn by Philippe Halsman and which featured on the cover of *Life* magazine (18 July 1955) shows her on an Italian farm in front of a dovecote, dressed in a slightly creased linen shirt, her short hair a little out of place across her forehead, her head turned over her shoulder, back towards the camera.[11] The details of this image suggest the taming of wild nature and the key combination of naturalness, sophistication, innocence and ordinariness I suggest above. The pose is typically Hepburn and can be related to the photojournalist style discussed above, that of a fashion shoot in progress. The model is caught at the moment of turning her head toward the camera, producing the lifted chin and slightly parted lips which are typically *Vogue* in the period. This pose is also typical of Hepburn in *Roman Holiday* and *Sabrina*, and also in *Funny Face*, which depends more self-consciously on the discourses, aesthetic and otherwise, of fashion photojournalism. This, then, is perhaps the basis of Hepburn's poised yet off-hand performance style.

In the films mentioned above (with the possible exception of *Roman Holiday*) and also in *Charade*, costume is not simply tied to character, functioning 'silently' in the mise-en-scène, but as 'fashion' becomes an attraction in the aesthetic in its own right, often outside the generic opportunities of melodrama or the musical, as in *Sabrina*, *Breakfast at Tiffany's* and *Charade*.[12] The 'Sabrina' neckline black satin cocktail dress (see figure 2.3) and the now famous debate over the identity of its creator offer a prime example of the significance of fashion in Hepburn's image, on screen and off. This dress, which is reputed to have prompted copies in department stores all over the world on the release of *Sabrina* in 1954, was claimed by Hollywood costumier Edith Head as her own creation, and indeed Head won an Oscar for *Sabrina*. It was, however, the work of Hubert de Givenchy which formed Hepburn's 'Paris' wardrobe for the film, albeit uncredited (Paris 1998: 114). Figure 2.1 shows storebought versions of the look shown in New York *Vogue* of 15 November 1954. This is described as 'the newest look for a black dress to have', available in 'junior sizes', and is clearly related to the new Paris look for the bustline showcased in *Vogue* in September of the same year (figure 2.4).

Charade is particularly interesting in that although it is an 'unspectacular' murder mystery, the presentation of Hepburn's Givenchy wardrobe proceeds in much the same way as a contemporary *Vogue* monthly feature on occasion wear. As the film progresses, Hepburn is shown wearing appropriate outfits for important social events of the season: skiing, a series of chic urban *ensembles* for Paris, day and evening wear. *Breakfast at Tiffany's* showcased her Givenchy creations in a similar fashion. The camera frequently catches Hepburn as Holly on the stairs or in the hall, on the point of going out or returning from a visit to Sing Sing or dinner at '21', and

Late-day choices—

choicest when hatted

This page, above: A camisole-top princesse
dress with its full skirt emerging from gores.
Black Du Pont rayon velvet, by Suzy Perette,
$40. Russeks; Hudson's. Accessory that
amounts almost to a necessary now: a coiffed-
looking hat—velvet beret by Madcaps.
Below: The newest look for a black dress
to have—the bare neckline very high, the
skirt fullness very low. By Anne Fogarty
of a Burlington fabric (rayon taffeta) in
junior sizes, $35. Lord & Taylor; Godchaux.
The plumed velvet hat by Lilly Daché.
Anne Fogarty bracelet: at Lord & Taylor.
Opposite page: One of the newest after-five
looks. Components: a beret-now-chignon-
cap, a black rayon satin sheath that's really
skirt ($10) and camisole ($6), and jacket of
silver fox and silver lamé (this—Lurex and
nylon—$35). The costume by Nelly de Grab.
Saks Fifth Ave.; Frost Bros. Madcaps
beret, Schreiner jewellery: Saks Fifth Ave.

VOGUE, NOVEMBER 15, 1954

2.1 'Late-day choices – choicest when hatted': store-bought versions of the
'Sabrina' look in *Vogue* (NY) (15 November 1954), p. 112

she is repeatedly captured at moments in which her silhouette and the details of her *ensembles* can be viewed to best advantage: press publicity for the film suggested that 'all told, Miss Hepburn is a fashion show herself as she scurries through *Breakfast at Tiffany's*'. In contrast to this spectacular visibility in the film is Hepburn's repeated appearance in what Ernest Betts in *People* magazine described as 'a series of towels, shirts, nightgowns and hats that no girl in her right mind would wear' (22 October 1961). *Two for the Road* is significant for its status as Hepburn's only major 'off-the-rack' film, and was promoted as giving her a new, 'sexy' image. The film features clothes by new young designers of the late 1960s: Mary Quant, Paco Rabanne, Foale and Tuffin, Ken Scott and Michèle Rosier. The work of these designers is centrally associated with the move towards 'boutique' wear which Horowitz notes as holding a position somewhere between elite, status-oriented *haute couture* and more age-differentiated mass fashion (Horowitz 1975: 289). As I suggest above, as a result of the non-linear narrative in *Two for the Road* Hepburn is fixed as neither girl nor woman, and this is underscored by the 'boutique' style of the costuming in the film. Perhaps the film was intended to secure her popularity for a new generation of young women:

> 'Audrey Hepburn swings? You're *kidding*. Well, she's got her image, hasn't she? You know: pure, dignified, ingenuous, impeccable – that sort of thing. Always wears couture clothes. No, she doesn't swing.' Is that what you'd have said? Well listen to what's been happening to her in her new film, *Two for the Road*. Okay, she's had an image people have raved about since she was twenty, but she hasn't been afraid to change it. She's gone for mini-skirts, vinyl shorts, whoops-gay clothes, hair, make-up: yes, it's gone-overboard-for-swingdom Hepburn we have now. In fact, a newly-golden girl.
>
> ('The newly golden golden girl', *Honey* (April 1967), p. 119)

At the same time, this is a period which sees the decline of the studios and the star system, and the rise of a new kind of star, typified by young European actresses like Julie Christie and Brigitte Bardot, who were seen as representing a newer, freer kind of femininity. It appeared from the pilot study I conducted around dressmaking and film-star fashions in this period that it was precisely Hepburn's ability, as representative of a significantly 'different' femininity, to cross the divide between the grown-up style of the 1950s and these younger female stars, while retaining elegance and 'class', that secured her continuing popularity at the beginning of the new decade. Hepburn's established status as the epitome of sophisticated femininity allowed her to carry off the range of outlandish outfits commented upon by Betts. The sheet is worn as a toga at the beginning of a cocktail party in Holly's eclectic apartment – the perfect precedent of the 1990s mood which has witnessed the revival of her image. The folds of her bathrobe are, naturally, perfectly arranged. As Tobin points out, 'Audrey Hepburn is the only comedienne capable of brushing her teeth while still maintaining her glamour' (Tobin 1991: 10). At this moment, as I discuss below, the difference of Hepburn's style was represented as a chic 'kookiness', and this, as I explore in Chapter 6, has carried her popularity through to the 1990s.

Breakfast at Tiffany's and *Funny Face* are useful examples of the way in which Hepburn comes to represent, as the material discussed in the chapters which follow demonstrates, an idea of 'acceptable difference' in terms of feminine style. Christine Gledhill discusses the operation of hegemony thus:

> capitalism cannot ignore the potential market represented by groups emerging into new public self-identity and its processes invariably turn alternative lifestyles and identities into commodities, through which they are subtly modified and thereby recuperated for the status quo.
>
> (Gledhill 1988: 71)

This process is clearly discernible in the way the identity 'Beatnik' is recuperated in these films through Hepburn's star image. Beatnik style (which was itself derivative and detested by the Beats who inspired it) was recently characterised in the following terms:

> you need to: wear berets, sunglasses, sandals and sweatshirts, striped jerseys or black turtlenecks; sport a goatee (male), heavy eye make-up and dark straight hair (female); drink espresso and red wine; smoke marijuana or cigarettes (in holders if a woman); hang out in darkened coffee shops or jazz clubs with candles stuck in Chianti bottles; listen to poetry read over jazz, baroque or avant-garde music; play bongos; read intellectual paperback books on conformity (the problem) and Zen Buddhism (the solution); stare at abstract expressionist paintings, experimental and foreign films; make ceiling mobiles; say, 'man, chick, dig, like, cat, ball, crazy, swing, pad, square, hip'; never work; largely eschew personal cleanliness; indulge in casual sex; and always have a cool, bemused, detached attitude.
>
> (Blackburn 1998: 4–5)

Funny Face directly satirises this, having Hepburn as Jo endorse a phoney philosophy, 'Empathicalism', whose originator is discredited, wear a lot of black, and dance a bizarre routine to discordant jazz in a subterranean Paris club.[13] Posters for the film carried the by-line 'Hepburn's a hep-cat now!' Beat culture becomes 'student chic' around Hepburn in this film, and, it seems from the accounts of women who admired her look in the pilot study, in *Sabrina*. Anne Hollander (1978) traces the meaning of wearing black, describing a 'mode, authentically European . . . radically anti-fashion . . . [which] originated after the Second World War among Parisian Left Bank intellectuals and their followers, and finally flowered in America among the members of the Beat Generation. This mode might be called Student Black or Modern Bohemian Black'. She points to the importance of the black turtleneck sweater and black tights for women, which produced 'a feminine antifashion variant describable as Dancer's Black' (387). In this respect, the look in both *Sabrina* and *Funny Face* – slim black trousers and fitted black sweater – was highly appropriate to Hepburn's persona in which dance was a key element, and was thereby naturalised and toned down at the same time as it was authenticated through her associations with ballet and French intellectual culture (playing Giraudoux's Ondine and Colette's Gigi). Something similar was at work around Leslie Caron in another musical, *The Subterraneans* (Ranald MacDougall, 1960), adapted from Jack Kerouac's novel and starring George Peppard. In *Photoplay* (9 January 1960) 'Miss Caron digs the lingo', the picture which accompanied a report on the star's research on Beat culture in San Francisco's North Beach emphasised her ballet slippers and 'Puritan' white collar which significantly sanitised the black 'Beat' ensemble she was pictured wearing. This antifashion mode, as Hollander describes it, becomes assimilated and accepted as 'one standard modern way to dress' (387). This is certainly one way to understand the continuing popularity of Hepburn's look for subsequent generations of young women. Beaton in 'The changing Venus' (n.d.) includes Hepburn amongst other 'Existentialist gamines [who] whirled out of Europe like wild leaves in the wind', including Juliette Gréco and Leslie Caron whom he saw as 'undisguised reincarnations of the revolutionary sprites who unfurled the banners and strode through the France of 1789' (169). As I suggest above, while it might be argued that the potential oppositional impact of Hepburn's and perhaps Caron's images is hegemonically negotiated, Hepburn certainly is nevertheless understood by women fans as 'alternative' in this way.

The next year, *Breakfast at Tiffany's* appropriated a version of Beatnik style for Hepburn's character Holly Golightly, significantly co-opting any alternative or oppositional potential and producing it as chic and 'kookie'. Advance publicity called the film Hepburn's 'first opportunity to play a character she described as a "kook"':[14]

> If you are an Audrey Hepburn fan – who isn't? – you may have some difficulty in picturing her as a New York playgirl. Miss Hepburn, an elegant thoroughbred, just doesn't look like the type of girl who would live strictly for kicks. Yet here she is, turning out the performance of her life, in a new picture, *Breakfast at Tiffany's*, as – what the Americans call – 'a real kookie dame!'.
>
> (*Photoplay* (July 1961), p. 54).

Holly lives on the edge of Beat culture, existing largely by night and sleeping by day, wearing lots of black and sporting 'the longest cigarette-holder since Harpo's in *A Night in Casablanca*' (Breen 1961: 41). Despite the fact that Capote's Holly is a high-class call girl, casting Hepburn the 'fairy princess' (ibid.) in the role negated any suggestion of casual sex. Above all, Hepburn is almost impossibly well-groomed in this film; she is different – 'kookie' – but always impeccable – eminently acceptable and clearly contained by the narrative resolution. This incorporation/recuperation of the identity 'Beatnik' within a cleaned-up notion of 'kookie' femininity is widely discernible in women's and film-fan magazines of this period. The British *Mirabelle and Glamour* magazine had a regular fashion and beauty page, 'The Mirabelle charm club', which showed readers through detailed information on make-up, hair and fashion how to 'Get the "Kookie" look!' It told readers '*you* can have it too – if you dare to look different, don't mind all eyes turning your way!' Notable here is the way in which this feature carefully constructs 'kookie' within, but also *against*, an idea of 'Beatnik':

> *Recipe for a kookie*
>
> Kookie means off-beat, striking, different. So people can be kookie, too. Film stars like Shirley MacLaine and Tuesday Weld are kooks, but not super-glamour girls like Elizabeth Taylor and Marilyn Monroe. Kookie girls avoid fussy, 'pretty-pretty' fashions, bird's nest hair-do's, chocolate box make-up. *But a kook is no scruffy beatnik* – she's right on the tip of her pretty toes when it comes to that smooth, bandbox look.
>
> (17 June 1961, p. 6) [emphasis added]

'Kookie' is simple, not fussy, and it is certainly not Marilyn Monroe. Hair is brushed and brushed until it shines – it's a clean and tidy look. Make-up is proto-mid-1960s Mod, with the focus on the eyes and pale skin and lips, but the denial that this is a Beatnik look necessarily references what it claims to exclude. Despite the disclaimer, the emphasis here is still on 'pretty' – a key discourse of femininity in this period. Similarly, *Picture Show and Film Pictorial* in a feature on Sandra Dee, 'A teenager with taste' who could 'set a good example to young film fans', encouraged readers to 'Aim for prettiness': 'the recent coffee bar, jiving era has done nothing to help her [the teenager] – slovenly sweaters, tight trews, straggly hair-dos are not assets to make her look pretty. And that is what she should aim to look' (28 June 1958, p. 14). Similarly, Brigitte Bardot is repeatedly discussed in the fashion pages of this magazine:

> Brigitte is considered one of the biggest launchers of fashion among the youth of France. And her influence is not unnoticeable in Britain! When she first flashed on the screen with her long, blonde tresses, perkily awry; all the pony tailed misses loosened the ribbons, and allowed their hair to run riot over their shoulders. What her copyists did not realise was that they were copying the reel, not the real Bardot . . . She is really quite a neat person. It was Roger Vadim who enticed her into allowing her glorious hair to flow, and to dress in off-beat clothes: much to the disapproval of her mother, who had brought up her two daughters very simply and strictly . . . The Bardot fans who allow their hair to look like rats' tails should be told that she is quite meticulous about her luxuriant golden tresses. She goes to the hairdressers *twice* a week; and, in private life, always wears her hair neatly piled on top . . . It is only for films, photographic sessions, publicity and holidays that it flies free.
>
> ('BB fashion leader', *Picture Show and TV Mirror*
> (16 June 1960), p. 15)

The advice in this and other such features didactically constructs the kind of femininity which is socially appropriate for young British women. While the 'difference' of Hepburn's neatly groomed chic 'Frenchness' is clearly acceptable, the freer, sexualised French femininity embodied by Bardot is not. The piece is concerned to discourage teenage readers from copying this look, stressing that *really* Brigitte is neat and well-groomed and not at all 'off-beat'. Similarly, 'Pat Gledhill's glamour' in *Photoplay* urged readers to 'Be meticulous' and 'Be feminine' amongst its '39 steps to glamour' (March 1959, pp. 40–41).

By looking at the discourses within and against which she is constructed in this way, Audrey Hepburn can be understood to represent
a kind of acceptable difference in terms of femininity. Any difference
she might represent in terms either of femininity or sexuality at this
moment, however, is even further displaced by her casting alongside
'kookie' Shirley MacLaine in *The Children's Hour* (William Wyler,
1961) as schoolteachers accused of having a lesbian relationship.
Publicity for this film featured an illustration (rather than a photographic image) of Hepburn and MacLaine with the by-line 'Different
. . . ', but included a short piece 'How to kook by Shirley MacLaine':
'Everybody says I'm a kook. All my friends thought it was "kookie"
to play Martha in *The Children's Hour*.' Hepburn as Karen, in contrast, is constructed precisely against MacLaine's 'kook' in this film.
The Children's Hour received mixed reviews, with the lesbian theme
of the film proving especially controversial. In this case, the idea
of 'kookie' femininity around MacLaine is clearly used as a way of
negotiating the sexual identity 'lesbian'.

Fashion: a gendered attractionist aesthetic

As I have begun to argue in a brief discussion of *Charade* and *Breakfast at Tiffany's*, costume, articulated as 'fashion', frequently functions in Hepburn's films as 'attraction' in the sense of Tom
Gunning's notion of the 'cinema of attractions'. Gunning discusses
spectacle as a key element in early cinema, one which goes under-
ground with the coming of sound, resurfacing in genres such as the
musical, and in the avant-garde (Gunning 1990). Spectacle in this
sense functions as 'attraction', halting the narrative and soliciting an
attentive gaze. The development of an aesthetic which foregrounds
costume as attraction, discernible across a number of Hepburn's
most familiar films, is largely the result of the construction of her
persona through the narrative of transformation and an association
with *haute couture* to which it is related.

Sabrina is the first of Hepburn's Hollywood roles where this
attractionist aesthetic operates; it is also the first in which she is
costumed by Givenchy, although he is uncredited. The film is particularly interesting in that as a romantic comedy it would not
appear a likely locus for the elaboration of an attractionist aesthetic.
I would argue that this aesthetic is both produced *around* Hepburn's
persona *and* constitutive of it in this and other of her films, thereby

producing an address which allows a significant space for a competent feminine gaze. In turn, this address in the aesthetic organisation
of the film facilitates the engagement of particular gendered competencies around dress and style. Sabrina Fairchild (Audrey Hepburn)
writes to her father from Paris with the details of her arrival home:
'If you should have any trouble recognising your daughter', she
writes, 'I shall be the most sophisticated woman at Glen Cove Station!' At this signal there is a shot of a French toy poodle, complete
with diamanté collar, sitting on a stack of luggage. The camera pans
slowly up an elegant skirt suit worn with heels to a pleated, white,
turban-style skullcap, short hair and gold hoop earrings, worn by the
new Sabrina. Transformed by two years in Paris, she strikes a sophisticated pose, looking to one side, head resting on hand. Hepburn's
performance prevents this sequence from producing her as pure
'image', despite the fact that the camera pulls back to give the spectator a head-to-toe view of the outfit, an image which is pure *Vogue*
fashion plate. The movement of her eyes when the camera comes to
rest on a head-and-shoulders close-up is enough to communicate her
self-consciousness. Sabrina walks away from the camera, turns and
retraces her steps, a move which offers the spectator a back view of
the suit and facilitates an attention to silhouette and the details of
cut, the tiny slit in the rear hemline and the 'kitten'-heel shoes
(figure 2.2). This is a fashion parade for the spectator, and importantly it is *not* about Hepburn's body, which a similarly organised
sequence might well have been, if, say, in a film starring Marilyn
Monroe – the wiggle would almost certainly have eclipsed the outfit.
Furthermore, this sequence and others in the film allow a significant
space for a pleasurable and non-voyeuristic gaze which emphasises
the details of her dress and accessories before David Larrabee does
a double take and screams to a halt in his sports car.[15]

   Short sequences such as these are motivated by the need to display
Hepburn's Paris wardrobe, which is of the latest style and is significantly different from the clothes worn by other female characters.
This is particularly evident at the Larrabee party, which showcases
the Givenchy evening dress she has repeatedly described with great
excitement, to her father, the other 'below stairs' staff, and to David:
'Yards of skirt and way off the shoulder!' Alone at the indoor tennis
court, she dances to the music coming from the party, sweeping her
skirts around her; the film allows a moment in which the details of
the dress and the rustle of the skirt can be displayed and appreciated

The camera pans slowly up from Sabrina's poodle and matching luggage . . .

. . . taking in the line of her Paris suit . . .

. . . and coming to rest on her face and perfectly adorned head.

Hepburn parades for the spectator, allowing her Givenchy ensemble . . .

... to be admired in detail.

2.2 A space for a competent gendered gaze in *Sabrina* (1954)

to full effect. Later, at Linus's office, this attractionist aesthetic is tied in to an economy of meaning in the film which throughout associates Sabrina with Linus's remark that with her return from Paris it is 'as though a window had been thrown open, and a lovely breeze swept through this stuffy old house'. The next sequence opens with a close-up of a fan blowing cool air onto the injury David acquired through sitting on the champagne glasses in his pocket, anticipating the shot which later introduces us to Sabrina in the controversial cocktail dress, spinning like a top in Linus's swivel chair.

The association of Sabrina at this point with the 'breath of fresh air' Linus has described emphasises not only her 'newness' in relation to her transformation, but indeed specifically the newness of her look in stylistic terms. This shot introduces another sequence in which the display of Sabrina's dress is prioritised and determines the camera movement, as in the earlier sequence at the station. Her walk towards the camera, pirouette to show the 'V' back, brief pause and then further walk are weakly explained in narrative terms by her 'exploration' of Linus's office, but seem in fact to be motivated purely by the concern to display costume, producing an aesthetic which facilitates an attention to the details of dress (figure 2.3).

These and other similar sequences in Hepburn's films cannot quite be described as 'spectacular', even as they arrest the gaze and halt the narrative. 'Spectacle' suggests distance (and fetishism), and I would argue that such moments are precisely characterised by the fact that the gaze solicited is a *close* and familiar gaze, one which is knowledgeable and attends to detail. In the conjunction of this gaze with such a particular aesthetic a space is offered in which gendered competencies might be engaged. In this sense Gunning's term 'attraction' is especially appropriate in its suggestion of a kind of drawing in.

Funny Face plays self-consciously on tropes and discourses associated with the world of high fashion, fashion journalism, photography and feminine culture as well as Hepburn's persona, which produces an innovative aesthetic. The narrative focuses on the transformation of Jo Stockton (Hepburn) from Greenwich Village bookworm to *couture* model, around whom an entire collection is designed by a Paris *couturier* (Givenchy) and photographed by 'Dick Avery' (Fred Astaire). This is a clear reference to fashion photographer Richard Avedon, who not only photographed Hepburn throughout her career

2.3 An aesthetic privileging the details of dress in *Sabrina* (1954)

but also acted as visual consultant for the film. A further shot in this sequence has Hepburn 'knowing' that she is playing a princess at a ball – clearly a self-conscious reference to this familiar aspect of her image, coming as it does soon after *War and Peace* (King Vidor, 1956). Avedon produced the special effects in the 'Paris fashion shoot' sequence, which, while referencing the style of photography alluded to in *Roman Holiday*, also 'freeze' each shot, manipulating the colour until a final 'print' version is reached. Not only is the colour manipulation spectacular, but the narrative is further arrested through the freezing of the image.

The opening credits of *Funny Face* feature a light box on which fashion and beauty plates for a women's 'glossy' are illuminated. Throughout the credits, the images become gradually more abstracted, with the details of a shoe or a made-up eye under a mag-nifying glass foregrounded in the frame. The production design is termed 'layout' in a further reference to the aesthetic of women's magazines.[16] The film opens in the office of Maggie Prescott, editor of the fictional *Quality* magazine (played by Kay Thompson and modelled on Diana Vreeland, editor of American *Vogue*), and firmly establishes the diegesis as a 'woman's world', a world of feminine culture. The spectacular 'Think pink!' number featured at the begin-ning of the film clearly references magazine aesthetics, being the-matically and formally related to a layout familiar from glossy women's magazines (see, for instance, 'In the pink' *Elle* (UK), Feb-ruary 1998, p. 32). The consumer tie-in, a feature of film publicity familiar from the 1930s and 1940s (see Gaines 1989), was a key publicity angle for this film, involving the 'classy' American teen magazine *Seventeen* and stores across the United States.[17]

The number features two-dimensional images of pink fashion and beauty consumables montaged in abstracted space: toothpaste, shampoo and details of fashion accessories are shown in isolation – a bag, a shoe, an earring, a hair bow. What may appear simply as spectacular montage might in fact offer an address to those spectators who are familiar with and competent in reading fashion magazine layout. The film is knowing about the discourses it mobilises: it addresses a particular audience – the woman with conventionally feminine interests, whilst also incorporating a proto-feminist discourse on the evils of fashion culture and the beauty industry. As I discuss in Chapter 3, *Funny Face* compromises Jo's intellectual aspirations in an interesting way, and yet despite this, a combination of intellect and beauty is frequently referred to by women as central to Hepburn's appeal.

'Can't do it with make-up': natural, democratic beauty

The musical number in *Funny Face* 'On how to be lovely' features Kay Thompson, who educates her protégée Jo, who has been chosen as the *Quality* woman for the difference and individuality of her looks, in being an authority on 'how to be lovely'; Hepburn clearly emerges throughout her career as a star who has indeed been an authority on this subject. Publicity for both *Funny Face* and *Breakfast at Tiffany's* featured lookalike competitions and consumer tie-ins. Girls who thought they had a 'funny face' like Audrey Hepburn's in the film were encouraged to enter the competition and win, amongst other things, a 'glamour build-up' like the one Jo receives: 'Any girl who thinks she looks like Audrey Hepburn – and you'll be surprised at how many there are around – is eligible to enter.' Despite the fact that competitions like this are clearly tied to commodity consumption in the same way as the 'Think pink!' aesthetic, publicity for this film played on a key aspect of Hepburn's image: that is the perceived difference, democracy, individuality and *naturalness* of her beauty.[18] As the words of the musical number 'On how to be lovely' suggest, 'Can't do it with make-up'. Edith Head, discussing Hepburn in this film, advised in *Picture Show and Film Pictorial* that 'The real secret to beauty – and popularity – is free' ('That certain something', 15 June 1957). 'Plainness' doesn't matter – 'that certain something' is individuality and charm – personality. The emphasis is on inner beauty, not on cosmetics and fashion. This discourse of naturalness is widely discernible in women's magazines and the fashion and beauty pages of film-fan magazines of this period, and often it is articulated specifically around Hepburn's star image. For example, *Mirabelle and Glamour*, a British magazine for teenage girls, featured 'Five golden rules for glamour':

1. Wear what *suits* you – don't just copy.
2. *Be yourself*. Don't try to look like Audrey Hepburn, if you're not the Audrey Hepburn type! Boys don't like anything phoney. A girl who is natural, gay, and true to her type, is far more fun than someone always worrying about trying to be somebody else. Dress to suit your personality and figure, too. If you're not sure what suits you, then take along someone older and wiser when you go to shop.
[. . .]
5. Look happy. (7 March 1959, p. 11)

The sleight of hand, of course, lies in the conjunction here of 'typing' with naturalness and individuality 'typing'. This kind of feature was common – Pat Gledhill's beauty page in *Photoplay* of February 1961 showed 'An ABC of glamour' which included 'N for Naturalness, which means you are never trying to be something you aren't . . . Be yourself'(39). In a piece in *Modern Screen* entitled 'What she doesn't need, she doesn't have', Earl Wilson (1954) emphasised Hepburn's 'lack of false modesty . . . her sincerity and her naturalness', and her discomfort at having her hair bleached for the role of Ondine: 'she felt it wasn't right. It was false' (94). In April of the same year, the journal featured a piece by Kirtley Baskette, 'Dutch treat'. The magazine was clearly addressed to women – all advertising space is dedicated to beauty (cosmetics and skincare) and fashion. The feature stresses her lack of conventional sex appeal – 'Audrey sports nothing up and down her chassis that would make the boys on the front row cheer [thus constructing her as "not for men"] . . . Neither pure beauty nor raw sex is what Audrey Hepburn gets across' and makes much of the unconventionality and unevenness of Hepburn's features: 'her teeth are not perfectly aligned, her nostrils flare and her dark hair seems carelessly cut'. At the same time, Audrey

can sit as primly as a princess, wearing a suit by de Givenchey [*sic*] and kicking off her patent leather pumps to reveal pink toenails peeping through her nylons. It seems so correct that you wonder if you shouldn't kick off your own shoes. She can slop her coffee over the cup and it looks as though that's the only proper way to handle a teacup. Audrey's undeniable attraction, in one word, is presence. Most Hollywood stars affect it but never quite attain it. That's why Audrey Hepburn has bowled them all over. With her it comes naturally, as it does with some other girls known as princesses . . . The girl who arrived on the spot left in the spotlight – simply by doing and being nothing but her enchanting self.

(Baskette 1954: 92, 94)

This account is significant for the way in which it offers detailed fashion information (pink toenail polish, patent leather shoes), but also places an emphasis on manners – social conduct. Particularly notable is the way in which Hepburn is seen to have an ability to make unconventional behaviour seem perfectly proper – the emphasis is on poise ('she is graceful yet informal' (92)) – and importantly, natural. Furthermore, she just *has* what other stars strive to *attain*. She is not artificial, not constructed; Audrey is simply herself. She is unique (94). Furthermore, she is understood to be 'the same girl she was before *Roman Holiday*', a star whose 'look is a glamorous projection of [her] true sel[f]'. Audrey is 'the girl from outerspace' – she is different – but despite being 'deliberately theatrical, she fools no-one – and never herself' (*Modern Screen* (September 1955), pp. 43, 46). Hepburn's transparency, the sense of closeness to her, has a different significance in these sites; rather than producing a sense of distance, for a certain audience competent in the production of femininity it offers an opportunity to deconstruct the look.

In an early piece on Hepburn in British *Photoplay*, Pauline Swanson referred explicitly to Hepburn's difference from Hollywood ideals of the day: 'too tall, too thin, and virtually, as she herself candidly admits, flat-chested'; Hepburn has never been constructed as 'sexy', and Swanson continues by according her a form of 'sex appeal' which is not corporeal, precisely through recourse to an idea of naturalness, simplicity and wholesomeness:

But if sex is the life-force, then, by anybody's standards, this girl is loaded with sex, for there has never been a girl so loaded with pure *vie*. She seems to get almost physical pleasure out of just plain breathing. The simplest things – things too many of us take for granted – things like food, and sleep, a new record or a small present, give her a lift and a bounce.

(Swanson 1954: 12)

The construction of Hepburn within these discourses of naturalness produces her look as eminently achievable as well as appropriate, evidenced in accounts of the popularity of her look amongst girls on the street and in contrast to Richard Dyer's suggestion that 'standards of beauty inevitably exclude the majority, and that "democratic" beauty such as Hepburn's may only induce a sense of misfortune or even failure in some in the audience' (Dyer 1993: 12) and to Stacey's notion of the 'impossibility of femininity' (1994: 212).[19] Even where accounts of 'doing' the Hepburn look are accompanied by the familiar disclaimer 'of course, I knew I could never really look like her . . .', the possibility of doing so, the accessibility of her style, remain in place.[20] Hepburn is frequently reported to have commented that her face was 'more personality than glamour' (*Photoplay* 27: 6 (June 1976), p. 60), and it is this emphasis on personality defining beauty, clearly expressed in *Funny Face*, which seems to have secured her appeal for many women. The emphasis on Hepburn's 'individuality' is particularly interesting in relation to the discourse of style and individuality discernible in the accounts of women who identified their period of young, fashionable femininity with the 1950s, as discussed in Chapter 3. Hepburn is frequently constructed as knowing what 'suited' her, a phrase which occurred repeatedly across their accounts.

Clever, not sexy: Hepburn and 'the Mammary Woman'

The discourse of achievability and ordinariness within which Hepburn's look is constructed is significantly tied to a notion of her 'difference'; in *Funny Face*, it refers specifically to the quality of her beauty, to her 'funny' face. It is significant that her body is not at issue in this film; indeed, Maggie Prescott explicitly points out that her body is 'good'. Hepburn has been frequently cited in retrospect as having represented for many women in the 1950s an alternative mode of femininity; indeed the pilot study bore this out (Moseley 2001). Her gamine look and slender figure are frequently contrasted with what has been described as the 'maternal' body of the 1950s feminine ideal, exemplified by popular Hollywood stars like Jayne Russell and Marilyn Monroe. This construction was in place from the beginning of her career:

> By Hollywood standards – and one must never minimize Hollywood standards! – Audrey Hepburn is flat-chested, slim-hipped and altogether Un-Marilyn Monroe-ish. Her measurements are: bust, 32 in; waist, 20½ in; hips, 34 in. Nothing sensational there, is there? And yet, Hollywood standards or no, Audrey Hepburn is the most phenomenal thing that's happened to the film capital since Marilyn Monroe.
>
> (*Photoplay* (March 1954), p. 22)

She is different, also, in her style of dress: 'a little lipstick, a man's cropped shirt, a full black skirt and ballet slippers' (23).

In *From Reverence to Rape*, Molly Haskell (1987) contrasts Audrey Hepburn, along with Grace Kelly, Doris Day and Debbie Reynolds, to Monroe. Her account of these stars, particularly of Hepburn and Kelly, although she does not use words like 'I' and 'we', seems as personal as it is critical. She is perhaps the first to address their importance as role models for young girls growing up in the 1950s; centrally, she suggests that through their androgyny they literally embodied an alternative to the maternal role. Similarly, Marjorie Rosen's account in *Popcorn Venus* contrasts Hepburn with what she calls 'the Mammary Woman' (1973: 285), and again there is a strong sense of personal investment in this writing. Barbara Hulanicki (1983), Alison Fell (1985), Molly Haskell (1991) and Elizabeth Wilson (1993) have all written accounts of Hepburn which focus on this aspect of Hepburn's appeal for them as young women growing up in the 1950s. Haskell remembers that Hepburn 'got what she wanted, and offered an alternative to the female biological and cultural imperatives of the Fifties' (1991: 12). During this period of Hepburn's popularity a significant amount of material was available in the press, emphasising her dedication to her marriage and family, for instance 'The secret of my happiness by Audrey Hepburn' in British *Photoplay*: 'If I had to make the choice, there is no doubt in my mind that I would willingly give up my career to devote the rest of my life to my family' (December 1961, pp. 10–11, 58). *Modern Screen* in particular worried over her marriage to Mel Ferrer, asking if he was right for her (January 1955, p. 30) and posing the question 'Will Hollywood ever see Audrey Hepburn again?' (April 1955, p. 52), after Hepburn was seen to be letting Ferrer take control of her career. Indeed, press publicity for *Breakfast at Tiffany's* noted that for her wardrobe, 'Miss Hepburn's husband, Mel Ferrer, flew to Paris, inspected the Givenchy collection, made his selections, and took them back to his wife'. This widely available aspect of Hepburn's personal life appears to be filtered out of her image in accounts by young women fans: the meanings made of her image by these women in relation to femininities in the 1950s are located in her body and her look. Alison Fell in a short autobiographical piece entitled 'Rebel with a cause' recalls figures are bursting out everywhere, particularly in the lower streams, or so it seems: it's as if the girls in the A class are saving themselves for better things. In the playground it's nothing but waspie belts and transparent blouses, a wiggle when you walk and a giggle when you talk, *really* vulgar, the lot of them. At home, Granny casts a grim eye over her skinny flatness and snorts: 'straight up and doon like a shit-hoose door.' Aspiring to femininity feels like imagining you could climb Mount Everest – all these film stars so impossibly hourglass and formed and grown-up, Lana Turner and Marilyn with their hips and hand-span waists and big cone-shaped breasts. (It's still years, remember, before Twiggy and flat chests, denim and the androgynisation of glamour. Only Audrey Hepburn gives cause for hope.)

(1985: 18–19)

This account is a complex articulation of ideas of femininity and intellect, where intelligence and conventional sexiness – as expressed in the display of secondary sexual characteristics – are produced as incompatible. She can either be 'Sexy Fell' *or* 'Brainbox'. Concomitantly, Hepburn's androgyny comes in some way to signify 'intelligence'. As one of my pilot interviewees put it: 'She looked as though she thought' (Liz). The undeveloped girls in the A stream are 'meant for better things'. Fell becomes a Beatnik. Elizabeth Wilson is also interesting on Hepburn's appeal as representative of 'sophisticated, existentialist Europe as opposed to the overripe artificiality of Hollywood' (1993: 31) – and her comment that 'she proved that a woman could have brains and still be attractive' (36–37) is significant in relation to my discussion of *Funny Face*, although as I suggest in Chapter 3, my reading of this film disputes her sense that 'the integrity of her earlier, intellectual self, is endorsed' (32). As I point out in relation to Hollander above, Hepburn's association with black clothing is perhaps a key way in which she has come to be understood as representing 'intellect', despite the negotiations made in the narratives of her films. These histories share not only a particular understanding of Hepburn as offering an alternative and in some senses oppositional femininity at this historical moment, but also a sense of closeness to Hepburn, of being addressed by her image, discernible in the personal turn of these narratives.[21]

A contemporary review of *Sabrina* commented 'Surely the vogue for asexuality can go no further than this weird hybrid with butchered hair?' (*Films and Filming* 1, 1 (1954), p. 20).[22] Constructed thus, Hepburn appears a less conventionally 'sexualised'

image and as such can be easily mobilised in the name of nascent
feminism, through her perceived embodiment of a freer, more independent femininity. However, unfamiliar as her look may have been
to the Hollywood screen and in relation to dominant discourses of
feminine glamour in the 1950s, Hepburn was the embodiment of the
Vogue couture ideal, in terms of hairstyle, body shape and fashionable
style, which produced her as representative of sophisticated Europe
and, importantly, 'class'. Hepburn's gamine haircut was a version of
a Paris style featured in British *Vogue* as early as January 1949 in a
feature called 'The small head'. Throughout her career, Hepburn
insisted on retaining this small, neat head shape, even when her
hair was long, as in *Breakfast at Tiffany's*, or in *Two for the Road*
which is so explicitly 1960s in terms of fashion and style.[23] Similarly,
Hepburn's extreme slenderness which is frequently cited as the
most explicit marker of her difference at the moment of her first popularity, was 'The 1950 bodyline' (British *Vogue*, March 1950). Figure
2.4 shows a feature from New York *Vogue* of 1 September 1954 –
the new sheathed, flattened ('flattered') 'Paris bustline', which was
accompanied by a Dior version of this new look, demonstrating
the extent to which Hepburn's style (and the 'Sabrina' dress) were
identical with the *couture* ideal at this moment.

At the same time, Hepburn was also able to represent casual,
Bohemian student chic in this film, wearing trousers, shorts and men's
shirts with panache. Hepburn's 'flat-chested' look was described in
my pilot study as having been a 'godsend' to some of those young
women in the 1950s. In this way, Hepburn brought together two
previously discrete ideals of beauty – the *couture* ideal with movie-
star glamour – and certainly in some respects democratised what had
until then been a clearly class-specific look. 'Class', of course, is a
key aspect of her image. My pilot study on dressmaking and star styles
demonstrated the way in which '*couture*' styles were available to
women whose finances would not have stretched to Dior and
Givenchy, through paper patterns and their own, or a dressmaker's,
skill. Nevertheless, it is imperative to recognise the hegemonic under-
pinnings of Hepburn's appeal; in many ways, her look was simply
another ideal which has become dominant in many cultures since
the 1960s.

Understanding Audrey Hepburn's persona to be constructed
within feminine discourses across film texts, press and publicity, I
would argue that she can be seen as a female star constructed

Vogue's eye view:

P A R I S   and   the   B U S T L I N E

First illustrated news

Now it can be told in pictures (Paris couturiers ask that no photographs
or drawings of French fashions be shown until now, September 1)—
exactly how Dior's new silhouette affects the bosom.
Flattening? The first frantic cables gave that impression,
but a glance at the Vogue sketches here would indicate that "flattering"
is the accurate word. For what Dior has done is this:
in many of his dresses, suits, and coats, he has sheathed the bosom closely,
making it seem rounder, smaller, younger.
No cleavage—the fabric holds the body like a close bandeau.
Then, in still other fashions (see below), he has created a new Anne Boleyn
kind of bustline. The bosom is lifted, but again, rounded
rather than pointed, and held closer to the body than heretofore.
On the following pages, first-time-shown photographs
of the new Dior fashion—bandeau bodices that flatter the bosom
with new subtlety; that indicate its beauty, but don't insist.

2.4 'Vogue's eye view: Paris and the bustline', *Vogue* (NY) (1 September 1954),
p. 149

as much for a female as a male, audience and gaze, if not more. Indeed, Molly Haskell's comment on the star's appeal for her in the 1950s suggests this gendered address quite precisely in relation to Hepburn's difference:

> best of all, she was, well, tiny-breasted. She was a triumphantly tomboyish figure in a rising tide of sex symbols . . . in the gang of giggling virgins to which I belonged, large breasts and menstruation were anathema, bras something to be postponed as long as possible. To an embryonic feminist, Audrey Hepburn was at the opposite pole from the bosomy stars then in vogue; she was alert, full of the ardor of an explorer . . . The qualities that made her more desirable to us were precisely those that made her less desirable to masses of red-blooded American men. A friend tells the hilarious story of seeing *Sabrina* on the Army post where his fellow servicemen much preferred the more curvaceous Martha Hyer.
>
> (Haskell 1991: 10)

I want to argue that the feminine address of the image-text 'Audrey Hepburn' which I have elaborated in this chapter produces a space in which the kind of skilled look at clothes, hair and make-up which emerged from the pilot study can be accommodated, and indeed might be said to be inscribed. Such a space allows for socially and culturally acquired gendered competencies to be engaged, this 'feminine' gaze coming into play particularly around the discourses within which Hepburn is constructed as a star: fashion, beauty and the details of the Hepburn 'look'. In this way, the visibility and spectacular display of the 'made-over' Jo in *Funny Face* before an assembled and predominantly female audience *in itself* reveals the work involved in the transformation to a spectator whose gaze is skilled and competent in feminine culture. British *Photoplay* of January 1959 featured an article providing 'training in poise and grace' – '*Photoplay's* glamour school' – which acknowledged the constructedness of this discourse, and the work involved:

> Here is your chance to walk – and look – like a star . . . Like them, you'll find that it takes more than just looking, to learn to move like a star. Like them, you'll have to practise daily, to make grace and poise a natural, unaffected part of your own glamour equipment. [You will learn] how to walk, to carry bag and gloves, hold a tea cup, bend down, sit, negotiate stairs and make an entrance.
>
> (44)

Similarly, 'Get the kookie look!' (*Mirabelle and Glamour*, 1961) noted 'A Kookie girl's make-up looks natural, but she puts a lot of hard work into it!' Such an intimate understanding of the processes involved in constructing these images produces a particular close-ness to them. As the lyrics to 'On how to be lovely' acknowledge, 'it's all in the know how'. This in turn allows a space in which par-ticular viewers might negotiate the ideological contradiction at work in this film and in Hepburn's image generally. The construction of the transformation in *Funny Face* as natural *and* magical, with the labour involved elided, can be side-stepped. A similar ideological sleight of hand is at work in the sequence from *Breakfast at Tiffany's* where Holly hurries to dress for a visit to Sing Sing. We witness the virtually effortless creation of perhaps the most familiar, sophisti-cated image of Audrey Hepburn. The film only allows us the merest impression of the labour involved in the production of this image; in the moment, however, when she appears in the door and asks, 'How do I look?', a space is opened up for the skilled spectator not simply to say 'perfect' but also to answer the question of just 'how' that look is constructed for herself. She might not be as 'amazed' as Paul (George Peppard).[24]

Although the effect of this scene is ostensibly to produce an idea of easily achieved, chic femininity, an intimate knowledge of the production of such images means that the female gaze which con-templates the feminine ideal on the screen cannot always fail to recognise the work of femininity it conceals, and hence the ideologi-cal sleight of hand in the discourses of natural, democratic beauty which surround Hepburn might not always be completely success-ful.[25] That gaze may also not, however, be *resistant*.

This discourse made Hepburn particularly suitable for 'Cinderella' type transformations – the key difference being that the 'before' Hep-burn, as in *Funny Face*, is often as acceptable as the after. Although the 'before' Hepburn is constructed as 'un-made-up' and natural, accounts demonstrate that women 'know' that cosmetics are involved in the production of Hepburn's look, and can competently decon-struct this 'natural' face in order to accurately reproduce it for them-selves. The 'know-how' was certainly available in the sites where her image was circulated: 'She never thins her eyebrows, just keeps them in shape and touched up lightly with pencil. No make-up base, rouge, powder. But lipstick – boldly applied' ('The Hollywood look', *Modern Screen* (September 1955), p. 46; see also Beaton 1954).

Lea Jacobs has argued of Hollywood narrative cinema that 'even when a woman is figured as desiring, the discourse works to figure her as desirable' (Jacobs 1981: 90), and *Funny Face* is a particularly good example of this formation. Jo's desire to visit Paris in pursuit of intellectual fulfilment leads her to become a fashion model, and she learns to love it: 'I like it! Take the picture, take the picture!' At the same time, this moment represents Jo's usurpation of Dick's role as artistic director, complicating her role and figuring her again as both art and artist. However, as I have argued above, I want to take issue with Stacey's (1994) emphasis on the production of images of ideal femininity for the male gaze. Indeed, I suggest that the argument I have presented in this chapter in relation to the specific construction of Hepburn for a predominantly female gaze throws this into question in important ways. Elizabeth Wilson has suggested that 'the most important thing about fashion is not that it oppresses women' (1985: 13) and Jane Gaines asks the important question 'What if self-decoration gives women a sense of potency to act in the world?' (Gaines and Herzog 1990: 6). Hepburn is noted as having held Givenchy's designs for her in this regard, seeing them as offering a kind of protection: this is clearly expressed in the poem she wrote in tribute to him (*Hubert de Givenchy* 1991: preface), and she commented 'They make me feel so *sure* of myself' (*Honey*, April 1967, p. 119). This is clearly also the case for many Hepburn characters: as I go on to suggest in Chapters 3, 4 and 5, the transformations I have discussed in this chapter are shown to facilitate an important sense of self, both on screen and in the lived experiences of some of the women in the audience who admired Hepburn's image.

Audrey Hepburn can be understood as a female star who addresses her audience as feminine through the constitution and circulation of her persona within discourses and sites specific to feminine culture. At the same time, this chapter has offered a context within which to read the accounts of Hepburn by female admirers presented in the chapters which follow. Particularly significant is the way in which Audrey Hepburn can be understood to have represented 'difference', individuality and acceptability in terms of fashionable personal style. This was accompanied by a sense of the achievability of the look produced through the discourse of naturalness within which she was constructed as a star. As the princess stands before the barber shop in *Roman Holiday*, she contemplates her own image reflected in the window, and compares it to the pictures of short female styles which frame it. Seeing a woman leave the shop with a similar new hairdo, her mind is made up and she goes in (see figure 7.1). At this moment the film offers us the literal creation of the 'Audrey Hepburn look', and the princess's new image as a modern young woman which enables her to take control of her life is constructed explicitly in relation to the ideal female images she sees around her. In retrospect, this moment stands as a delightful, ironic reversal of the relationship between Hepburn and her female fans – the taking up of the gendered address that I have suggested in this chapter. In the next chapter I begin to consider more precisely the nature of that relationship, looking in more detail at the narratives of transformation which mark the image-text 'Audrey Hepburn', their place in constructing discourses of subjectivity and self, and the ways in which they relate to the accounts of Hepburn which form the basis of the following chapters.

Notes

1 Poovey (1984: xii–xiii) discusses the role of conduct books which provided models for 'acceptable behavior, legitimate values, and even permissible thoughts'.
2 I argue in Chapter 4 that Hepburn's positioning in this respect is more complex than this familiar 'child-woman' construction suggests.
3 This line, not included in the screenplay, hints at the central difficulty of Hepburn's casting in the role of Holly: the character's relation to sex. Holly is supposed to have had eleven lovers '"not counting anything that happened before I was thirteen"'. Barry Paris quips, 'One could believe that of Monroe [whom Capote wanted for the part], but never of Hepburn' (1998: 171). A fuller discussion of Hepburn's relation to discourses around sex and 'sexiness' can be found in Chapters 4 and 6.
4 Holly Golightly (Hepburn) as described by her agent O. J. Berman in *Breakfast at Tiffany's*.
5 *Cinémonde* (25 September 1962)
6 *The Cinema Studio* (January 1951), p. 16.
7 Hence the resonance of the slogan used for the launch of Chanel's recent fragrance, 'Allure': 'Difficult to define, impossible to resist'. Audrey was offered as the epitome of feminine allure in tie-in articles.
8 'She's the kind of girl you want to protect – and yet she gives the impression that she can take care of herself in almost any kind of tight squeeze' (Conolly 1954).
9 I discuss particular instances of such modern Cinderellas in Chapter 5.
10 See Moseley (2000).

11 This image can be viewed in the cover archive of the *Life* website, at: www.lifemag/Life/.

12 Gaines (1990) and more recently Bruzzi (1997) offer interesting arguments about the significance of dress and its relation to narrative and meaning in Hollywood cinema.

13 See Dyer (1980) 'Entertainment and utopia'.

14 Press publicity for *Breakfast at Tiffany's* emphasised the contrast between Patricia Neal's 'more New Yorky, smart, chic, simple and outrageously expensive' wardrobe designed by Edith Head, and Hepburn's rather more 'on edge' and 'kookie' Paris wardrobe by Givenchy which was accessorised to the point of excess.

15 Since this research was completed, Gaylyn Studlar (2000) has published an interesting piece which also comments on the feminine address of Hepburn's image, and makes a similar argument in relation to the gaze in *Sabrina* (2000: 164–165).

16 *Harper's Bazaar* (September 1959) featured a photo shoot, 'Paris pursuit' which in an interesting reversal used a film-style narrative with its title page laid out like film credits. The piece played on elements of Hepburn's image such as romance with an older man (played by her husband Mel Ferrer in the photospread) and a Paris in which an Audrey lookalike appears at every corner.

17 *Seventeen* of January 1956 did indeed feature a 'pink' fashion page, but there was in fact no linked copy or specific reference to the film.

18 *The Nun's Story* (Fred Zinneman, 1958) played heavily on Hepburn's 'individuality'; the stark black and white habit which framed the faces of all the nuns, and the symmetrical organisation of the shots, made her difference particularly noticeable.

19 'Nobody ever looked like her before World War Two. Now thousands of imitations have appeared. The woods are full of emaciated young ladies with rat nibbled hair and moon pale faces' (Cecil Beaton, quoted in Collins 1995: 169). Collins also draws attention to the new generation of Audrey clones' as he puts it, who 'aspire not only to look like her but to dress the part as well' (169). On the occasion of the London première of *War and Peace*, the *Daily Mail* (17 November 1956) commented on Hepburn's new hairdo and the 'girls all over England [who] strove to be mistaken for Audrey Hepburn by looking angular and wearing fringes'.

20 Stacey acknowledges that 'similarity became an imaginable possibility through consumption in the 1950s' (1994: 223), but there are, as I suggest here and in Chapter 4, other factors at play which make Hepburn 'possible' as a star.

21 Valerie Walkerdine (1997) also offers a fascinating personal perspective of the importance of Audrey Hepburn for her as she grew up in this period; I discuss this account in Chapter 5.

22 Publicity for *Funny Face* used two alternative posters to advertise the film, both showing Hepburn in her 'existentialist' outfit from the scene in which she dances in a Paris club. Significantly, though, while one showed her true silhouette, in the other (which is a drawn rather than a photographic image) her hips and breasts are greatly 'enhanced' to give her curves more readily associated with Hollywood feminine glamour.

23 This point is made in a comment by Hepburn's hairdresser on the film, in 'The newly golden golden girl', *Honey* (April 1967), p. 119.

24 At the time of writing, the current advertisement for Pantene shampoo on British television has a transformation narrative structure and features music which incorporates this 'How do I look?' 'Very good' soundbite from the film. After using Pantene, the female shopper decides against her original choice of a grey dress, opting instead for a more frivolous shocking pink cocktail dress similar to the one worn by Hepburn in *Breakfast at Tiffany's*.

25 Smith (1988) makes an argument for the competent female gaze in 'Femininity as discourse'; see also Partington (1992) for a discussion of the skilled gaze of the female consumer.

Chapter 3

Dress and subjectivity: remembering Audrey

There is a moment in *War and Peace* (1956) which is emblematic both of a significant motif around Audrey Hepburn as a star and also of the nature of the relationship between the star and the women who spoke to me about liking her. Natasha attends her first ball, and dances with the prince. Later, as her family prepare to leave Moscow under threat from Napoleon's advancing armies, Natasha discards everything she can manage without. Coming upon the beautiful dress she wore to that first ball, she holds it to her body, caressing her face with the fabric before the mirror. She sways and pirouettes to the dance music in her head as she remembers that important moment in her life, but as the music fades she drops the dress to the floor and walks away (figure 3.1). The enormous significance of that first ball is beautifully captured in Hepburn's performance, and this is a key moment in the film which signifies not only Natasha's growing up but also the ephemeral nature of the moment she remembers.

I want to do two main things in this chapter. On one hand, it will offer an introduction to the material from the main body of interviews which is discussed in Chapters 4, 5 and 6. It will consider, for

3.1 Natasha remembers her first ball in *War and Peace* (1956)

instance, the ways in which the women who spoke to me about liking Audrey Hepburn discussed their favourite star, and how they talked about her in relation to their own identities and histories. At the same time, I intend this chapter to function on a more methodological and theoretical level. Throughout the central films of Hepburn's Hollywood career a significant relationship between dress and subjectivity is repeatedly expressed, as in the moment from *War and Peace* described above in which subjectivity is signalled formally – music is used to signal memory and interiority – around dress. Subjectivity is repeatedly articulated *through* dress around Hepburn. My central methodological concern in this work is to attend to both text and audience, and it is precisely in this key relationship between dress and subjectivity that the central problematic of the project is encapsulated. This motif, central to the star-text 'Audrey Hepburn', also structures the accounts which are discussed in the following chapters. It is through talk about dress, in relation to Audrey, that the women who took part in this study articulate their own identities, their own senses of self. It is through remembering and talking about clothes, and the importance of clothes in the main structuring events of their lives – dances, weddings, work – that they tell their own stories in this study, in talking about their favourite star. As Annette Kuhn has argued in *Family Secrets*, 'telling stories about the past, our past, is a key moment in the making of our selves' (1995: 2). While such remembered events may seem ephemeral, as in Natasha's memory of her first ball, it is through the details of dress that they are given concrete existence in the accounts which form the main part of this study.

Dress and desire: the articulation of self through style

First then, I want to explore the ways in which subjectivity and interiority are ascribed to Hepburn characters, and the textual inscription of this in key films through point-of-view structures, voice-over and the representation of desire. At the same time, I want to look at the way in which this subjectivity is articulated in relation to dress and stylish transformation, and the specific shifts in that relationship in relation to the changing historical contexts of the films' moments of production.

In *Roman Holiday*, transformation in terms of personal style is indisputably marked as a positive and enabling process; at the conclusion of the film the princess has clearly 'grown up', taken charge of her self and managed to negotiate this with her public role and identity. In its first moments, the film announces what will become a complex articulation of the private or subjective within the public. Documentary-style footage of the princess's European tour which inscribes an explicitly public gaze at her, is followed by her appearance at the embassy ball, where everyone turns to watch her entrance.[1] As I discuss in Chapter 1, the intimate view of the princess attempting to retrieve her shoe in this sequence affords the viewer an access to her subjectivity which continues in the film, eventually becoming aligned with her self-transformation, which replaces the formal inscription of subjectivity around her during the rest of her free day in Rome.

Later, point-of-view shots show her gaze wandering around the ornate room which represents her imprisonment within the proper, serene and conventionally 'pretty' femininity she will temporarily escape. The non-diegetic music fades out, to be replaced by the strains of dance music from a party on a moored barge on the Tiber. As she jumps out of bed and looks longingly at this scene from her window, we are allowed to share her optical point of view, and the princess's subjectivity and desire are clearly inscribed. Her desire is immediately linked to the outward signs of her femininity – her clothes – as she puts on a pared-down outfit of a plain shirt (with necktie), skirt, low-heeled court shoes and gloves – an outfit which, whilst still perfectly proper, is nevertheless in direct contrast to the ornate surroundings which seem to overpower her. As she escapes in a laundry truck, her delight is evident, and once more we are allowed her optical point of view as she is driven out into the streets of Rome. In anticipation of these shots, her eyes appear above the tailgate: Hepburn's eyes framed above a horizontal are a perpetual marker of subjectivity ascribed to the characters she plays in almost every film. *The Nun's Story* is exemplary in this respect: the nun continually fails to observe 'modesty of the eyes', and her struggle to contain her subjectivity within the social identity she has taken on as a nun is central to the film (indeed her powerful sense of self wins out as she leaves her order to join the Resistance).

Having passed out in the street as a result of a sedative, later, in Bradley's room, the princess removes her gloves and is presented with his pyjamas – the first of her wishes to come true.[2] Propriety is retained, however – 'Have you lost something?' he asks as she checks beneath the covers to see if she is wearing the bottoms. 'No,' she replies, relieved and excited at the same time by the daring of the situation. As she wanders through Rome, secretly observed from a distance by Joe and the viewer, she swaps her 'court' shoes for a pair of open Roman sandals. Arriving at a barber's, she decides to have her long hair cut very short in response to the pictures of fashionable new feminine styles in the window, against which she compares her reflection – an interesting anticipation of the kind of relation which will link Hepburn's female fans to the familiar 'Hepburn look', the creation of which we witness in the following scene (see figure 7.1). In *Roman Holiday*, and, as we shall see, in *Sabrina*, it seems to be the case that clothes offer Hepburn's characters 'a sense of potency to act in the world' (Gaines and Herzog 1990: 6). Princess Ann's determination to lose her long hair ('All off!') in favour of a new, boyish style, while created and later touched up by the barber, produces her first true close-up in the film – a further sign of subjectivity – and her new look gives her access to the barge dance, the scene of her initial desire which motivated the narrative. Gradually, she sheds the last vestiges of her 'princess' style as she adapts her outfit: her sleeves are rolled up and now appear short and casual, the necktie is loosened and is eventually replaced by a jaunty striped neckerchief: she becomes 'Smitty' – an androgynous diminutive of the name she chooses for herself. On her eventual return to the embassy and her public role, it is clear that the princess/Smitty has 'grown up', and that the fulfilling of her desire during her day off and the stylish transformation which accompanied this have been instrumental in that process. She refuses the milk and crackers which were a sign of her childishness, rebukes and dismisses her staff so that she can be alone. She has taken control of her image, her life and her public role.

The moment at the opening of the film where we witness the princess losing her shoe precisely articulates the anxiety around the maintenance of a publicly visible, proper femininity. 'Control yourself', the princess is told when the strain of keeping up this public face becomes too much: she must appear 'calm and relaxed for the press conference' the next day. This discourse around the maintenance of a particular serene public femininity is resonant in its address to a female audience; indeed, advice on posture in '*Woman's Weekly* whispers' (thus explicitly coded as a 'feminine secret') later in 1961 urged that '[f]ace muscles must be relaxed, too, and this is the hardest lesson of all. However cross you feel, remember that your public face must always be pleasant' (*Woman's Weekly*, 19 August 1961).

Part of the power of the hegemonic work this film performs through Hepburn is in allowing her to retain the subjectivity and selfhood she has acquired through her day of freedom, whilst she struggles to negotiate this with her 'public face'. The highly emotive final moments of the film, in a mirroring of the opening scenes, are powerful precisely through our understanding of the princess's struggle to maintain her composure whilst conducting a very private exchange with Joe Bradley under an extremely public gaze. While ultimately this public face takes precedence, the princess does manage the private face, which has been aligned from the opening of the film with her desiring subjectivity, within the restrictions of her public identity more ably than in the opening scenes, where she literally stumbled and had to be aided in the retrieval of her shoe. On her return she is self-possessed and decisive, breaking away from her prepared speech to proclaim Rome as her favourite city.

The stylish transformation of the eponymous heroine of *Sabrina* is equally aligned with the acquisition of selfhood. Subjectivity is formally inscribed around Sabrina – her retrospective voice-over opens the film and announces its fairy-tale status. We first see the young Sabrina helping her chauffeur father wash the cars – as strains of diegetic dance music waft in, she looks screen right and walks out of shot. A cut to the source of this music – the Larrabee party – is followed by Sabrina climbing into a tree to watch – again, the dance is explicitly marked as the scene of her desire, along with David Larrabee, whom she watches flirting with the giggling Gretchen van Horne, from the tree. Shots of the couple from Sabrina's point of view are cross-cut with ever closer shots of Sabrina, until she turns away in disappointment. Again in this film, great emphasis is placed on Hepburn's eyes, as Sabrina peers out of the tree and over window sills. While her desiring subjectivity is carefully inscribed in these ways, it is also made clear that the young Sabrina has no sense of self, no self-possession. 'Oh, it's you Sabrina,' David remarks as she jumps out of the tree behind him. 'No – it's nobody,' she replies. Later, as she peers over the tennis court window at David and Gretchen, David prepares to open the champagne, aiming the cork where there is 'no-one' – and it hits the window squarely in Sabrina's face. On the balcony at her father's quarters, she looks away as he tries to reassure her, and as the strains of music return, she goes into her own room, her private space, and sits in the dark to listen. 'Isn't it romantic' begins to play, and the camera moves in towards her face, at which point there is a dissolve to David and his giggling partner which we understand to be motivated by her subjectivity. Sabrina makes a half-hearted suicide attempt, but is saved by Linus Larrabee and goes away for two years to a Cordon Bleu school in Paris.

While Sabrina is away, we are given access to her through the letters she writes to her father, and which he reads to her 'family' – the downstairs staff. It is clear from these letters that her desire for David remains although she struggles against it. While she clearly wants him to see and desire her ('I have a lovely evening dress . . . if David could only see me in it – yards of skirt and way off the shoulder'), the last scene in Paris introduces an alternative and yet equally strong discourse around her selfhood, which is slowly being loosened from its dependence on David. Until this point, our access to Sabrina's letters has been through her father's reading of them. Now, however, her interior voice reads her final letter as she writes it. We see Sabrina's new look for the first time – her chic new short hair is apparent, but the spectacle of her new outfits is held back; typically for an Audrey Hepburn character, she wears a white robe. She sits at a desk before an open window through which Paris – the Sacré Coeur at night – can be seen. She opens the window to let in the city, the accordion music which has been faintly heard in the background. She writes: 'Someone across the way is playing "La vie en rose" – it's the French way of saying "I'm looking at the world through rose-coloured glasses", and it says everything I feel.' This tune will accompany her throughout the film, and is related not just to love and David, but also to life. This evocative expression of her sense of the possibilities which lie ahead for her is further explained: 'I have learned so many things father, not just how to make *vichyssoise*, or calf's head with *sauce vinaigrette*, but a much more important recipe. I have learned how to live; how to be *in* the world and *of* the world, and not just to stand aside and watch. I will never again run away from life, or from love either.' This scene ends with Sabrina forewarning her father that should he have difficulty recognising his daughter, she will be 'the most sophisticated woman at the Glencove station'. There is a dissolve to the transformed Sabrina, and the upwards pan which reveals her new look is accompanied accordingly by a more fully orchestrated reprise of 'La vie en rose' –

a particularly affective expression of the realisation of earlier potential which this moment represents.

Our access to Sabrina's subjectivity changes from this moment, in
precisely the same way as in *Roman Holiday*. While formal point-of-
view structures largely disappear, our access to Sabrina's interiority
continues in two main ways. On her return to Long Island, she is
witty, confident and entirely self-possessed. 'Hello Linus – I'm back!'
she cries; from now on her speech is littered to references to 'I' and
'me' – she has found a voice. Sabrina's new-found sense of self is also
clearly expressed through her dress and the relation of her body to
it – her demeanour. She is poised and in control, and her pleasure in
her new self – her enjoyment of her ball dress when she stands waiting to enter the party, oblivious of the dropped jaws of the men on
the terrace; her solitary dance in the tennis court; the spinning ball
of energy she becomes in the '21' dinner dress – is unmistakable.
Furthermore, after her arrival at the Larrabee party, our access to the
events and conversations taking place around Sabrina is aligned
almost exclusively with her perception.

By the time of *Funny Face* (1956) the relationship between
subjectivity and transformation has become more tortured – Jo
Stockton has to be physically forced into her new look by *Quality*
fashion editor Maggie Prescott and her female team – and her eventual wholehearted acceptance of the more conventional femininity
she represents as the 'Quality' woman is accompanied by a distinct
circumscription of her subjectivity. This subjectivity has previously
been signified through her 'intellectual' Beat style of dress, constructed in the film as unfeminine and unattractive, and which ironically has subsequently become a key element in her appeal to
women. Significantly, in contrast to *Roman Holiday* and *Sabrina* this
film does not inscribe Jo's subjectivity in a formal, textual way, but
limits it *solely* to her appearance from the beginning. While the film,
as I discuss in Chapter 2, addresses conventionally feminine interests, at the same time it attempts to address those women who may
not share these concerns through Jo's initial protestations and critique of the fashion industry as 'chi-chi, and an unrealistic approach
to self-impressions as well as economics': its project is to reconcile
the two by having Jo happily become a successful model, whilst still
ostensibly retaining her intellect. Jo's interest in philosophy, however, is compromised by the film in parallel with her gradual acceptance and increasing ease with her new look. While photographer

Dick Avery produces a fashion spread designed to show that 'a woman can be beautiful as well as intellectual', this is undercut by the presence of a model who struggles to look as though she appreciates modern art and reads 'Minute men from Mars' during her break. She is replaced by Jo – 'a woman who can think as well as she looks', 'a cutie with more than beauty'. Jo agrees to go to Paris merely as a means of meeting her intellectual hero Professor Flostre, originator of Jo's chosen philosophy – 'Empathicalism'. While the professor is ultimately discredited, revealed as 'just a man' who is interested in Jo's body rather than her intellect, the philosophy remains intact and indeed is the means by which Jo and Dick find each other at the end of the film: this scene has Jo dressed in the wedding gown which was the finale to her catwalk show. Furthermore, this philosophy is revealed simply to be 'empathy', which like most emotional work is commonly perceived to be a feminine attribute. While Jo is ostensibly allowed to retain her intellect after her transformation, then, she is at the same time placed firmly within the realm of the feminine and apparently marriage precisely through it. However, Hepburn characters in the central films of her career do actually remain unmarried; in this respect, it is significant that the final 'wedding' scene of *Funny Face* is explicitly marked as fantasy through the use of soft focus and contrived iconography: fairy-tale setting, doves, the peal of church bells. There is a way, then, in which despite the film's attempts to confine her within conventional femininity, the ideological process is perhaps not so secure.

Eliza's subjectivity is clearly inscribed in *My Fair Lady* – again this is most evident at the beginning of the film. In response to Henry Higgins's claim that he could 'pass her off as a duchess at an embassy ball . . . even get her a job as a lady's maid, or a shop assistant, which requires better English' there is a cut to Eliza's face (she has thus far been excluded literally and visually from this exchange) which shows that her interest is caught by the latter part of this boast. After Higgins and Colonel Pickering have left Covent Garden, Eliza's desire is made clear through the song 'Wouldn't it be luverly?' which informs us of her yearning for love, domestic comfort and a move inside from her current existence on the London streets ('All I want is a room somewhere, far away from the cold night air . . .'). The viewer is privileged with Eliza's subjective thoughts and desires – the repetition of Higgins's boast in her head, accompanied by the camera moving in closer to her face as she thinks about the possibilities of this claim: what she wants is 'to be a lady in a flower shop, 'stead of selling at the corner of Tottenham Court Road'. Higgins will also claim to make her marriageable – the guarantee of her upward mobility.

Eliza's transformation in this film is exceptionally difficult; not only is she physically forced, kicking and screaming, into the bath, but her vocal training to remove her (working) classed accent in Higgins's laboratory resembles medieval torture. The results of this enforced labour are more conventionally feminine than in any of her other film roles – and are equally the most circumscribing of her subjectivity and sense of self. Having finally achieved the required pronunciation, she joyfully sings 'I could have danced all night' in her bedroom, dressed in a flounced nightgown reminiscent of the one she so forcefully rejected in *Roman Holiday*. Stern (1988) and Starks (1997) have both argued that the presence and performance of Audrey Hepburn in *My Fair Lady* foreground femininity as 'performance'. Throughout the film, however, Eliza gradually becomes more 'like Audrey' in appearance and demeanour, and when she descends the staircase dressed for the embassy ball in the most minimal outfit of the film, an elegant white gown of long, clean lines and simple coiffure, the modulation of her voice as she says '*Thank* you, Colonel Pickering' clearly reveals her as 'Audrey Hepburn'.[3] I would argue, then, that despite the emphasis on learning in this film, Hepburn's image ensures that her presence precisely marks her acquisition of hegemonic femininity as both 'natural' and inevitable: in this moment of her 'coming out', and in this outfit, the simplest in the film, she becomes herself.[4] Instantly, however, the film negotiates the power of this moment; at Higgins's comment 'Not bad, not bad at all' she looks at her feet and the camera pans swiftly right, excluding her from the frame and privileging Higgins. This staircase has throughout the film been the visual site of Eliza's struggle and achievement between the class associations of upstairs and downstairs: initially she has to be dragged up it, and she is figured at its base while Higgins stands above her halfway up. It (and others in the film) can now be ascended and descended with ease, but simultaneously it has become site of both her visibility and exclusion.

The relationship between selfhood and personal style becomes increasingly tortuous and circumscribing as this discourse in Hepburn's films continues out of the 1950s into the 1960s. In *Funny Face* and *My Fair Lady* her characters are increasingly difficult to bring into line through transformations which are less and less joyful and more and more limiting in terms of the representation of their subjectivities and their sense of self. These transformations contain her characters within increasingly traditional femininities with intensifying urgency, across an historical period in which gender roles begin to shift, and in which women's expectations of work and marriage change; there is certainly much at stake ideologically in women 'being in the world and of the world' at this moment, and the relationship between dress and subjectivity is often, as this research shows, fundamental in this respect. It is not surprising, then, to find that the representation of this relationship becomes increasingly problematised, and that while the transformations in *Roman Holiday* and *Sabrina* are of a modern, urban, pared-down kind and enabling to the character in question, in the two later films the opposite is the case and the characters are increasingly trapped in conventionally feminine garb, the representation of their subjectivities seriously curtailed. Dress, for Hepburn's characters, is in turns enabling and constraining.

There is, then, a significant, if shifting, relationship traceable across Hepburn's Hollywood films between the acquisition of fashionable style or *transformation*, self, and the formal inscription of subjectivity/interiority in those films.[5] The accounts of Hepburn offered in the interviews are informed by a similar relationship – these stories of growing up and forging an identity frequently centred around dress: shopping for clothes and fabric, adapting and making clothes, wearing them, behaving in them. Emerging from the accounts is a profound sense of the importance of the relationship between self and dress; as I discuss in Chapter 5, clothing can facilitate an increased sense of self, and indeed often functions as social protection (cf. Skeggs 1997). I want to go on to consider the ways in which the women who took part in the study talked about Hepburn, about themselves, and about the relationship they perceived between the two, telling their own histories and identities through their memories of significant events and clothes in growing up with Audrey Hepburn.

Growing up with Audrey: dress and subjectivity

In the introduction I discuss my use of the term resonance throughout this study as way of describing the relationship between Audrey Hepburn as discursive formulation/image-text and the women who spoke to me about her. Accounts of Hepburn seem to be focused around key events and experiences in the women's lives which resonated with Hepburn as an image-text – with understandings of her image and discourses and narrative structures such as the Cinderella motif which I discuss in Chapter 5.

Two of the main interviews with women who grew up in the 1950s and 1960s initially seemed unproductive, and in one case even difficult. Despite offering herself to me as a research subject, Bernie seemed reluctant to talk about Audrey Hepburn, and for some time the discussion centred around her memories of growing up during the explosion of American music and fashion in Britain in the late 1950s. It came through powerfully that as a young teenager, Bernie was strongly invested in American culture – films and music, rock 'n' roll. The memories she offered of this period were fascinating, and indeed emerged as very rich in relation to the complex ways in which she understood Audrey Hepburn to be 'modern', as I discuss in Chapter 4. The point at which Hepburn does occur in her story is revealing, however; Bernie had previously identified her interest in Hepburn as beginning in her late teens, 'you know, when you're just, sort of, smartening up a little bit'. The conversation turned back towards Sandra Dee (a star she favoured as a younger teenager), coffee bars, music and having a Saturday job which gave you money of your own to buy clothes and records. She told me about the Dansette she loved as a teenager:

> Bernie: Yes, I remember that, I loved it, I had it for years – in fact – I had that record player right up until I got married . . .
> RM: Did you?
> Bernie: Yes, and probably long after.
> RM: What happened to that?
> Bernie: Oh, I should think I just wore the thing out! [both laugh] . . . What else . . . Fashion-wise, for me, anyway, it was her. And her hair! [sharp intake of breath]

This is the point at which Bernie began to talk in an extended way about Hepburn – and clearly she is identified through her positioning in this woman's narrative with putting away the period of youthful, carefree femininity which she associates with American youth culture in the 1950s, maturing and getting married. Although it was clear from the rest of our discussion that Bernie was aware of Hepburn before this point in her life, as this example illustrates, the ordered flow of memory and talk can be essential to a nuanced picture of how, in this case, an image is recalled and understood. She returned to Hepburn again after she had spoken about the emergence of the new (American) identity 'teenager', describing her as representative of a mode of femininity she chose in her late teens and early twenties, and she shifted immediately to a recollection of the influence of what she described as Hepburn's 'Italian' style on her wedding gown. The moments which the women who took part in my research recalled and spoke about in relation to liking Audrey Hepburn are often key emotional events: a first dance, a social occasion, starting work, marriage, shifting class. Audrey Hepburn became important for many of these women at a significant moment of growing up – their late teens and early twenties. At times they spoke about admiring her style of dress at this point in their lives; in others the association is rather more oblique, emerging through the kind of patterning I discuss in relation to Bernie above.

Across these accounts, Hepburn comes to occupy a rather complex position in terms of age and identity, somewhere between child and adult but not, I would argue, the same as the term 'child-woman' which is frequently offered in relation to her. A consideration of the construction of Marilyn Monroe in *Let's Make Love* (George Cukor, 1960) is instructive, marking precisely the distinctions between Hepburn and Monroe who have nevertheless both been described as 'child-women'. While both stars play characters who are 'motherless', and who have significant relationships to older men, in *Let's Make Love* the simultaneous infantilisation and sexualisation of Monroe which is characteristic of her roles (for instance in the number 'My heart belongs to Daddy' where she is clearly presented as a Lolita figure in tights and a sweater), could not be further from the construction of Hepburn's characters as young women learning to be in the world. While Monroe's character struggles to improve herself by acquiring her high-school diploma, the education of Hepburn characters is usually of a more genteel, social kind. Hepburn is never sexualised in relation to her body – the only erotic charge around her is an attraction engendered by beautiful clothes. Where Monroe is manhandled quite roughly in musical numbers in this and other films, the comparative delicacy of touch with which Hepburn is treated is telling. It is significant that Hepburn is frequently offered in this study in opposition to both Monroe and Brigitte Bardot, who occupy similarly sexualised positions.

While for Janet, Audrey Hepburn represented a completely grown-up style, in Bernie's account, for instance, she is constructed against 'teenager' Sandra Dee, as a smarter, more grown-up version – more of a 'young lady'. For slightly younger women like Liz, Rosie and Barbara, Hepburn offered a femininity which enabled them to negotiate between the 'young lady' of the 1950s and the youth styles of the 1960s: the social and historical moment when 'young ladies' became 'girls'. Hepburn is equally elusive with regard to her national identity; while for Bernie Hepburn represented modern, urban, classy East Coast American (although this interviewee was aware of her European origins), for Janet, Caroline and Rosie she is distinctly European. While emblematic of 'Left Bank Parisian cool' for Rosie, for Janet and Caroline (as well as in the pilot interviews), Hepburn's Europeanness is constructed in direct opposition to 'brash American starlets' and indeed to the sex-ualised Frenchness of Bardot. For Janet, indeed, she was 'typically English', representing 'the college girl look', and through this a star 'you could relate to'.

The interview with Janet was also in some ways rather difficult; she was reluctant to talk about liking Audrey Hepburn, and during the first part of the interview she gave single-word answers to all my questions. Again, during the process of transcription it became apparent that her recalcitrance was linked to two central issues. First, the question of not being 'a fan' which was also apparent in the interviews with Liz ('I wasn't a *fan* in that sense') and Caroline ('I'm not an Audrey Hepburn groupie'), occurred around not having cer-tain kinds of knowledge about Hepburn, and also in relation to dif-ficulty with the potential for an erotic attraction between women suggested in the relationship between female star and female spec-tator. Second, in the interview with Janet a difficulty emerged which had also been an issue in one of the pilot interviews: the delicate question of subjectivity and, in relation to this, the notion of indi-viduality. Commenting on an earlier short piece of work I had done on Hepburn to which she had contributed her memories, Helen had told me in one of the pilot interviews:

You see, when I read your thesis, the bit that I – that made me a bit cross – I don't think it was you – it was you quoting someone – was this idea that we all wanted to be Audrey Hepburn. And I just don't think that was true . . . I mean, *I* didn't want to be Audrey Hepburn, I wanted to be a history student, which is what I was . . . I might have quite liked to have been a history student who *looked like* Audrey Hepburn, but that's a bit different.

Helen makes an important distinction here, between 'being' and 'looking like' or indeed 'producing oneself to look like' which involves a profound awareness of the difference between self, and self as image. Furthermore, through the direct challenge she makes here to academic approaches to the study of feminine cultural practices, she pinpoints precisely the unequal power relations involved in the analysis of interview material. She continued, 'Generalisations are interesting, especially if you're making them, but if you're one of the individuals, that – you know, it takes your individuality away'.

The notion of individuality emerged as central to the slightly uneasy discussion I had with Janet – clearly, it is also at work in the emphases on 'not being a fan'. Later on in the interview, I asked her if she thought Hepburn's style still affected her own: 'I don't suppose so, I mean, as I've said to you, I don't go by fashion, I wear what I *like* and what I think *suits* me. Whether it's in fashion or not. That's why I'm still wearing clothes now that I bought when I was nineteen.'

In the pilot interviews, the idea of 'wearing what suited you' – in which a discourse of individuality is central – emerged as significant across the accounts of those women who identified their period of fashionable, youthful femininity more closely with the late 1950s than the 1960s. As I discuss below, this periodisation which relates to 'style' as opposed to 'fashion' also operated across the main study.

Earlier, in response to a question about the stars liked by her friends, Janet had told me that she did not go to the cinema or talk about films with friends or in a group – she placed emphasis on her cinema-going and interest in films as a solitary activity which was not shared by her peer group. Similarly, when I offered my understanding that Hepburn was very popular with young women of her generation, she immediately countered this with, 'There was another film star that I used to like, that – wasn't at all like Audrey Hepburn, and that was a film star called Loretta Young, which you wouldn't – probably never heard of'. A resistance to being identified as part of a group is clearly discernible in this comment – certainly the notion of individuality is key here. One of the central things I learned through the process of interviewing was that offering phrases like 'influence' and 'role model' as ways into talking about women's relationships with stars was unproductive. Talking about

Hepburn's short hair, for instance, Liz offered 'I think it was more like mine', rather than 'I had mine like hers'. In this way, she is able to construct herself, through Hepburn, as 'different' in a way which is satisfying because that difference is located in herself, before it is located in Hepburn: it is not about 'role models', 'copying' or 'being influenced by'. As I discuss in Chapter 2, Hepburn was a star around and through whom a similar discourse of individuality circulated, and this may have been key to her appeal for some young women. That very discourse may paradoxically make it difficult to discuss the relationship between the star and women to whom she appealed. When eventually Janet did begin to talk about liking Audrey Hepburn, her account fluctuated continually between a characterisation of her relationship to the star as one of direct influence, and a denial of this in favour of an idea of shared taste and physical features (cf. Stacey 1994: 161), or even coincidence. She began by telling me:

> Janet: Obviously she must have had some . . . sort of lasting effect on my thinking, because I was always told that I looked like her, the way that I used to – when I got older – the way that I used to do my hair and the clothes I used to wear . . . so . . .
> RM: How much older?
> Janet: Oh – quite a lot. When I was in my early twenties, and even when I was in my late twenties, because I was the same sort of build as she is – *was* – is – whatever.

She went on to tell me that the clothes she married in were 'exactly the same sort of clothes as she used to wear', admitting that this was a conscious, deliberate choice. Recognising similarities of build and hairstyle between herself and the star, and remembering being told that she looked like Audrey Hepburn, she continued in a way which suggests the complexity of the relationship between female star and female spectator: 'I don't know whether it was because I used to dress and wear my hair the way that I did that made me look like her, or whether . . . I did anyway. I don't know.' The direction of influence and appeal is anything but simple, and again, the indeterminacy of the term 'resonance' seems appropriate here, with its suggestion of recognition, pattern and harmony. This is not to suggest that the relationship is a straightforward or even a conscious or readily acknowledged one. Again, Janet insisted that she couldn't remember very much about Hepburn – only the things that were important to her: 'Well, I've told you – I mean, the fact that obviously I'd got some sort of . . . *rapport* with her, because she was the same build as I was, and we'd got similar sort of features, and I obviously built on it, didn't I?' Later, the same complex relationship was reiterated around a specific instance:

> I think the outfit that made the most impression on me, was probably the one that prompt – well, I mean, it wasn't done intentionally – I didn't go out looking for a wedding outfit that looked like an outfit that Audrey Hepburn wore, but it just turned out that the one I picked, was very like the outfit that she wore in that film that she was in with Cary Grant [*sic*]. Where she was a princess . . .

Similarly, when I asked if Hepburn's style had affected her own, Caroline told me:

> *Yes*, I would – whether she – whether her style has affected me, or whether I just *liked* that style and therefore – you don't know which comes first, really, or whether . . . it was coincidence that I happened to like that style, and therefore the outfits I've tended to buy – but even now, yes, I'm just thinking, you know, I go for a very plain, tailored look, now.

Janet went on to describe in detail the similarities and differences between her own wedding outfit and the dress worn by Hepburn in *Roman Holiday*. The main interviews repeatedly offered examples of the kind of detailed talk and joyful memories in relation to dress that had come through so powerfully in the pilot study focused specifically around dressmaking – perhaps suggesting that this kind of skilled gaze and detailed memory is not linked *exclusively* to this practice. As I argue elsewhere, this gendered, detailed gaze is a culturally produced competency related, for instance, to the aesthetics of girls and women's magazines (Moseley 2000). Furthermore, it has also been suggested that memory can be understood as 'gendered' (Leydesdorff, Passerini and Thompson 1996: 1; Schor 1987), in the sense that gendered experience produces different qualities of memory; the kind of detailed memory and talk about dress I encountered during this research is indeed also suggestive of certain gendered competences in looking. Bourdieu's notion of habitus as a set of dispositions, as a 'practical sense' and 'a feel for the game' (1990, 66), re-read by Toril Moi (1991) and Beverley Skeggs (1997) in relation to gender, is useful here. I would add that if we exist in the social field as necessarily gendered individuals, then a notion of gendered habitus can be understood as the process of learning to be a social woman (or man) part of which is the acquisition of attributes and dispositions which are socioculturally gendered feminine (or masculine) and which enable us to 'play the game' effectively. The kind of detailed looking, talking and remembering I suggest here can be usefully conceptualised in this way.

Style, 'the look' and 'being a girl' in the 1950s and 1960s

In the pilot study a significant periodisation was discernible in talk about dress, distinguishing those women who identified more closely with the late 1950s from those who saw themselves as having grown up in the 1960s. This was suggestive of the shift from a notion of stylish dress for the 'young adult' to a simpler idea of 'young' fashion with the move into the 1960s and 'youth culture'. Furthermore, the idea that the 1960s could be more clearly associated with the idiosyncrasies of fashion, rather than an objective notion of 'good style' identified with the 1950s, came through in this material. '1950s' young women operated through a discourse of style and individuality, and '1960s' girls through fashion and an idea of 'the look' in which shared feminine culture and girlfriends played an important role. This periodisation was also a feature of the interviews in the main study.

Perhaps predictably, the accounts of those women who crossed both periods were especially interesting. While Liz, for instance, talked about 'good cut' and what was 'fitting' to wear as a young woman starting work, she shifts to talking about fashion and 'the look' in relation to her later teens and early twenties and the youth culture of the mid-1960s. Her reference to fashion icon Twiggy at this point as another 'boyish' figure she aspired to is emblematic, in some ways, of the shift. Janet, who identified more closely with the tailored styles popular in the 1950s, denied an interest in mass-produced 'fashion', as I note above, in favour of what she perceived as an individuality of style – what suited her, what was a good fit: 'They looked as if they're made for *you*. They look as if they are *yours*, they fit *your* figure' (pilot interview).

Both Liz and Bernie talked explicitly about the overwhelming mood of optimism that characterised the post-war period in Britain; Liz linked what she describes as a sense of the 'opening up of possibilities' explicitly to clothes, and to the desire to be different. She described dress as 'A sort of, *sign* of being, well, moving on, and being different from your parents' generation', and having your own style. Bernie expressed the excitement of that moment after the war when 'things started to look up, your parents, things started to . . . to get *good*'; she associated this with a 'slight loosening of the rigid rules' which is linked to the explosion of American youth culture in Britain in this period.

Ang and Hermes in 'Gender and/in media consumption', however, warn against making over-simplified and reductive analyses which do not account for inconsistencies and contradictions (1991: 315). Subtleties of generation and historical period were not the only factors at play in these women's memories of dressing female in the 1950s and 1960s. It is interesting, for instance, that Barbara, who from the points of reference she offers in discussion in some ways identifies more strongly with the 1960s than the 1950s, nevertheless talks about dress in a way which suggests a residue of the 'fitted' dress and 'matching bag, gloves and shoes' discourse of 1950s feminine style than the youth-oriented fashion/look of the 1960s. Telling me how she used to make all her own clothes, she remembered, 'Yeah – I suppose my, I was more into the, I was the more classic look, well, you could – at my age, you couldn't get the classic styles, if you went to the class – they were old, for older women, so I would, I would adapt it, and then, and make my own patterns and things'. Barbara's understanding here of the 'classic' styles she preferred as 'for older women' precisely suggests the periodisation I offer above; as I suggest in chapters 4 and 5, she was clearly much less invested in the youth culture of the 1960s than other women of her generation who contributed to this research, and more concerned with producing herself in terms of a more conventionally 'proper' femininity. Subjectivity is formed and decisions made in relation to a multitude of factors including generation, gender, social class, regionality, relationships and individual psychology. In Barbara's case, it was clear that her relationship with her mother had played a major part in the investments she makes around personal style. Whatever the specificities of each case, it is clear across the accounts I gathered in this study that not every woman could afford socially to 'be a girl' in terms of dress and demeanour in the historical sense of the word – for some women, it may have been more important to remain a 'young lady'. For instance, it is often imperative that working-class women produce themselves as 'respectable' in this way (cf. Skeggs 1997). As I argue in Chapter 5, for those women taking part in the study who experienced social changes and shifts in status in this period, dressing 'appropriately' was paramount. For some, then, there was clearly more labour – physical and emotional – involved in producing an acceptably feminine self in this period than for others who were able to embrace more openly the 'freer' femininities of the 1960s. Hepburn's image, as we will see, was flexible enough to offer and enable both.

Talking about Audrey

In the pilot interviews about dressmaking I looked closely at the kind of talk which was generated around questions of dress and identity between female researcher and interviewee – the shared repertoires and negotiations which made the process so enjoyable on both sides. I want to make a brief observation about the modes of response I encountered in the main body of interviews. Generally, our discussions were characterised by an intimate, almost confessional mode of talk, in which personal issues and stories were spontaneously shared. The majority of the women who spoke to me shared my social background, as women who grew up working-class but in many cases had shifted class through education, work, marriage, or a combination of all three. The interviews with Liz and Rosie, for instance – both women academics working in the field of cultural studies and cultural/film studies respectively who had grown up working-class but shifted through education – often operated on a more critically sophisticated register than other discussions. It was notable, though, that both discussions were also characterised by the same kind of detailed, intimate talk as interviews with women who had not shifted, or had not shifted through education.

For many of the women who spoke to me about liking Audrey Hepburn in the 1950s and 1960s, films and the cinema were not the primary site of access to her image. Rather, Hepburn is remembered by them as having been available largely through women's and film magazines. Liz's comments were interesting in this respect – she remembered Hepburn as featured not only in these sites but also in dressmaking pattern catalogues.[6] While this might not be the case (as she in fact indicated), as I suggest above, 'mistakes' of this kind are extremely revealing – and in this case not only suggest the centrality of Hepburn's 'look' in stylistic terms, but also hint at the importance of dressmaking as a practice around Hepburn and other stars. Indeed

Janet, while an avid cinema-goer in this period, could remember almost nothing about Hepburn's films, but was able to offer detailed accounts of her look and of the similar clothes she made herself.

Audrey Hepburn was repeatedly remembered in these interviews through the idea of key 'moments'. Rosie stated this quite explicitly, as did Bernie. 'She was – always struck – she always left you with . . . a vision. It was always – whatever film – there would be . . . a little vignette, somehow or another, in the whole, you'd come away with something.' This is something akin to the form of memory also noted by Jackie Stacey in *Star Gazing*, who terms it 'iconic' and relates this to what she understands as the central importance for women of 'being an image'. Some of the women I spoke to did remember Hepburn in precisely the way Stacey describes, focusing on the details of dress; Bernie, for instance, remembered Hepburn in *Breakfast at Tiffany's* 'flouncing out of some apartment, and she's got this hat on ... outrageous! But fabulous'.

Similarly, Caroline recalled Hepburn 'as Holly Golightly wrapped in a towel. Which is probably a stereotypical reaction!' Her comment here perhaps points to the way in which memories of stars who have become cultural icons are inflected by widely circulating images of them. At the same time, the words she uses are common to many accounts: Hepburn is often remembered *as* Holly Golightly, *as* Eliza Doolittle, but also as 'the princess', as 'a nun' – as living characters, but also as ideals of femininity. What is more, the moments through which Hepburn is often recalled are frequently moments of activity – as in the example above. Two such moments, for example, are Hepburn whizzing round Rome on a scooter, and the scene in which as the princess in *Roman Holiday* she put her hand in the 'mouth of truth', both recalled by Rosie and Bernie. While Bernie remembers that this moment was 'unscripted' and links this to what she describes as Hepburn's 'naturalness', Rosie mentioned both of these as something she would like to do if she found herself in Rome: 'I always wanted to zip round Rome on a little motor scooter, and see all these things, you know, and I'm sure I would sort of go to that point and try and stick my hand in that, you know . . . mouth in the sculpture on the wall.' Rosie particularly remembered the moment from *Breakfast at Tiffany's* where Hepburn sings 'Moon River', and while as we talked I simply associated this scene with the television mourning of Hepburn's death, Rosie's comments on this scene were insightful:

I think actually it might be – that sort of might be how I'm thinking about it now . . . I think it was just like a combination of . . . the point it got to in the film in terms of emotions – the fact that I always responded emotionally to that particular music anyway . . . I just thought it was – for a film where she isn't honest, throughout most of it, it's moment of honesty. [RM: Oh right, I see, it is] And you know, and I always – it always used to really upset me, that she wasn't who I thought she was, or she was constructing this idea – I just always wanted her to be, sort of, truthful . . . and I think, I think, as a small child as I probably was, I just didn't quite understand it. I really, I liked her, so I liked to watch it, *but* it was sort of 'I don't quite understand' you know, why she's sort of left this situation, why she's doing all these fantastic things and she hasn't got the money, and you know, she's changed her background, and she's forgotten everything, and it sort of seeped in on a level that, I think, you know, maybe uncomfortable with her as a character. That you know, she had to, sort of win me over again.

In contrast to the inscription of interiority around Hepburn's characters in the films I discuss above, in *Breakfast at Tiffany's*, our *lack* of access to Holly's subjectivity and her isolation is formally marked by the repeated device of a screen which prevents her from being clearly seen separating her from the other characters in a scene, and us from her. In Paul's apartment, she is seen through a hanging room divider which both separates her from Paul and us, and at the same time reflects the constant references in the film to Holly as a caged 'wild thing' – a state, it is suggested, she has brought upon herself. She talks to Paul through the mirror – a repeated device which suggests the difficulty of working out where the 'real' Holly might be found – as suggested in the description of Holly as a 'real phoney' at her cocktail party. Asleep next to Paul, she is again seen through the screen, but as she begins to dream about her brother Fred and a reprise of the 'Moon River' theme comes in there is a cut to a closer shot which moves beyond this barrier. This refrain is a sign, throughout the film, of the 'real' Holly, and the words (and indeed the fact that she sings it on a fire escape) are significant: 'Moon River, wider than a mile, I'm crossing you in style, someday', reflecting the shift in identity and status she has made before the film begins, and her aspirations to move onwards and upwards.

The moments chosen by the women in my study, then, are emblematic of those aspects of Hepburn as a star which are particularly significant – resonant – in that person's understanding of her, and which may also emerge as important in that person's self-narration –

in their understanding of the construction of their own identity. As Janet put it: 'I've just taken out things from it, that were important to me, haven't I?'

Hepburn is understood in these accounts as overwhelmingly natural and authentic: she is seen to always be 'herself'. The discourse of transparency to which I drew attention in Chapter 2 is echoed in these interviews; for instance, Bernie told me, 'That was another thing about her – I never felt . . . she was act – I always felt she was being herself, I never felt she was ac – she, she was *play*ing a character, I appreciate *that* [. . .] she was just *so* natural. *So* natural'. At a later point she returns to this quality she perceives in Hepburn: 'And she . . . you know – she would look at the camera – if she was talking to the camera she was talking to you, and her eyes – you know – she looked straight at you – just, sort of, the whole . . . everything was up front, hiding nothing, and I think she was just wonderful.' Bernie links Hepburn's 'naturalness' to the transparency of her image through her performance style here, emphasising her eyes, which are a key signifier of her characters' honesty, integrity and naturalness across her films. Similarly, Barbara links this to her understanding of Hepburn as innocent: 'It was – I think it was her pure innocence, wasn't it. She was – what you saw *on* the screen, was what she was *off* screen – that was her. She never pretended to be an actress, she never put a face on, she never – *that* was *her*.' Clearly, this is related to the way in which several of the women I spoke to understood Hepburn to be different from other stars in the sense that her private life was never part of her image – there is no 'gossip' or scandal attached to her. For instance, there was often surprise when I offered stories of Hepburn's broken marriages: while Caroline imagined her to have been married to the same person for many years, Janet insisted that magazines like *Picturegoer* never featured information on Hepburn's domestic and romantic life (they frequently did). Her image seems so powerful that certain elements are filtered out: 'Because you never heard, you never heard of any scandal attached to her, *ever*, like you did with all the others, and I think that is probably what set her apart. I can't ever remember her being associated with any men, at all' (Janet). Certainly, this is linked to the way in which Hepburn is so often described as innocent in these accounts, and understood as 'nice'.

Hepburn is also understood in these accounts to be both ordinary and special. While Bernie knows that in *Breakfast at Tiffany's*

Hepburn wore an exclusive and expensive Givenchy wardrobe, nevertheless stylistically it seemed 'obtainable' to her as a young woman, largely through her understanding of Hepburn as ordinary: 'She made you feel, oh, I don't know, it was just a lovely, *comfortable* . . . I know it sounds ever so daft, you know Lady Di? [RM: Yes –] It was that same sort of . . . Yes . . . You fel . . . she was very . . . *ordinary*. Do you know what I mean? . . . Just – *ordinary*.' She is often referred to using phrases such as 'she was one of the girls' – and the younger women in this study often referred to her as Audrey, and sometimes as 'Our Aud'. As Richard Dyer has pointed out, the combination of ordinariness and specialness is a key element of stardom (Dyer 1979: 49), but in these accounts of Hepburn the sense that she is both ordinary and herself produces a closeness to her which is diametrically opposed to the rhetoric of untouchability which pervades the small body of (largely male-authored) critical writing I discuss in Chapter 2. The impression of familiarity and intimacy which characterises both the oral accounts of Hepburn presented here, and writing about her by women academics, appears to be based in a sense of shared cultural competency – an understanding of certain discourses of femininity which is exemplary of the notion of gendered habitus I suggest above. While there was often a sense of the difficulty of saying anything concrete about Hepburn – summed up in phrases like 'I don't know, she was just . . .', in fact the interviews revealed that the women I spoke to had a very precise sense of why they liked Audrey Hepburn, and this was articulated through extremely detailed talk about the production of femininity, of self, and of the practices through which this was achieved. Barbara, for example, told me about an edition of *Style Challenge* (BBC1, 1996–98) she had recently seen on which they attempted to create an Audrey Hepburn look:

Barbara: Young – Audrey Hepburn eyes, the big eyes, yeah . . . But I
    didn't think they succeeded, *at all*.
RM: Did you not?
Barbara: No I didn't [RM: Why?], no. Because her outfit – she just
    wasn't . . . it wasn't.
RM: Tell me about it – what they did –
Barbara: I can't, I can't remember what she wore, but I know at the
    time, I know at the time . . . 'cos I was working away, and they said
    – oh, they wanted to do her with Audrey Hepburn eyes, I thought,
    no, they've got that wrong.

RM: How'd they got it wrong –

Barbara: I mean there was the eyeliner, and, wasn't there – they used to do the eyeliner with the flicks at the side, and they did them *straight*. [RM: Oh, did they?!] And I don't think they – I don't know whether it was . . . it just wasn't *her*, it wasn't right – [RM: But, I mean, you just know by looking –] I think they put too much pencil underneath, or something – it wasn't – they didn't have it right.

RM: She didn't really have it underneath –

Barbara: No, it was more on the top, wasn't it, than underneath –

RM: Mascara and her, and her . . . eyebrows.

Barbara: That's right – more above than under – and I think they did it more *under*, they did it more like Dusty Springfield – with the big black kohl eyes – which it wasn't like that *at all* – no, but I was interested that they – that they picked it up, they were going to use it.

This is an excellent illustration of the very particular way in which women are trained to look at the construction of femininity; Barbara has a very detailed knowledge of the distinction and periodisation of different make-up looks ('flicks' versus 'straight' eyeliner), and indeed, memory of the programme itself. This is not to say that all women look in this way, of course, but for women who are invested in producing themselves as feminine in particular ways, an eye trained for detail is essential, and is produced by years of close scrutiny of images in films, on television and in magazines. Furthermore, Barbara confirmed my sense that the 'magic' of a moment of transformation such as that in which Holly gets ready to go to Sing Sing in *Breakfast at Tiffany's* may be negotiated by this kind of detailed understanding and closeness to the image (see Chapter 2): 'But she's put together perfectly, yeah, it's all the little – it all comes together. [RM: It all happens] Very quickly. [RM: Very] Now if I did that, you know, it would take about two hours' planning!'

Janet, in particular, gave extremely detailed examples of the dresses she made which were like those worn by Hepburn. Dressmaking emerged as a key practice around Hepburn particularly, but also more generally, across all the accounts of this period – the main body of interviews as well as the pilot study. The simplicity of the styles worn by Audrey Hepburn meant that they could be made at home with reasonable ease. Adapting store-bought clothes was another way in which looks which were desired but were unavailable (literally or economically) were achieved. The interviews are full of wonderful stories of hunting and shopping for exactly the right clothes. Rosie, for instance, told me how she managed to get some flat black Audrey Hepburn-style shoes to fit her large feet – she bought Vietnamese men's pumps from a market in Paris. In the pilot study, Helen told me a similar story of having to buy costly ballet shoes which weren't designed to be worn outside to achieve the look. I found out about going to the hairdresser's – and the labour involved in maintaining particular looks; while Barbara, who was a hairdresser, explained to me how in practice one lived with the hair-pieces which were fashionable in the late 1950s and early 1960s (by going to bed with the head wrapped in toilet paper!), Bernie told me how she and her friends washed their underskirts in sugar water and dried them over an umbrella in the garden to get the desired effect. While for the most part this is a study about Audrey Hepburn, through talk about this well-loved star the research generated exciting historically, nationally and often class-specific material on many aspects of feminine culture and the production of femininities in the 1950s and 1960s. Sadly, it is impossible to include much of this wonderful material here.

Audrey Hepburn is often constructed through discussion of other female stars of the period – I discuss her relation to the Monroe/ Bardot axis in Chapter 4. However, she is also frequently discussed alongside or even on occasions confused with stars such as Leslie Caron and Katharine Hepburn.[7] Through the association with Caron in these accounts, Hepburn is produced as embodying a certain waif-like, balletic 'Frenchness' – a Frenchness which is precisely not the Frenchness of Brigitte Bardot, for instance. Through Katharine Hepburn, a connection is made between trouser-wearing and feminine elegance, modernity, strength and independence. It is interesting to note, furthermore, that Audrey Hepburn is often characterised in terms of both strength and frailty (often simultaneously), and that this understanding of her is common across generational, if differentiated, lines in this study. For instance, while Barbara, who as I suggest in Chapter 4 has particular investments in delicate, 'old-fashioned' femininities, reads Hepburn's performance in *Wait Until Dark* (Terence Young 1967) largely in terms of her frailty and vulnerability (as a blind woman under attack in her own home), only hinting at the fact that 'it doesn't matter if she's in the dark', Rosie, by contrast, places great emphasis on her ingenuity, and her saving of herself: 'Because she knew every, every piece of furniture, every pathway through – she was very independent, which I think I always liked about her as well – she just took all the light bulbs out, and turned the electricity off so when he came after her in the dark, she was actually in control and he wasn't.' In many ways Hepburn can be understood to reconcile contradictions in exactly the way Richard Dyer suggests is key to stardom (Dyer 1991).

While mother–daughter relationships may be significant generally in women's accounts of growing up, as mothers are a structuring absence in Hepburn's films – she is definitely a 'daddy's girl' – the centrality of mother–daughter stories in interviews about her have an interesting compensatory status. Mothers (and in one case a father) are formative figures in the majority of these accounts. Women often remembered coming to Audrey Hepburn for the first time through sharing a love of musicals with their mothers, for instance, or in the case of the younger women, through watching old films on television together. Dressmaking was another shared activity, and the role played by mothers and aunts in passing on skills and knowledge about femininity to their daughters was clear. Rosie, for instance, remembered hunting with her aunt for exactly the right shade of black fabric with which to make a pair of Audrey Hepburn trousers to match a black sweater for a family celebration; she also recalled having jewellery placed on her by her great-aunt as a finishing touch to this outfit – emblematic of this 'passing on' of skills and tastes from older to younger women. The importance of the skilled, professional gaze of another woman was a key feature of the pilot study. In Barbara's case, this was a more difficult memory; her mother's attempts to impose femininity on her daughter are clearly remembered with some discomfort and resentment.

'Oh, please God – let it happen to me!'[8]

Lisa Starks (1997), critical of what she describes as the 'Pygmalion film' – particularly *My Fair Lady* – and hostile to films which foreground women's relationship with dress and towards the 'cute but rather silly'(53) Hepburn, has argued of *Sabrina* that the protagonist's

> metamorphosis does not seem to extend much beyond a new look and self-confidence in her physical attractiveness; Sabrina seems just as child-like upon her return than she did before her two years abroad. What Paris has taught her is, of course, how to wear her hair, how to shop, and how to accessorize to project the image of a sophisticated,

elegant woman of leisure. Apparently, these skills are all our 1950s
Sabrina needs to elevate her station in life.

(51)

Starks here disregards the potential emotional resonance of narratives which dramatise the complex and significant relationship
between women and dress. As I discuss in Chapter 5, the transformation scenario looms large in feminine culture and experience.
At the beginning of our discussion, Barbara remembered Audrey
Hepburn in *My Fair Lady*:

> Barbara: I mean she was just . . . she was just the perfect image, it was
> just how – she was just perfect for the part, and her whole image just
> bowled me over, and I think – I suppose I can remember when I was
> tiny . . . I was always . . . I don't know, I was always – I always felt I
> wasn't . . . right – something was always wrong – I was a bit plump,
> or – you know [RM: Mmm], or I wasn't – I didn't act properly, and
> I'd – you'd got to sit correctly, and you'd got to close your legs when
> – and mum was always – you know, I mean, she gave me this great
> big folder of . . . erm . . . beauty tips.
>
> RM: Your mum did?
>
> Barbara: Yes, yeah – [puts on haughty voice] 'Now this is what you
> should –' – you know. So I'd sort of got – I always felt totally inad-
> equate, totally, you know, out of place [RM: Yes], and then, when I
> saw her being transformed from this – so that's why I suppose – I
> liked the play at school, but then when I actually – when you see it
> visually on the film, she was [laughs shortly] transformed from this,
> sort of, guttersnipe, wasn't she? [RM: Yes] From this little flower
> person . . . to this very . . . *beautiful*, stunning – and I suppose that
> image – that was it – Audrey Hepburn. She was – magic.

Barbara's story is framed by her recollection of not living up to a
particular mode of femininity. Towards the end of the interview she
returns to this, remembering how her mother disapproved of her
liking other stars such as Marlene Dietrich and Eartha Kitt, who
were representative of a type of femininity that was completely
unacceptable: 'I suppose it all goes back to what – my mum saying I
was frumpy, and I was a lump, and then you see this very *elegant
lady* and this – I just *wish* I could always be.' Audrey Hepburn in *My
Fair Lady* represented something that she wanted to be: 'I mean,
from everything, from, you know – she's just – total make-over, isn't
it, from talking, you know, to be able to speak like her, as well, to
talk properly, nice, you know, and everything, yeah.' Barbara would

go on to become professionally involved in the production of femininity, running a hairdressing salon and taking part in competitions
across Britain. Her account is suggestive both of the appeal of the
transformation scenario, the relationship between dress and subjectivity, but also the significance of the conjunction of class and gender
in relation to this. I discuss the question of dress and status in relation to the Cinderella motif through which Hepburn and accounts
of her are structured in Chapter 5.

Text and audience: resonance and address

How, then, can we theorise the relationship between text and audience – the way audiences relate to and respond to texts? In pointing
to this complex structuring of both star-text and audience account by
the same motif – the articulation of subjectivity through dress – I
want to bring together the notion of gendered address which I
discuss in the previous chapter and the idea of a resonance or recognition between such an address and the lived experience and/or
memory of the audience member.[9] In that respect this chapter can be
understood as a bridge between Chapter 2 which elaborates that
address in the star-text Audrey Hepburn, and chapters 4 and 5 which
present and discuss accounts of taking up that address: doing the
Hepburn look. In giving those accounts, the women who took part
in this study told their own histories, structuring their stories around
significant events and outfits, and it is here that the notion of resonance comes into play. It is the resonance of that relationship
between dress and subjectivity in a particular form – the Cinderella
motif which structures both 'Audrey Hepburn' and audience
accounts – which is the focus of Chapter 5, suggesting the difficulty
of satisfactorily extracting any idea of 'text' from 'audience'. The
relationship between them seems both structured, but at the same
time essentially emotional or affective. It is a question both of the
structuring of subjectivity in discourse, habitus in the Bourdieuian
sense, and investment, but the relationship is also complicated by
the process of remembering, by emotion and experience. If we
understand the text 'Audrey Hepburn' as discursively produced, and
subjectivity as structured in discourse, then it is possible to see the
text as simultaneously constitutive of and working to engage female
subjectivities. It is in trying to understand the nature of this relationship between text and audience member that the terms resonance and

recognition are so useful. 'Resonance' is suggestive of the 'back and forth' movement between the two (as Penny Summerfield (1998: 15) suggests, between 'the voice that speaks for itself, but also the voices that speak to it') – a kind of perpetual 'this is mine, this is me'. In a similar way, 'recognition' might be understood as the reactivation in memory of earlier moments of the constitution of that subjectivity, in the face of the replaying of those moments in texts. This might be a way of understanding how 'gendered' texts engage subjects; for instance if one key way in which female subjectivity is constituted discursively is in relation to dress, and one of the ways in which this happens is textual, then in the confrontation between a thus constituted subject and, for instance, 'Audrey Hepburn', a star around whom this discourse is firmly inscribed, there is a moment of resonance, recognition and engagement: 'This is me, this is mine.' In a study such as this, memory may play a key part in the process, and in the interviews, stories are told which then again replay the constitution of the subject, through this establishing a composed and acceptable self (Summerfield 1998: 16). This may be especially important in this study in relation to the notions of feminine respectability and acceptability that repeatedly re-emerge. 'Resonance and recognition' as a way of understanding what may go on in the encounter between audiences and texts is a then a shifting and refracted, rather than a rigidly determined relation, perhaps best described by Raymond Williams's term 'structure of feeling' (Williams 1977).

Audrey Hepburn emerges from the stories I was told during this research as an ideal femininity: the perfect nun, princess and even the perfect bride (although as I discuss in Chapter 5, the relationship of Hepburn's characters to marriage and domesticity is far from simple). At the same time, she is understood as having represented a femininity that was largely attainable, in social and economic terms, and which offered a way to be which was simultaneously different and acceptable. In the next two chapters, which consider the material generated in the main body of interviews, I consider these aspects of Hepburn's appeal for young women growing up in the 1950s and 1960s, and in Chapter 6, for young women in the 1990s.

Notes

1 The film announces its 'realism' in these terms in the opening credit sequence: 'This film was photographed and recorded in its entirety in Rome, Italy.'

2   See figure 4.1: Paper pattern for 'Audrey in *Roman Holiday*' style
    pyjamas.
3   'Let's not buy her anything too flowery,' says Higgins to Pickering. 'I
    despise those gowns with weeds here and weeds there – we want to buy
    her something – sort of simple, and modest and elegant, is called for,
    perhaps with a bow . . . '
4   I would argue also that Bruzzi's claim (1997: 6) that one of the results
    of Hepburn's screen relationship with Givenchy is that *couture* cos-
    tume became more intrusive, that it 'no longer had to remain sub-
    servient to character', is significantly complicated by this kind of
    understanding of Hepburn's image and its relationship to dress.
5   Mary Ann Doane has argued in relation to the woman's film of the
    1940s that the particularly strongly marked address to the female
    viewer in these films makes them a privileged site for the exploration
    of the inscription of female subjectivity (Doane 1987: 3). While Hep-
    burn's films are not 'women's films' in the precise historical sense of
    Doane's study, I would argue that the strong feminine address of her
    image, and the discourse of authenticity which is a key element in it
    makes these films interesting in relation to the formal inscription of
    subjectivity around Hepburn as a star. Indeed, *Kinematograph Weekly*
    emphasised of *Roman Holiday*: 'Excellent general booking and a mar-
    vellous woman's film . . . Grab it at all costs!' (20 August 1953).
6   One respondent to my letter in *Sewing with Butterick* sent me a number
    of her old dressmaking patterns from this period, those which for her
    were particularly suggestive of Audrey Hepburn (See figure 4.1).
7   This kind of confusion is most evident in letters and questionnaires
    where there is no possibility of two-way conversation. In one case I
    received a follow-up letter from a woman who had written a long letter
    about Katharine Hepburn, and suddenly realised her mistake.
8   Barbara remembers how she felt on first seeing *My Fair Lady*.
9   I use the term subjectivity rather than identity to suggest a sense of the
    discursive constitution of the subject in and through discourse (see
    Chapter 1) – in this case the constitution of female subjectivity through
    discourses of femininity such as these which emphasise dress and
    deportment. Equally, it is essential to retain a notion of *investment* in
    such discursive positions.

Chapter 4

Doing the 'Hepburn look'

'I used to think, "Oh, I could almost sort of manage that" because she was sort of slightly boyish, but terribly feminine'.

(Rosie)

Chapter 2 explored the ways in which Audrey Hepburn as image-text, through film, publicity and extra-cinematic material from sources such as women's magazines, can be understood to address a feminine audience. The mobilisation of discourses conventionally associated with women's culture, such as the narrative of fashionable transformation and the Cinderella scenario, can be understood to work simultaneously to constitute and engage feminine subjectivities. In the chapters which follow I draw on audience accounts of Hepburn to explore the ways in which that address is taken up, producing Hepburn as an ideal of fashionable femininity which is both practicable and socially appropriate from the 1950s to the 1990s. In every discussion I had with women who liked Hepburn in the 1950s and 1960s, her 'look' was a continual point of reference for their recollections about growing up in that period. Thus it was predominantly through talk about dress and 'doing the Hepburn look' in practice that subjectivity was articulated, that the women who spoke to me told themselves and their personal histories. At the same time, through their understandings of that look, their stories of 'doing' it – through shopping, adapting garments, dressmaking, grooming – and using it for themselves, 'the Hepburn look' emerged as a particularly rich site through which complex ideas about femininity, modernity, national identity, class and generation were being articulated. As Pam Cook has convincingly argued in *Fashioning the Nation* (1996) in relation to film costume, clothes are key markers of identity – national, sexual, gendered, ethnic – and also of its potential fluidity and instability.

I consider this interview material in detail here, beginning with the varied yet structured ways in which Hepburn's look is understood in relation to femininity. The accounts consistently produced stories about achieving 'the look' and its attainability, and I go on in this chapter to look at those narratives, and the precise ways in which the look was used in practice – often as a means of negotiating the perceived gap between social propriety and a sense of self. I also draw upon textual analysis of a number of key Hepburn films and material from contemporary women's and film-fan magazines as a way of sketching in a discursive historical context. In the juxtaposition of these different sources and methods of analysis, significant contemporary discourses around femininity are brought to the fore.

Difference

Common to almost all of the accounts was an understanding of Audrey Hepburn as offering a femininity which was perceived as 'different' from other dominant modes available through the cinema, magazines and music at that moment. A primary way in which Hepburn's perceived 'difference' was articulated was through a rather complex understanding of Hepburn as 'boyish'. Liz, for instance, told me, 'I suppose that sort of slightly vulnerable look that she had, but also quite boyish, and I think that was the other, the other dimension that I really liked, and I still like, that kind of look'. Caroline similarly recalled:

> And I think what appealed to me about her, is her, her type of beauty, I think, I think that's what – I mean, obviously, knowing I was coming to talk to you about her, I thought, well, why is it I *do* like Audrey Hepburn, what is it about her, and I think it's her type of beauty, it's a sort of femininity that isn't *excessively* feminine, in that she's slightly an androgynous look . . . I like her sort of – I think at that age I wanted to be like her, I mean, if you look at me now, I'm probably a middle-aged, overweight version of her [laughs] – you know, the short dark hair, the sort of slightly boyish face, *ingénue*, gamin – that sort of person – and I loved the style of clothes that she used to wear – I think it's Givenchy? Or Courrèges, or something – [RM: Mmm, it was] yes – very understated, very firm, clear, clean lines, nothing *frilly* or fussy – although I know in *My Fair Lady* she wears . . . I'm thinking of in the scene where she goes back to, runs away to the mother, and she's in this lovely, sort of, chiffon – [RM: Cecil Beaton –] yes – lovely, but even then, she doesn't, it doesn't seem cluttered [RM: No] – I suppose

I would have liked to have been as thin as she was, but I never obtained that! [laughs]

Key here is the understanding of Hepburn's femininity as 'not frilly or fussy', but rather as pared down, even when, as in *My Fair Lady*, the mode of dress is more conventionally feminine. In such accounts, Hepburn's femininity has a simplicity which allows these women to understand her as both 'different' and yet at the same time acceptable in terms of hegemonic definitions of femininity. This is also key to the modernity of her look – Courrèges is cited here.[1] Significant, too, is the sense of distance between 'then', when this interviewee was a young woman, and the 'now' of the interview, which is suggestive of what Stacey describes in *Star Gazing* as the 'impossibility of femininity' (Stacey 1994: 66–7). However, also evident in this interviewee's account is a sense of achievement and similarity which is common to a number of other women's perceptions of their relationship with Hepburn. There appears to be something about Audrey which is precisely 'possible', even in the light of the distance between 'then' and 'now'.

In a similar way, Rosie talked about *Funny Face* in terms of Hepburn's different 'androgynous' look in the film:

Rosie: I don't particularly like it as a film, but I love *her* in it. [RM: Do you?] And I love her *style* in it.
RM: Her style of dress?
Rosie: Yeah – just like, sort of . . .
RM: Or of being?
Rosie: Both, both, definitely, but I always remember, she always seemed incredibly androgynous to me in that film, which I suppose was something I always found very attractive, or it was, you know, 'cos I'd never been very sort of . . . I'd never really understood, you know, make-up, femininity, clothes very much [RM: Yeah], but I used to think she was *wonderful*, and when I was sort of, younger, she was perhaps, I used to think, 'Oh, I could *almost* sort of manage that' because [RM: Yeah] she was sort of slightly boyish, but terribly feminine.

Liz and I began to discuss Hepburn's look around a photograph of her in an outfit from *Sabrina* on the cover of Barry Paris's biography (Paris 1998) which I had taken to the interview. An extract from this interview is reproduced in Appendix II (pp. 225–226), and I want to begin by commenting on this extended quotation, because it introduces a number of broader discourses and areas of interest which I will draw out from other discussions throughout the chapter. First, Liz's association of Hepburn with 'little flat shoes' was shared by Bernie and Rosie, and here begins a rich vein of associations which are discernible across a number of the interviews. She contrasts this explicitly here with the stiletto heels which the women around her and she herself wore at that time – a significant way in which Hepburn, then, was 'different' – so different, in fact, that Liz felt unable to step into those shoes until much later. As the conversation continues, it emerges that the stilettos are representative for Liz of a mode of 'excessive' femininity of which Audrey Hepburn – and a number of other film stars and female celebrities – were the antithesis, and to which indeed she aspired. The flat shoes worn by Hepburn and by Natalie Wood in *West Side Story* (Jerome Roberts 1961) are explicitly associated in this account with female mobility, action and freedom – 'she was *running* and *dancing*' – something that recurred towards the end of our discussion:

> But I think the other thing about her – when I – sort of, just looking at these pictures, is that she looks *balletic*. That's the other – [RM: Is it?] – because I think *ballet* was the one – now – you know, every little girl dreams of being a ballerina, and I remember being very struck by that, sort of, *dance*, and – [RM: were you?] yes – I never did it, 'cos my – my parents couldn't afford it – but it had that, sort of, female . . . I suppose, it was a way in which females could use their bodies [RM: Oh right . . .] – more expressively, and I think she had this look of that kind of – a kind of a ballerina.

The idea of female movement is common in discussion around Hepburn, and is frequently linked to her slenderness – to her body. Similarly, Caroline talked about the familiar (in both cases unfulfilled) feminine dream of being a dancer. We were discussing the films in which Hepburn danced:

> Caroline: And again, that's probably something why I like her, [much more quietly] I wanted to be, to do ballet, and I was quite tiny when I was small, and quite good at dancing, my ballet teacher wanted me to, you know, enter me in – sort of, my parents were anti it.
> RM: Oh –
> Caroline: [more loudly] And as it was I would have been too tall, and too fat. But I suppose there's always been a sort of, thwarted ballet dancer inside me, so I'm attracted to people that – look as if they're dancers.

Janet remembered being a similar build to Hepburn, but while she recalled feeling self-conscious about being flat-chested, she also offered her love of athletics, gymnastics and dancing as an explanation of her shape: 'I've never had hips, I haven't really now. I've never had them, but that didn't bother me, at all. And when you were as athletic as I used to be, I mean you just didn't have any spare flesh on you at all'. In these accounts, then, Hepburn is clearly associated with activity and movement; *Roman Holiday* appealed to Rosie because she 'always wanted to zip round Rome on a little motor scooter' and as she put it, 'there's an energy to her'.

As the comment by Liz above illustrates, this sense of energy and freedom is often tied, through a recourse to body shape and fashionable style, to an understanding of Hepburn's difference from the more conventional femininity of the time:

> Liz: I remember thinking that she was the, one of the film stars that I really th . . . sort of, identified with, because she wasn't like the other ones.
>
> RM: In what way?
>
> Liz: Well she appeared much younger, and I suppose I was quite young then, I mean I can remember really – I suppose in my early teens – thinking that she was the kind of woman I'd like to be [laughs], it was sort of, you know, she wasn't, she wasn't very . . . *glamorous* in a – in that conventional sort of 1950s way, which was what the other films stars were, and she was much less *curvaceous* – all the others were rather sort of – *large*, and [both laugh] which I didn't particularly like . . . and I always liked her *hair*.

The perceived difference of Audrey Hepburn from the feminine ideal of that moment comes through clearly here – these extracts begin to illustrate the way in which Hepburn takes on meaning through accounts of other female stars, as I discuss below. Here, though, Hepburn is explicitly contrasted to what is seen – and here experienced – to have been the dominant feminine ideal of the time – blonde hair and curvaceousness as a conventional notion of feminine glamour. The glamour represented by Hepburn for these women will emerge as something rather different. Hepburn's short hair was frequently offered as a point of appeal: Caroline remembers 'having this very stylish, *chic* . . . almost *boyish* look' herself, as does Rosie: 'I think, I think it was that, it was that blend between the sort of, androgyny . . . because she always had very short, or sort of, hair, which I, you know, I certainly had at that point.'

Similarly, Liz's account of Hepburn's short hair above emphasises its 'boyish' quality. She remembered how she had her hair cut short by her mother's friend and then went on to describe how she and her brother, who looked alike, were dressed alike, and how she was once mistaken for a boy at the age of twelve or thirteen:

> Liz: Yes – it was amusing, but it was quite – it was quite revealing, I think, as to what I looked like, and . . . at that . . . stage . . . But yes, *short* hair – I remember when I had my hair cut very *feathery* and short – the . . . the girls in the typing pool were . . . *nobody* was . . . had hair like that.
>
> RM: Really?
>
> Liz: Yes – it was – they were all very, sort of, *set* – they used to go to the hairdresser and have – you know – *perms* and rollered hair, and so on – I suppose it was slight rejection of that.
>
> RM: So you wouldn't have had to have had any of that done, once you'd had your hair cut short, would you?
>
> Liz: No – no, I didn't – I used to use – I remember using curling *tongs* at one point – just to get some 'lift' [laughs], but – no – it was – yes – it was quite unusual, I think. And there – you see, Audrey Hepburn, Una Stubbs and Petula Clark – to a certain extent, all had that kind of look.

Again, Hepburn's 'difference' comes through here – and Liz's use of the word 'set', to describe the hair of the women around her, although it is obviously a common hairdressing term – seems apt in the light of her earlier association of Hepburn's look with mobility and freedom. Similarly, Bernie's account of Audrey Hepburn's hair is fascinating, partly for the way in which it engages with my analysis in Chapter 2 of the star's short hairdo as a version of the 'small head' showcased in *Vogue*. This extract begins, as I discuss in Chapter 3, at the point where Bernie begins to talk about Hepburn in an extended way for the first time, and she remembers being amazed when she first saw Hepburn's short hair:

> RM: Was that quite different then, to have really short hair?
>
> Bernie: Ooh, *yes*.
>
> RM: Was it?
>
> Bernie: Yes, yes. I mean, prior to that, when I was *much* younger, the only time I can remember a girl having really short hair at school was 'cos she'd had nits or something awful, and she'd had it all . . . !
> [both laugh]
>
> RM: Oh right! So it was a bit of a stigma!

Bernie: And then we'd go to . . . The Gaumont . . . yes it was, she had
her hair cut very short. I'm trying to think, there was someone else
who had their hair cut very, very short . . . You see, some *models*, if
you like, in the early fifties, had their hair cut, but it wasn't . . . it was
still sort of, 'mumsy' – you'd see people my mother's age with that
haircut – well we didn't want *that*. And suddenly, this . . . fabulous
woman, this Audrey Hepburn, she'd got this very cropped . . .
RM: What was different about it then, from the women of your mum's
age?
Bernie: From her, her?
RM: Yeah, I mean what if, if they, I mean if she had, if they had short
hair – I mean, I'm really interested in that, that there's –
Bernie: It was almost boyi – the way she had it, it was almost like
boyish. It was *totally new* [emphasises each word]. Quite *daring*.
[. . .] But yes, it was quite the thing, it was *quite daring*, really. Terri-
bly *modern*.

Again, coming through strongly here is the difference of Hepburn's look, but the emphasis in this account is also on its modernity, its daring, its *newness*. Whereas in Chapter 2 I suggested the
similarity between Hepburn's look and earlier styles, this woman's
experience emphasises its distinctness, relating this to a generational
shift – Hepburn's short hair is not 'mumsy'. It is in this way that she
is able to construct herself in retrospect as a 'modern'. She goes on
immediately from this point to remembering this period as the
moment when young people had their own money and culture for
the first time. Having this 'modern' haircut meant breaking away
from your parents' generation, striking out, becoming an individual.

I want to make two main points about the rather lengthy quotes (it
is impossible to offer shortened extracts and still preserve the rich-
ness of this kind of talk). First, common to these accounts is a way of
understanding Hepburn which constructs her precisely in opposition
to notions of 'frilly', 'fussy' and 'excessive' femininity associated with
other female stars of the period, and within a discourse related to
modernism which emphasises 'clean lines' and simplicity. Caroline,
for instance, talked about *The Nun's Story* and Hepburn's association
with Givenchy: 'In a way, her habit, her nun's habit is almost as geometric and simple and elegant ... it is a very uncluttered femininity.'

Penny Sparke in *As Long As It's Pink* (1995) discusses the notion
of 'frilly femininity' which was in place in this period, contrasting
this to what she describes as the '"true" canon of aesthetic values of
the dominant culture'(3) a pared-down, minimalist modernism

which she associates with the masculine. Sparke offers Art Deco as 'a distinctly feminine version of the modern', the 'streamlined moderne' (127; see also Hebdige 1988). Anne Hollander (1978) relates this earlier modernism in feminine style – short hair, lean bodies – to movement: 'a vibrant, somewhat unaccountable readiness for action but only under expert guidance. This was naturally best offered in a self-contained, sleekly composed physical format: a thin body with few layers of clothing. . . . Women, once thought to glide, were now seen to walk' (153). In a sense, then, the alternative femininity which Hepburn represented for these women in the 1950s, her ability to be both feminine and boyish at the same time, might be seen similarly to offer a way into this legitimate aesthetic notion of 'good taste', without necessitating a complete relinquishment of the conventionally feminine.

Second and in relation to this, an understanding of Hepburn as offering a style which was both 'boyish' and 'feminine' at the same time was key to her significance for a number of the women who spoke to me, having made her 'look' both appealing, attainable and in most cases largely appropriate both socially and to the girls' own senses of themselves, as the epigraph to this chapter illustrates. Despite, or indeed because of the kind of different femininity Hepburn represents in these accounts, the femininity she embodies becomes hegemonic. It is precisely the possibility for this kind of negotiation within Hepburn's look which enables consent to be secured around it (see figure 4.1).

Being a girl

Bernie moved on from talking about the influence of Hepburn's style on her wedding dress, to thinking about more everyday looks. While for this woman Hepburn was associated with growing up, taking on responsibility, as I discuss in Chapter 3, her style simultaneously suggested freedom:

> Bernie: But when she wore casual things . . . it . . . it was *feminine*, but *tomboyish*. [. . .] *Yes*, you could – you had the *freedom* of – *putting* a pair of trousers on and jeans, and so you could . . . go riding your bike and *not* have to keep holding your frock down and all this crap –
> RM: Yeah! [laughs]
> Bernie: You know – 'cos I mean you could be as free as the lads, and

4.1 Boyish, but still a girl: Audrey-style paper pattern for pyjamas like those worn in *Roman Holiday*, supplied by a *Sewing with Butterick* correspondent

have a laugh, and run and do whatever we wan – you know what I mean – but still be . . . a *girl*.

RM: Yeah.

Bernie: And it – and it looked *nice*. It looked nice. I can remember us all – what we did was – with rolling these jeans up sometimes, we would sew gingham . . . so they'd be blue jeans, but the turn-ups would be, like pink and white gingham!

RM: A little 'girlie' . . . edge.

Bernie: Yes, and it was just a little . . . yes, that was just a . . .

RM: Touch –

Bernie: Yes, yes, yep.

RM: So would she be one of the people you'd associate with – you know, like the fact that you could wear trousers –

Bernie: But be . . .

RM: But be a girl?

Bernie: *Yes.*

RM: And have short hair, but –

Bernie: *Be a girl*, yes.

RM: And that was important to you?

Bernie: [at the same time] And all this . . . yes because, I mean, it was a pain in the arse, bloody washing your hair, and it took hours to dry. I mean we didn't *have hair*dryers – *I* didn't have a hairdryer.

This is a particularly rich extract: it brings out very well the shared understanding of Hepburn as both boyish and feminine, and at the same time is a wonderful instance of this aspect of the 'Hepburn look' in practice – edging a pair of turned-up jeans with pink and white gingham is a rather nice concrete example. In this case, the mode of femininity represented by this star offered a literal mobility and freedom which had previously been impossible within the constraints of more traditional 'frilly' feminine styles: 'you could . . . go riding your bike and *not* have to keep holding your frock down.' Coming through here too is the inconvenience and labour of maintaining this kind of femininity in contrast to the ease of the look Hepburn offered these young women – short hair was easy to care for. A hairdryer, perms and sets were unnecessary. Bernie had told me about a weekly magazine she used to read, which I subsequently discovered in the British Library and which became a rich source for investigating discourses around femininity in Britain in this period. *Mirabelle and Glamour* (4 July 1964) ran a story 'Good Old George', a 'Cinderella' narrative which similarly focuses on the process and negotiations entailed in 'becoming a girl'. 'George' is a tomboy mistaken for a boy by a boy she likes, and who decides 'to become a girl at last!' Her mother helps with her hair, dress and make-up but she falls down the stairs in her high heels – walking and talking 'feminine' are difficult: 'It was sheer murder trying to behave like a girl,' says George. Her new boyfriend likes her for not putting on airs and graces 'like other girls' (she is 'natural' like a boy, and different, but still definitely a girl). He changes her name to Gina and kisses her at the end of the dance: 'Now I really have made the Girl-grade – and I like that the best of all,' she says – the pay-off for the difficulty of the labour of becoming feminine. The negotiation in this story is exactly that expressed in the account given by Bernie above of the appeal of Hepburn's style. Her sense that this look meant that 'you could be as free as the lads, and have a laugh, and run and do whatever we wan – you know what I mean – but still be . . . a *girl*' is especially significant, for it underscores the way in which for this woman being 'like the lads' – having equal freedom and fun – is precisely not the same thing as being 'not feminine', not a girl. Edging your jeans with pretty fabric still 'looked nice' – it was tomboyish but with a feminine edge. Hepburn is understood to be boyish – she is 'like' a boy. Certainly this is related both to her body shape and to her style of dress; both Liz and Bernie refer to Hepburn's wearing of men's shirts and the habit of turning her collars up. These women's understanding of Hepburn as 'boyish' is not a negation of femininity: it does not produce her as in any way *masculine*. Rather, 'boyish' in these accounts refers to a stylishness which signifies naturalness, freedom and the pre-sexual – the moment just before a girl becomes a woman and is thus less differentiated from her male peers – when her body does not display the secondary sexual characteristics which will mark her as 'sexual', a point which is particularly interesting in relation to the way these women so often constructed Hepburn in their accounts through their dislike of other, more 'excessively feminine' stars like Marilyn Monroe. Furthermore, the idea of boyishness is also related to her indistinctness in terms of age – she is understood as both grown up, and yet very young compared to other stars. Perhaps this is what is meant by the term 'waif-like' which is often used of her – it suggests delicacy and vulnerability but is not an exclusively feminine term. Flat shoes are still understood to be 'waif-wear' and were clearly advertised in this period as footwear for the young.[2]

Several of the women I spoke to told me of the inappropriateness of women wearing trousers in the 1950s. Bernie associated Audrey (and Katharine) Hepburn strongly with wearing trousers: 'You see, we all wanted to, but it was very sort of . . . I mean . . . you *didn't*.' What is more, she remembers the difficulty of getting them:

> There was no such thing as girls' jeans! . . . You had to buy boys' jeans, and you had to get someone to come with you to go into Foster Brothers

or whatever it was, to buy a pair of jeans to fit me, oh, and it was so embarrassing, going to buy them, 'cos you felt *silly*! [. . .] You wanted to try them on, and you had to go into the men's changing rooms to try them on. I mean, it was all very difficult.

Trousers were completely unacceptable at work; Janet told me 'you only wore trousers when you went on holiday [. . .] they weren't acceptable any other time'. Liz remembered how 'wearing trousers was quite different. It was – particularly in . . . the north of England, I have to say [laughs] [. . .] but trousers were always rather sort of, *daring* [. . .] and I think there was something good about that as well'. There is also the suggestion here of the important role played by region in women's relationship and access to style. All of the women in this group of interviewees grew up outside London, and many of them in the North or the Midlands. Looking back at women's magazines and the fashion pages of film magazines, there was certainly something going on around the issue of women wearing trousers in Britain in this period. There is an identifiable discourse which combines an anxiety about the potential empowerment of women and threat to traditional definitions of femininity which might accompany women wearing this more 'masculine' garment and a degree of hegemonic negotiation. While flat shoes are indeed desirable before the age of eighteen, in particular (Hepburn-style) versions they are also acceptable for evening wear: 'Keep to the flatties, choosing dainty ballet slippers' ('Trouble a-foot', *Picture Show and Film Pictorial*, 3 November 1956). A fashion feature entitled 'Women wear the pants!' (*Picture Show and Film Pictorial*, 21 May 1955) pictured Audrey Hepburn, Grace Kelly, Cyd Charisse and Virginia Mayo wearing trousers, informing readers: 'Like garments are purchasable in shops here'. All, apart from Hepburn's, are shown to be beach or holiday wear, and Kelly's are worn with an overskirt: 'Slim Audrey Hepburn wears sleek black jersey pants and sweater reminiscent of those she wore for ballet practice' – Cyd Charisse's and Audrey Hepburn's trouser wearing is also made acceptable through a relation to dance as an appropriately feminine mode of movement. 'More women than ever will 'wear the pants' this summer-time', it continues, 'there is no doubt about that! Fortunately, it is only in the fashion sense.' There is an interesting shift towards the new, more approved style of trouser: women are no longer to wear the same style as men, as they have previously, 'for alas, women themselves are not modelled on the same lines as men.

They have more curves, and these showed themselves to great dis-
advantage in sleek breeks'. The new trousers are 'feminised' but still
'a provocative fashion, one that can be slim and chic, or fanciful to
an amusing degree'.[3] The piece warns against 'hippy' women wearing trousers: 'just leave the pants to the men and look pretty in skirts
. . . one would have to be as slim and youthful to wear the sleek,
severe pants favoured by Audrey Hepburn.' Similarly, Rosie remembered wearing this Hepburn look as a young woman: 'I must have
been about fourteen 'cos I was skinny enough to do it then.' Despite
the fact that the piece above showed this outfit from *Sabrina* (which
appealed particularly to her) with the warning 'this is her favourite
lounging housewear', and indeed the fact that Sabrina herself turns
down an evening at the theatre in this outfit, saying 'Oh, I couldn't
possibly go anywhere', Liz nevertheless, perhaps as a result of the
'daring' she expressed above, loved wearing trousers and flat shoes:
'I always felt very . . . *glamorous* . . . in them. I still do [laughs].'
Audrey Hepburn, for a number of the women, offered a new, different way to be – a way of wearing trousers and short hair, but still
understanding oneself, and indeed being understood, to be a girl.

A discourse which constructs Hepburn against 'frilly' femininity
and as pared-down and modern is also discernible in both *Roman
Holiday* and *Sabrina*. In *Roman Holiday*, Hepburn's character
escapes from the fairy-tale femininity within which the film places
her from the start, transforming herself into a pared-down, mod-
ernised and more casual version. 'I'm not two hundred years old!'
she complains, unhappy with her fussy nightgown (she would prefer
pyjamas) and underwear. "Everything we do is so wholesome!'
'Sweetness and decency', 'white lace and very small pink roses' are
the very antithesis of her youth and freshness in this film, and as she
lies in bed, her gaze at the rococo mouldings around the ceilings and
her headboard appears to prompt her escape, a tiny figure against
the ornate grandeur of the embassy building as she makes her flight.
She names herself 'Smith' – 'Smitty' – and becomes ordinary for the
day. 'I hate girls that giggle all the time,' she declares in *Sabrina*. Her
new look in this film is not only more beautiful than the conventionally feminine styles which surround her at the Larrabee party,
but very different; it is simple and elegant. Despite the floral embroi-
dery, her Paris ballgown is strapless and combines a slim skirt with a
fuller overskirt. She manages a rejection of a particular mode of
fussy femininity with supreme elegance and propriety. In *Roman*

Holiday and *Sabrina*, Hepburn's characters reconcile a new, modern, youthful look with an absolutely socially appropriate femininity. Later in our discussion, Liz summed up:

> I mean, I've talked about the hair and stuff, which was important, but she also had this *wonderful*, kind of, *simple* elegance. *Not frilly* – you know, there was nothing *frilly* about her, nothing sort of, *outrageous* about – you know when you said about other icons, they always were 'overdone', and she was always *very* simple, and I think that I associated her with a *look*, rather than anything else – I mean, I can hear her voice, now, I can – I know what her voice was like, and I know, you know, what her face looked like, but she, she actually just represented that, really *wonderful* . . . image of, you know, just *so* stylish.

Caroline saw her 'in very clean cut, probably, short or capped sleeves, or short sleeves, just a simple round neck [. . .] – just very simple, very straight, plain, sort of, *classical*'. Bernie, too, summed her up: 'There were no frills, no nothing! Beautiful, clean and – obtainable.' Earlier, she had told me 'she wore a band in her hair. I mean, we all had *ribbons*.' Although I can't think of an instance where Hepburn wears this kind of accessory, it is significant for its positioning in Bernie's comment as a new, simple alternative to the ribbons that the girls around her usually wore. This, perhaps, is what Rosie meant, when she described *My Fair Lady* as 'not . . . an Audrey Hepburn film to me.' As I discuss below, this film struggles to contain Eliza in the most 'frilly' and perhaps the most conventional femininity of her film career.

The understandings of Hepburn generated through these accounts are complex. Particularly interesting is the way in which Hepburn was frequently constructed as 'not sexy' in the more conventional sense associated with stars such as Marilyn Monroe and Brigitte Bardot. In Bernie's account, this discourse emerges in relation to the more conventional femininity of the 1950s she associates with another young actress she liked in this period, American teen star Sandra Dee. Typical of these discussions, her understandings of these stars and of herself in relation to them are expressed through talk about dress. Discussing a film she saw with her friends as a teenager starring Troy Donahue and Sandra Dee, *A Summer Place* (Delmer Daves, 1959) she described the dirndl skirts, tight, wide belts and 'gypsy' tops worn by Dee: 'You know, sort of, you know, with a bit of luck it'd slip off your one shoulder, and be terribly sort of, oh, *yes*, (both laugh) and your jeans would roll up, right, so you'd

have them just below your knee.' The feminine style Bernie associates with Sandra Dee here is contrasted directly, here and in other
discussions, with the pared-down style Hepburn represented for
these women. Janet, for instance recalled Hepburn's style thus:

> RM: What is it about those kinds of styles that makes you think of
> Audrey Hepburn?
> Janet: I dunno – it just did, because everything that she seemed to
> wear, was that shape [indicates a tailored, tapering silhouette].
> RM: Right, I see.
> Janet: It wasn't – she never wore *that* shape [indicates a flared shape].
> RM: Oh, right, I see – so they were all slim fitting, rather than flared.

At the same time, notice the way in which in Bernie's account, this
kind of femininity is subtly but definitely associated with a conventional notion of sex, 'sexiness' and feminine glamour – the clothes
she associates with Dee emphasise female secondary sexual characteristics: breasts, hips and waists accentuated by waspie belts, full
skirts and 'gypsy' tops which fell off your shoulders. The high heels
worn with this style of dress are again contrasted by this interviewee
to the newness and difference of Hepburn's 'flat, slipper-type' shoes.
In a similar way, Caroline made an interesting observation about
Hepburn's wearing of the habit in *The Nun's Story* and her usual
Givenchy outfits:

> but almost, in a way, her habit, her nun's habit is almost as geometric
> and simple and elegant, as ... it is a very uncluttered femininity . . . and
> I mean, his styles were, they were slightly, sort of, shift dresses that
> didn't cling to waist and boobs, you know, it just *skimmed.*

Clearly, here, Hepburn's 'purity' in this film, in both aesthetic and
moral terms, is linked to her simple, 'uncluttered' femininity, which
again is understood as not conventionally 'sexy': 'shift dresses that
didn't cling to waists and boobs'. In a similar way, Caroline remembered going to her first 'grown-up' parties when the fashion was for
big skirts and tiny waists, but then it went to the modern 'Twiggy
look, the very slim look, the Mary Quant, Biba' of which she understands Hepburn to have been 'a high-fashion version'. Bernie goes
on to talk about the much-discussed slim black trousers and sweater
worn by Hepburn in *Sabrina*. This interviewee's understanding of
Hepburn as 'modern' is both complex and illuminating. The discussion occurred in the context of her memories of there suddenly
being a style, a space for young people in the late 1950s: this she

associates explicitly with the explosion of American youth culture in
Britain in this period – coffee bars, music, fashion, films – and having
money of your own to spend on these things. She offered an illuminating account of the shifts taking place at this moment:

> Bernie: Yes – instead of being a young replica of your mom, or your dad,
> you were . . . it was the first time, really, you were . . . *teenagers*. I can
> remember first – the first time I ever heard the word *teenager*, was
> from a record! Which was . . . again, a Negro, American, Frankie,
> Frankie someone and the Limes, Frankie . . . and it was 'Teenager in
> love' or something [sings] 'Why must I be a teenager in –'
> RM: Oh right!
> Bernie: – and it was the first time I heard 'teen*ager*'!
> RM: Was it!
> Bernie: There was no such thing!
> [. . .]
> Bernie: *Yes*, it gave, it gave you a *space*, to *be*, not a school . . . 'person',
> and not a *young* adult, you know.

She associates Sandra Dee with this moment of modernity, which is
bound up in her account with the 'risqué' – wearing jeans, all things
American, being a teenager, and sex. She referred particularly to the
film *Blue Jeans* (Philip Dunne 1959) which 'was terribly risqué
because it was about this young couple . . . and she got pregnant [. . .]
and that was when I, that was the first pair of jeans – I saw a girl in
jeans, rolled up [sharp intake of breath]'. However, she also understands Hepburn as 'modern' in a distinct way which is revealing.

Hepburn's modernity is a generational shift which is also about
growing up – not just about being young and different from your parents – a teenager – as with Sandra Dee. For this interviewee, Audrey
Hepburn occupied a position somewhere between 'teenager' and
'young lady' – she offers both the modernity of the former and the
acceptability of the latter. Hepburn's short hair is modern, as are her
flat shoes and, as I discuss in Chapter 5, her association with the city.
She is modern, and about modern urban America, but she is not
Sandra Dee-beach-sex-and-jeans modern. 'She was *modern* because
she was *different*.' Audrey Hepburn, as I discuss in Chapter 3,
becomes important in Bernie's narrative at the point where she discards this particular kind of youthful femininity and gets married: 'I
think, we – in my later teens, she was – you know, when you're just,
sort of, smartening up a little bit.' She goes on to talk about her
Audrey-style wedding dress. Hepburn also wears trousers and men's

shirts, which makes her modern, but Bernie uses her understanding of Hepburn's particular version of trouser wearing as more grown-up and smart as a way of legitimating her wearing of jeans – edged with pretty fabric as I discuss above: 'I mean her first, the first, when you saw her, she was very, she was . . . a Sandra Dee-type figure, but smarter, older, if you like. Do you know what I mean?' She also uses her construction of Hepburn against Dee to legitimate her wearing of cardigans in a way which was not seen to be proper. Gillian Gilles's regular film fashion back page of *Picture Show and Film Pictorial* carried an article, 'Good companions for the teenager', which featured Janette Scott (British). 'A lesson in cardigans':

> follow Janette's lead – put it on properly and carefully button it right up the front (Janette does that, though she is opening it to disclose the frock in her picture here), pull the sleeves up well so that it sets correctly on the shoulders; and see that it matches the dress in colour
>
> (4 May 1957).

This fashion page regularly warned young British women against wearing jeans to go out dancing, instead advocating the 'pretty frocks' which Bernie found so limiting. When she spoke about going dancing 'with the girls', she remembered wearing trousers, flat shoes and a cardigan, worn without putting the arms in the sleeves: 'And in fact, I think she was the first one I ever saw, that had the sleeves of her cardigan tied round her neck! And that was in one of her films. So that's what you'd do, you'd do the top button up of this cardigan, and oh, *yes*, terribly . . .'

Bernie can use modern Audrey Hepburn to negotiate certain other versions of modern Americanness which appealed to her – cardigans with trousers, and tied around the neck or unbuttoned and over the shoulders – because she, like the other women who spoke to me, understands Hepburn to be 'not sexy' in the way that other stars were, and *classy*.

Classy, not sexy

'She was one of the stars that I really . . . sort of, identified with, because she wasn't like the other ones.'

(Liz)

An especially interesting way in which the women who spoke to me expressed their understanding of Audrey Hepburn and the particular appeal she held for them was through other female stars of the 1950s and 1960s. As the extracts I quote above begin to show, she is clearly constructed in these accounts as significantly different from other popular female stars of the period, in terms of the modes of femininity, style and glamour they represented: Marilyn Monroe was a recurring point of reference in this respect. A significant discourse emerges in this material in which Hepburn is figured as 'not sexy' but rather 'classy' – these two are presented as diametrically opposed – interesting in relation to the formation 'clever, not sexy' offered in Chapter 2. This was also the most significant discourse to emerge from the pilot study. Janet's reaction to my question about whether she liked Monroe is telling in this respect:

> RM: I just wonder why, you know, you were attracted to her as a role model, as opposed to, say, er . . . Marilyn Monroe –
> Janet: Ugh! [RM: Or –] To me, Marilyn Monroe was just *tarty* [RM: Really?], absolutely and utterly.
> RM: What, why, do you think?
> Janet: Well, she just looked it. And all the films that she acted in portrayed that type of person. And – she did absolutely nothing for me, at all.
> RM: So why wouldn't you have gone for that? I mean, that sort –
> Janet: Because I wouldn't want to look like she looked – even though blondes were supposed to be more attractive to men, that wasn't important to me, because I just wouldn't have wanted to look like a tart. And Audrey Hepburn was totally oppo – was absolutely opposite to that, I mean she looked . . . a really nice sort of person. She may not have been, but she, she gave that impression, and people would – well . . . *girls* would want to be like that, I would have thought, rather than like Marilyn Monroe.

This exchange began with Janet referring to Hepburn's perceived innocence ('doe-eyed'). Monroe, by contrast, is described as 'tarty' – a term in which dress, sexuality, class and character are conjoined. Hepburn, in opposition, 'looked . . . a really nice sort of person'. There is a strong sense here of social mores, of propriety, of the imperatives of acceptable, socially appropriate, respectable femininity understood by this woman to have been in play in the 1950s and 1960s. Furthermore, she offers an idea of Monroe as 'for men' and Hepburn as 'for girls' or women, which is echoed throughout the accounts and suggests the idea of Hepburn's address to an audience of women in Chapter 2. Indeed, Bernie also discussed stars like Brigitte

Bardot, whom she described off tape as 'made for men' as 'role models
out there, that we women – *girls* – took no notice of at all!' Stars like
Monroe and Bardot were 'the enemy'. Earlier she had told me:

> Yes – I mean Sophia Loren was gorgeous, but she was older somehow . . .
> and then she had these huge boobs, and it was a bit like, she was more
> . . . the men would fall over Sophia Loren. They didn't seem to notice
> Audrey Hepburn. Audrey Hepburn was one of the *girls* – that's some-
> thing as well, you know what I mean? You could really relate to her.

She later used an idea of Hepburn's perceived address to women
rather than men as a means of deflecting any suggestion of sexual
attraction in her admiration of this star, emphasising the repeated
use of close-ups of Hepburn's face in films rather than shots which
emphasised her body.

Hepburn, through her body shape, is again seen as 'not sexy' like
other stars, and this makes it acceptable, 'comfortable' as Bernie puts
it, to admire her. Significantly, while Bernie described *Blue Jeans* as
risqué, she obviously recalls this film with pleasure while talking
about the modern American culture she associates with Sandra Dee.
In contrast, she talked about Hepburn's role in *The Nun's Story*,
which she disliked because it was 'too naughty'. Although she insisted
that her dislike of Hepburn in this film is due to her Catholic upbringing, it seems significant that she has this reaction to the Hepburn film,
and not to *Blue Jeans* which is far more risqué, suggesting the incom-
patibility of the ideas 'Audrey Hepburn' and 'sex'. In the same way,
Caroline related Hepburn's type of beauty – 'a sort of femininity that
isn't *excessively* feminine, in that she's slightly an androgynous look'
– her simplicity, to her not being 'over, overtly *sexual*'. She continued: 'I mean, obviously, she is erotically attractive, perhaps that's
something that appealed to me because I could feel I could be
attracted to her, without there being anything *lesbian* about it, I think
perhaps that – I don't know.' This is interesting particularly because
Caroline uses a notion of Hepburn's androgyny – a term which carries with it an idea of sexualisation – as a way of 'making safe' her
attraction to Hepburn. Stella Bruzzi argues that while the androgyne
has been theorised as 'a pre-sexual Platonic' ideal, it is important to
see androgyny as a 'diminution of difference', an 'eroticised ambigu-
ity' which may carry a sexual charge (1997: 176–178). Again, then,
Hepburn's status as 'both/and' in relation to gender makes her at
once both safe and yet potentially dangerous.

Like almost every woman I spoke to, Janet told me she also liked
Doris Day:

> RM: Did you like her clothes?
> Janet: Yes, I did. But you see, they were a – well, they weren't similar
> to what Audrey Hepburn wore, but
> RM: They were later on, weren't they? I mean, there were sort of,
> dresses and coats and things –
> Janet: Well Doris Day's clothes were the sort of things that you used
> to try and emulate when you went dancing. [RM: really?] Yeah –
> because they were feminine, and well, they were nice, the sort of
> style dresses that she used to wear, were nice.

This is a clear example of the periodisation of style I suggested
in Chapter 3 – for this woman, slightly older than Bernie, who
identifies her period of growing up more distinctly with the mid-
than the late 1950s, dance wear is dresses, rather than the jeans, flats
and cardis Bernie remembered. Significantly, Janet *and* Bernie and
Liz (who identify their moment of growing up with the last years of
the 1950s and the beginning of the 1960s) all think about dress
through an idea of 'looking nice' which is evident in magazines
across these moments. 'Nice' is also used here in contrast to the
more sexualised femininity represented by Monroe, in contrast to
whom Janet offered her admiration of Doris Day. To look 'nice' is
also to be a 'nice girl' in sexual terms, in terms of respectability (cf.
Skeggs 1997).

Audrey Hepburn was often referred to as 'classy' in the discussions I had with women who grew up in the 1950s and 1960s. Caroline, for instance, described her as 'ladylike and 'too classy' for
the 'Pop, sort of, Mary Quant types – Biba stuff' of the mid-1960s,
which is interesting for the way it figures the styles of this period
as 'not classy'. Barbara was particularly invested in the idea of
Hepburn as 'ladylike':

> I think she was a, she was just this *elegant*, she was a *lady*, wasn't she?
> And I – I don't know – she was just so unique, I mean, I suppose when
> I think sort of back to the films in those times, like *Georgy Girl*, and all
> those that were popular then the women were more . . . well – they
> weren't as feminine – and they were rowdy, weren't they, but she
> always had this – this *innocence*, I suppose, which I liked, I suppose
> that people were becoming more aware of their independence, weren't
> they, the women, of them times, whereas she wasn't, she was always
> like the person who had got to be looked after at the end of the – you

know, the end of the, and I suppose that's how I'd been brought up, perhaps I – more old-fashioned, isn't it?[4]

Hepburn is constructed as 'a lady' here in contrast to what Barbara describes as the 'more rowdy', independent – perhaps proto-feminist – women of the 1960s. She repeats this later in the interview, in relation to contemporary stars such as Sharon Stone, Kim Basinger, Michelle Pfeiffer and Demi Moore: 'She's not a lady! She's not elegant, she's not . . . could she play an elegant – could she play *My Fair Lady*? Could she play *Charade*, or *Breakfast at Tiffany's*?'

There is a significant discourse evident here in the association of modern, 1960s femininities with independence and sexuality which Barbara herself understands to be 'old-fashioned'. What appeals to this woman is Hepburn's innocence, vulnerability and a more conventionally 'classy' mode of femininity which is significantly different from that pared-down look which Bernie, Liz, Caroline and Rosie associate with Hepburn. It is no coincidence in this respect that Barbara's favourite Audrey Hepburn film is *My Fair Lady*. Indeed, in a move similar to Bernie's use of Hepburn to legitimate her improper wearing of her cardigan, Barbara uses Hepburn to legitimate her wearing of a colour and style she has earlier associated with the 'more rowdy' 1960s women:

> RM: What sort of colours did you, would you have chosen for those kinds of dresses? Were they like, day – day dresses, or evening, like when –
> Barbara: No – day dresses. Yeah, yeah . . . in *fact*, I bought one in Cheltenham . . . er, and I was still at school, and that was an Empire line, but that was orange, *bright orange*, but that was based on her look. [RM: Was it?] Yeah, yeah – almost like a 'baby doll' thing.

Clearly, then, there is something more at stake in the use of the term 'lady' here by a woman who identifies herself as working-class, than there is for Caroline, who self-identified as upper-middle-class.

In Bernie's account, Hepburn becomes classy through her difference: Bernie offers an association between Hepburn and 'Italian style'. She recalls seeing Hepburn for the first time in a book of Italian-style knitting patterns in the late 1950s. To begin with, she associates this with newness and modernity: 'You see *Italian* fashion, and *Italian* . . . was terribly . . . *the thing*, 'cos up until then we'd all worn what our mothers wore . . . I mean you did, you wore what your mom wore. And then suddenly, you know, you all had your own

style.' She explains this further: 'Anything *Italian* – Italian fashion
meant . . . it was *expensive*. [RM: Mmm] But anything, but – so that
was, sort of, you know, really nice. But casual, it had to be very American [. . .] which was blue jeans, and you know, all that type of thing.'
'Italian', then, is understood here to be modern, smart, unlike American fashion and, importantly, *nice*. She remembers Hepburn's short
hair style as being called 'The Italian', and similarly she recalls her flat
shoes being known as 'black Italians'. These shoes didn't last long,
and their life was prolonged by using 'Phillips stick-on soles'.

For Bernie 'she was *classic* [. . .] You could put any picture of her
up, and her face – just her face – blanked out, but leave her clothes,
her *stance*, whatever, and you'd say "Audrey Hepburn". You could
pull her out, you *know*. It's like looking at a piece of Royal Minton
– you *know* that that's what it is.' Here Hepburn is placed within a
discourse of quality and value – and like fine china, she is instantly
recognisable.

Similarly, both Janet and Bernie talk about Hepburn in relation to
the wedding dresses they chose, and both, through this, construct
her and themselves within a discourse of 'classiness'. Bernie expresses
this through an idea of 'Italianness', and as I have suggested, Hepburn
is explicitly linked, for this woman, to 'growing up', not only through
the particular kind of femininity she represented, but also in the order-
ing of her memory – Hepburn occurs in her narrative around getting
older, smartening up, getting married:

> RM: So I'm quite interested in that, 'cos she, in some ways she was
>   quite a, sort of, a 'young lady'? Wasn't she?
> Bernie: Yes.
> RM: Sort of – *after* the teenage stage?
> Bernie: That's right – I'd say, eighteen, nineteen, twenty.
> RM: Right – that's really interesting.
> Bernie: Because a lot of our wedding dresses – I mean my wedding
>   dress, that I had, was very sort of . . . Italian. Again. It had the tight
>   bodice, it had the – what was that lace – that . . . bro –
> RM:*Broderie Anglaise?*
> Bernie: [at the same time] *Anglaise* top . . . you know, all the very fitted
>   sleeves, and quite a high neck, very, again, Italian looking – very sort
>   of – what she'd wear – she wore these lovely mandarin – don't know
>   why – but she wore – I don't know, it was just *classy* – and *different*.

Bernie may be thinking about Hepburn's dress in *Roman Holiday*
at this point, but as I have suggested, the fact that Audrey Hepburn

may not actually have worn a dress like this is in many ways imma-
terial. What matters is that through her description Bernie produces
a particular understanding of Audrey Hepburn in relation to what
she knows to be 'classy and different' at that moment: 'Italian' style.
Janet also produces Audrey as an ideal, 'fairy-tale' femininity around
a description of her wedding dress:

> Janet: Well, you've only got to look at the clothes that I got married in,
> and they were exactly the same sort of clothes as she used to wear.
> RM: In what way?
> Janet: Well, the sort of dress that I wore, which was a pure silk, 'A'- line
> shift dress, without any sleeves in it and just a round neck, and the
> coat that went over the top of it, which was an A-line coat, which
> was exactly the same sort of things that she wore.
> RM: What year was that?
> Janet: 1966. I wore, erm, a little tiny hat that was made up of three
> satin roses in a line, with swansdown over the top that just fit on top
> of my head, and I used – and I wore my hair up in curls all round it,
> which was how she used to wear hers . . . at times.

Again, Janet relates this to the dress Hepburn wore as the princess
in *Roman Holiday*, and uses 'pure silk', 'satin roses' and 'swans-
down' to give an idea of quality – producing herself in relation to
this notion of taste and quality through her relationship to the star:
'exactly the same sort of things that she wore'. This continues
through the description of the store where she bought her wedding
outfit: 'It was, it was a store in Birmingham, it was called Marshall
and Snellgrove, which was very high class . . . and I bought that
outfit, just probably a couple of weeks before the store closed.'

Pat, who had grown up in Birmingham, mentioned this store in a
way which similarly constructs a discourse of quality and, importantly, class.[5] Through Janet's description her dress becomes an
expensive item of rarity which guarantees the appropriateness of her
look on the big day: 'just . . . before the store closed'.

Undoubtedly, it is also an understanding of Hepburn as an ideal
femininity associated with purity, quality and class that makes her
both an appropriate choice of image at moments like this, simultaneously constructing her as such *through* those choices.

Negotiating the social:
growing up, looking 'nice', wearing black

As the epigraph to this chapter from Rosie's account suggests, one of the most interesting findings to emerge from this research is the way in which the 'Hepburn look' is understood as both achievable and appropriate in the late 1950s and the 1960s around the axis boyish/feminine and not sexy/classy. This conjunction of terms appears in varying combinations in the accounts according to differential factors including generation, education and social status, so while in some cases the 'Hepburn look' emerges as a means of reconciling all four of these contradictory terms simultaneously (Bernie, Liz), in others an idea of Hepburn as 'classy' (Barbara, Janet) or 'boyish' (Liz, Caroline, Rosie) might be more or less important.

For Liz, then, as we have seen, Hepburn was significant because in terms of her femininity 'she wasn't like the other ones'; she was 'boyish' – which is for this woman understood as a mode of femininity which was 'more available, more accessible'. Rosie, too, was attracted by Hepburn's 'androgynous' look; having never felt an investment in the accoutrements of conventional femininity, she felt that Hepburn's ability to be 'slightly boyish, but terribly feminine' at the same time was a femininity she might be able to manage. She goes on to tell me about a particular instance when she achieved and used the 'Hepburn look' to cope with a social situation of a kind she had previously found difficult to manage:

> Rosie: So I always remember when I was about fifteen, and I was incredibly skinny when I was fifteen, and my family always despaired of me in France, because I'm half French and half Irish [RM: Right] and it was my father's cousin's golden wedding [RM: Right] and there was this great dilemma about what we were going to do with me at this occasion, 'cos I never dressed appropriately! [both laugh] I could never – no matter what I tried, I just never was comfortable in what they considered being, sort of, a suitable thing to wear.
>
> RM: What would they have liked you to have worn on that occasion, do you think?
>
> Rosie: Some sort of co-ordinated, you know, outfit that was – preferably either a dress or a skirt, but I actually wore a black, very very thin cotton polo neck sweater in black, and some sort of black equivalent of ski pants, and, which I think very much came from the whole sort of, Left Bank *Funny Face* type, sort of Audrey Hepburn . . . and it worked! I mean, you know, they actually thought I'd found some style

at that point! [laughs] So I think, that was the sort of image I locked into, but I think it was just much more than the way she looked, I think it was, I thought, 'Well that's the *sort* of acceptable –' because it's on the big screen, and everybody thought she was wonderful [RM: Of course] – femininity, that I could just about cope with.
RM: One that you could do?
Rosie: One I could do, and one that didn't confine me too much.

Rosie's experience was of being able to use the 'Hepburn look', which she associated very much with contemporary Parisian 'cool', as an 'appropriate' and 'co-ordinated' ensemble in the late 1960s. In contrast, she talked about Hepburn's ultra-feminine look as Holly Golightly in *Breakfast at Tiffany's*:

Rosie: That incredibly cool party that she has, sort of swans through it in the little black number, with the long cigarette, which was the sort of Audrey Hepburn I knew I could never do. [RM: Really?] That's where she, sort of, crossed over.
RM: Did it appeal, though?
Rosie: Oh, well – it appealed to me to watch, but it was sort of, quite distant from me . . . so, you know, it was like, that must be incredible to do that, but no way – [RM: That's not for me –] – yeah, that's not a thing I could ever do, or . . . pull off, or . . . it's fascinating.

For Rosie, it was the ability of Hepburn's 'Bohemian' Beatnik look in *Funny Face* to be both boyish-feminine and socially acceptable which was the basis of its appeal; she felt she 'was never very good at fitting into what everyone else was meant to be', preferring trousers over skirts even as a very young girl. She used and uses a version of the Audrey Hepburn look, both then and now, as a way of negotiating socially defined notions of appropriate femininity with her own strong sense of self.

Today, this woman, like most of the women who spoke to me from the different generational groups, continues to use the wearing of black as a strategy for coping with formal occasions; in the case of the young women I spoke to, this was often through the 'little black dress' aspect of her look (not just hers, of course), but for Rosie, despite the disapproval she experienced for being dressed all in black at a Golden Wedding, nevertheless it worked, and continues to work for formal and professional occasions:

Rosie: But yeah – it's still my strategy to any do, now [RM: Black?] – always to wear black. [Both laugh] [. . .] If I'm trying to – it depends what image I'm trying to put over – but that is my 'conforming' image.

RM: But is it still acceptable to you though?

Rosie: It's not completely alien – I think – yeah – it's not alien – it's not alien, I think it's my acceptable compromise – it's the one I feel the best about doing, that doesn't rock the boat, doesn't cause problems for other people. And probably in other people's eyes I'm still not actually making enough of an effort, [RM: Oh right, I see] but – do you know what I mean?

RM: Yeah, I do.

Rosie: But it's the sort of – as far as my effort goes for it. Mmm.

While Liz recalled how she would at one time have chosen light, feminine colours, particularly interesting is the way in which this woman discusses her social shift around the idea of wearing black:

RM: Was black not really 'in', do you think?

Liz: It *was*, but it was sort of – it was much more grown up.

RM: Was it?

Liz: Yes, and it was much less likely to see young people wearing black until – well certainly, again [laughs] I have to qualify this by always saying 'in the North!', in Leeds!

RM: But it's very important.

Liz: Yes, you know, the – *black* was I mean, I did get into black, but it was *much* later, when I was in my twenties [RM: Right] . . . but when I was a teenager it was hardly ever . . . I remember one of my boyfriends, one of my boyfriends who went to university, in fact I got engaged and married to him, in fact, but he had a black polo necked sweater, and that was the great [both laugh] the great thing to have, you know, this very sort of, bohemian looking, and I think I got one then, I can't remember exactly – but black wasn't a colour that you would have worn, and my mum would have looked at me – ever so strangely . . . if I'd thought of wearing black.

RM: That sort of bohemian look was really – I mean from what, from what I know, from what I've read, it was a – a very *alternative* thing –

Liz: Yes.

RM: – to do, to go for that bohemian look, wasn't it?

Liz: Yes, yes and I think much more middle-class.

RM: Do you think so?

Liz: Yes, I think so, and I think the thing about *black* for *my* family was, that you were in mourning, if you wore black.

Coming through strongly here is a sense of the generational, regional, intellectual and class dimensions of the wearing of black, which persist today. In Liz's experience, black was not only considered 'inappropriate' by her mum, but is also understood to be more 'middle-class'. Liz's account, like Bernie's, is particularly interesting around dress, as I suggested in the previous chapter, as her period of growing up precisely straddles the shifts which took place between the 'matching shoes and gloves' period identifiable through these accounts with the late 1950s, and the burgeoning of new youth cultures and styles in the 1960s.

Janet, whose period of growing up and thinking about Audrey Hepburn comes just before these kinds of shifts in the late 1950s, discussed a very different aspect of Hepburn's look to that identified by Liz and Rosie. She offered detailed accounts and descriptions of making and buying 'tailored', 'fitted' dresses in quality fabrics which she understands as being 'like Audrey Hepburn wore', and which would take her from a day at work to going out in the evening. Likewise, for Barbara it was also this smart, tailored, 'ladylike' aspect of Hepburn's look which appealed. Neither Janet nor Barbara made any reference to the 'modernity' of Hepburn's look which came through so strongly in other accounts. I bring *Funny Face* into this discussion, mentioning Hepburn's 'pared-down' style in this film as a point of reference for many of the women I have spoken to, but while Barbara admits to having worn a similar style of trouser on occasions, when I press her she offers her dislike of jazz as a reason for not liking the film, and is uninterested in discussing this aspect of Hepburn's look. Rather, Barbara was especially taken with Hepburn in *My Fair Lady*. In particular, she remembers Beaton's designs for the ball, and the Ascot scene:

RM: What about it – what was it about that one?
Barbara: Well I mean – I just loved it – I'd just love to go back – I'd like to be in that – I mean, I'd love to wear them clothes now, you know.
RM: That was Edwardian period, wasn't it –
Barbara: Yes, yeah – I mean, they'd er – even the men looked elegant, you know, and the ladies, I mean, it must have *killed* them to *wear* the fashions, I mean, absolutely horrendous, but – but I'd love, I'd love to wear them now. The trim waists, and the –
RM: Can you imagine the corsets –
Barbara: Oh God! [both laugh] it'd be awful, wouldn't it – they were all very upright, and very elegant, because they couldn't bend!

In contrast to the accounts of Hepburn's modernity and ease of movement discussed above, this account is significant for its emphasis on rigidity and an inability to move. Barbara had a nostalgic desire for this mode of femininity which was the ideal decades before she was born. As I suggest above, she finds modern 1960s femininity unappealing and in some cases 'rowdy' in contrast to the more 'ladylike' demeanour she understands to be embodied by Audrey Hepburn – as I discuss in Chapter 3, for instance, at one point she juxtaposed Hepburn with Dusty Springfield. She picks out and discusses this element of Hepburn's look as a 'classic' look she still uses today, noting the prevalence of styles in the shops at that moment – November 1997 – similar to those in *My Fair Lady*:

> RM: So then you would say then, that her style has affected –
> Barbara: Oh yeah!
> RM: – yours?
> Barbara: Even today. [RM: Today?] Oh *yes*, yes.
> RM: Tell me – tell me how . . . why, how?
> Barbara: Well, I still, I still look – if I go in a shop, well, I can still pick things up which I can associate with her, you know. [RM: You can?] Oh, yeah.
> RM: What sort of things, for example, would stick out as – you know, that makes you able to associate that with her, particularly? What elements?
> Barbara: Well, now I suppose, the Christmas stuff's coming in, so – the glittery stuff, and a lot of it, are in the styles of those ballgowns, those gowns she wore, and the long – the s – the – even in *My Fair Lady* when she's got the suits on, with the jackets, the long, the line – jackets, with the belts – I mean, you can actually get them *now*, and the long, the long skirts with the pleat – the split up the back, people are wearing them today, and the boots, the little boots . . . the colours are different, I mean I used to wear, she wore pastels and things, but, you know, [RM: Of course . . .] you can almost, you could almost . . . copy that, today.
> RM: You could find it, couldn't you? [Barbara: Yeah, yeah . . .] And particularly, I suppose, the party, the party wear, as you say, very similar, so I mean –
> Barbara: The only thing, I suppose, you wouldn't wear the hat – you wouldn't wear the hat!
> RM: No – it's a bit of a shame, really!
> Barbara: Or the gloves – people don't wear gloves now, and the little bags, but I mean, yeah – you could get a suit, and the long skirt, and the little boots. [6]

Here, again, is a reference to the 'bags, shoes and gloves' aspect of Hepburn's look common to the accounts by women who associate their period of youthful fashionable femininity with the 1950s. It is interesting to note that although Barbara herself identifies this as the period she associates with growing up, her points of reference suggest that like Liz and Bernie, in this respect she in fact crossed both decades. If her attraction to these elements of Hepburn's look are not entirely the result of generational factors, perhaps, as I suggest in Chapter 5, there is something more at work here around the relationship between feminine dress and social status. I go on to discuss the resonance of the transformation/coming-out narrative of this film around dress and status for young women in Chapter 5. Towards the end of our conversation, Barbara tells the following story about her relationship with her mother and other potential female role models:

> I don't know, and I suppose it all goes back to what – my mum saying I was frumpy, and I was a lump, and then you see this very *elegant lady* and this – I just *wish* I could always be . . . I can always remember, when I was tiny watching a film with Marlene Dietrich in – now I thought she was *wonderful*, I really did, I just thought – I can remember sitting watching films, and sort of singing along, and her saying 'Oh, no you don't want to watch *this*' – [. . .] and it was also – I always used to like Eartha Kitt, 'cos she was – made me laugh – this *outrageous* woman, she used to sit on this *chaise longue*, with this cat suit on, and *purr*, and swing the tail, and er – I used to think she was really good, you know, and this unusual voice, and I remember my mum saying, 'But you shouldn't like people like this' – you know, 'you shouldn't –', and then the first film I can remember going to see at the pictures was *The King and I*, and those *huge* dresses, with Deborah Kerr, yeah – crinolines, and I was just – these people on this screen, I was just totally . . .

This is a powerful evocation of the way in which as a young girl this woman learned certain femininities as appropriate models, and others as off limits. This was not a subtly learned disposition in Bourdieu's sense, but was rather experienced and remembered as *taught*, and this interviewee expressed great pleasure in the memory of these other stars ('wonderful', 'outrageous' compared to her restrained description of Hepburn as an 'elegant lady'). Marlene Dietrich and Eartha Kitt were seen as inappropriate by this woman's mother – perhaps because they share a certain blurring of gender boundaries (and Kitt is represented here as feline and 'animalistic' in her sexuality), so it is significant that this woman refuses the notion of Hepburn as androgynous. Deborah Kerr, on the other hand, in her crinoline, was fine . . .

'She was everything.
And it was all within reach, if you like.' (Bernie)

I want to end this chapter with a discussion of a more extended extract from the longest and the most detailed of my interviews – the one with Bernie (see Appendix II, pp. 226–231). She talked very interestingly about the accessibility and appropriateness of the kind of femininity she understood Audrey Hepburn to represent through a discourse of realism, telling me that Hepburn's clothes, what she describes as 'The Italian look', were what 'we could get at'. 'We could reach it,' she told me, 'it was obtainable, you could obtain that look.' This, as I discussed in Chapter 3, was partly due to the simplicity of making or adapting clothes to look like those worn by Hepburn. There is something else going on in this woman's understanding of Hepburn's look as attainable, however. The discourse of realism in this account not only draws together the presentation of Hepburn as in this sense different from other stars of the period, as I discuss above, but at the same time constructs her as 'classy' and as 'not sexy' in a very precise way.

Bernie's is an extremely rich, socially and historically situated account of Hepburn's appeal for a young woman growing up working-class in the British Midlands in the late 1950s and early 1960s. Although Sandra Dee was also a great favourite of Bernie's, it is made clear that not only the kind of femininity, but also the lifestyle and behaviour Dee represented through her films, felt beyond Bernie's reach at this time in her life: 'I would have loved a pink sedan with Troy Donahue in it', she told me, 'but . . .'. Today, she travels to America on holiday regularly, and in many ways has achieved what seemed impossible then. Hepburn, too, was 'modern', but she was also 'different'. Somehow, for Bernie, growing up in an inner-city suburb of Birmingham in the late 1950s, Audrey Hepburn came, in contrast to the 'cute', 'beachy' Americanness of Sandra Dee and Doris Day, to represent something plausible, something *possible*. Audrey Hepburn and Sandra Dee are constructed oppositionally in this account as obtainable/unobtainable through her understanding of them as classy/not classy. In this sense, then, Hepburn comes to represent the possible for this interviewee, because she seems to represent the *socially* possible: Sandra Dee and her companions, for instance, got into cars without opening the doors – Bernie couldn't imagine herself being able to do this. She goes on to discuss Hepburn's body shape through the same discourse of realism and possibility in relation to sex and sexiness. Not only were the bodies of Bardot, Monroe, Gardner and Russell outside the realms of physical possibility for a teenage girl, they were also outside the realms of social possibility: 'There's *no way* we could walk around the streets like that! . . . Everything you've been told, "You can't, you mustn't, it's not – and if you do, they won't love you anyway".' They represented something which was socially impossible. In contrast, Hepburn represented a type of sexiness which was both physically, practically and socially attainable and appropriate, as expressed in the conjunction of terms 'she was *sexy*, she was *sweet*, she was *smart* . . . she was *everything*. And it was all within reach.' She has 'class', because she is not 'about sex' in an obvious way – she didn't have to emphasise her breasts to get ahead. She was modern and different, but at the same time classy and attainable.

It is interesting to compare Caroline's comments around the Hepburn/Monroe axis that emerged from this research. In the extract that follows, Caroline has told me that Hepburn's was the kind of beauty she aspired to as a young woman, and I have just asked her if she felt that this was an achievable kind of beauty:

> Caroline: *No*, not really, 'cos I'd never ever had the slight frame that she had, but I thought it – I was . . . *yes*, I think I probably felt it was, it was worth *trying* – because, it wouldn't be quite so – it wouldn't be totally ludicrous, the effect, [RM: Of course . . .] so I thought well I could – perhaps, *halfway* there.
> RM: Perhaps she *was* a more accessible kind of femininity?
> Caroline: Yes – perhaps she was –
> RM: Than, say, Marilyn Monroe –
> Caroline: Yes, *yes* – and I would have thought that trying to be someone like Marilyn Monroe you'd end up looking a bit *silly*, whereas because, perhaps, Audrey Hepburn was a slightly *ladylike*, understated form of femininity, you know, if you missed it, you're probably – on the good, on the good side of taste, rather than the bad! [both laugh]

By juxtaposing these two accounts of the difference between the contrasting modes of femininity seen as offered by stars like Marilyn Monroe and Audrey Hepburn, it becomes clear that these two women, from radically different social backgrounds, have a rather different understanding of and investment in terms like 'classy' and 'ladylike'. When Bernie discusses the potential appropriation of these identities, there is an issue around propriety and

social acceptability which registers a concern with the practical consequences at stake in doing certain types of femininity. For Caroline,
meanwhile, the question is one of restraint and 'taste'.
Hepburn *embodies* class in Bourdieu's sense. She speaks it
through her body:

> Taste, a class culture turned into nature, that is, *embodied*, helps to
> shape the class body. It is an incorporated principle of classification
> which governs all forms of incorporation, choosing and modifying
> everything that the body ingests and digests and assimilates, physio-
> logically and psychologically. It follows that the body is the most indis-
> putable materialization of class taste, which it manifests in several
> ways. It does this first in the seemingly most natural features of the
> body, the dimensions . . . and shapes . . . of its visible forms, which
> express in countless ways a whole relation to the body, i.e. a way of
> treating it, caring for it, feeding it, maintaining, which reveals the
> deepest dispositions of the habitus.

(Bourdieu 1986: 190)

In her demeanour – her controlled, even *mannered* use of her body
and her slenderness – Hepburn speaks (high social) 'class' through
her corporeal form.[7] Marilyn Monroe in *Some Like It Hot* (Billy
Wilder, 1959) provides a useful contrast: she performs 'I want to be
loved by you' in a sheer dress which clings to every contour of her
body, her nipples barely covered with the briefest of pale embroi-
dery. She appears as if naked – this is a body unfettered, uncorseted,
uncontrolled, sexual. She represents excess – the undisciplined
female body which signifies low social status (Skeggs 1997: 100).

Hepburn's 'class' is also linked repeatedly to her national identity in
these accounts; both Caroline and Janet describe her as 'not brash' –
Caroline adds 'not a starlet' around her perception of the lack of 'dirt'
available on Hepburn in the press. Janet takes this further in relation
to her sense of Hepburn's Europeanness; while she describes Loretta
Young as 'a typical American girl', she says she would call Hepburn

> Typically English! [laughs] [RM: Would you?] Yes! Like a college –
> well, sort of, portraying a college girl type, when she used to wear the
> trews, and tops – I mean I've got a photograph of me somewhere,
> where I could have copied exactly the sort of clothes that she used to
> wear, I'd got trousers on that sort of came to there [indicates mid-calf]
> that were tight fitting, I'd got a short-sleeved blouse on that was all
> little tiny-weenie pleats, that was buttoned down the front, with
> reveres, and I'd got a chiffon scarf folded, with my hair up and the

scarf tied, and in – sort of tied here [gestures under chin] – and the ends
sort of floating down. Which is exactly the sort of thing . . . .

I ask her why Hepburn seems 'English':

> Janet: I don't know . . . I don't know, I mean, American girls were
> always brash, and far more mature than English girls, and I think
> Audrey Hepburn was – you could relate to the sort of person that
> *she* was, because she didn't give that impression.
> RM: Of being brassy?
> Janet: Yeah. Well, not brassy, but *brash*. Which is different. I mean . . .
> she was, she portrayed – or gave the impression – that she was very
> clean living, and goody-goody, and all that sort of thing.

For Janet, then, Audrey Hepburn's student style represented something that was properly English. When she is discussed in terms of
the 'American', it is against the West Coast 'beachy' Sandra Dee and,
as I discuss in the next chapter, in relation to the modern East Coast
American city – New York. In other accounts, Hepburn is constructed, again against American femininities, as acceptably European
– more like Leslie Caron than Brigitte Bardot, for instance, and 'Italian' in a way that is precisely unlike Sophia Loren's Italianness. Dick
Hebdige's account of the significance of Italian style in young British
working-class culture in the late 1950s and early 1960s is illuminating in relation to Bernie's emphasis on the Italian as new, different and
representative of 'quality'. Italy represented 'everything that was chic
and modern and "acceptable"' – and in good taste:

> Step by step, through various deviations, the clothes and haircuts grew
> less eccentric and extreme, until at the end of the 1950s they had
> become unified in the rather attractive 'Italian Style', which had
> become normal walking-out wear for the working-class boy; and by
> 1960 this had blended with 'conservative cool' or just very ordinary
> but well cut clothes.[8]

Bernie's story completes this picture, suggesting the significance of
Italian style for girls in this period. A key element in Mod fashion,
'Italian' style was encapsulated in the scooter – the Lambretta and the
Vespa. Hebdige notes how the 'new Italian woman' was pictured
with a scooter which enabled her to zip around freely, this in turn
encouraging a new fashion for the 'urchin cut', narrow skirts, turtleneck sweater and flat shoes which facilitated scooter riding. We can
see how while Bernie's account of Hepburn's 'Italian' look ties in
clearly with this – particularly in the way it facilitated movement and

greater freedom; however, while the article in *Picture Post* entitled 'A new race of girls', referenced by Hebdige, featured Gina Lollabrigida on a scooter, Bernie's choice of Hepburn as 'for women' and as 'one of the girls' over the stars mentioned in Hebdige's account (Anna Magnani, Loren and Lollabrigida for instance) is significant, and is shared by the other women who offered me their memories of Audrey Hepburn.

I want to suggest, then, that in the material I have presented here, Hepburn is understood as a star who offered the possibility of reconciling certain key contradictions which were significant for women in this period, for instance in her ability to be both boyish and feminine, and for one woman, both classy and sexy in a way which was completely acceptable. At the same time, there is a distinct sense of achievement in these accounts around 'doing' the Hepburn look. Not only was hers an attainable look in practical terms (simple, and sometimes, but not always – depending on the aspect of her look chosen – affordable), it was also within the realms of physical possibility for girls on the verge of womanhood: 'I think I looked like a lad when I was fourteen, fifteen – I think I looked like a lad 'til I was about twenty-two, actually' (Rosie).

What is perhaps most interesting about the material on Hepburn's look, though, is the way in which as a sign she is flexible enough to appeal across subtle lines of generation, class and periodisation. While she could appeal through what I have called the 'matching shoes, bag and gloves' element in her image to aspiring working-class women who identify their youthful selves more definitely with the 1950s (Barbara, Janet), other more 'modern' aspects of her image could be used by younger working-class women to negotiate and produce images of socially acceptable femininity which did not clash too violently with their own sense of self (Rosie, Liz, Bernie). For the former, the 'boyish' element of her image was irrelevant, while for the latter it was of prime importance as they began to seek 'freer' femininities. At the same time, while Barbara could negotiate a 1960s femininity which she felt was inappropriate through reference to the 'classic' aspect of Hepburn's look (bright orange 'baby doll' becomes 'Empire line' in relation to *My Fair Lady*) and Bernie could legitimate the way she wore her cardi through the propriety of Hepburn's image, the 'modernity' of Hepburn's 'college girl' look was appropriate for Janet because it was acceptably 'English'.

It is clear that these divisions are not discrete – a complexity emerges from these accounts along and across lines of generation, historical moment and social class. For instance, Audrey Hepburn's 'ladylike', 'Italian' *Roman Holiday* look was the model for Bernie's wedding dress, but her wearing of trousers and flat shoes (also Italian) offered a femininity which allowed literal mobility – bike riding – while being perceived at this later moment as smart enough to go dancing in. Janet, although also identifying herself as working-class, would not have dreamt of going dancing in trousers; in quite a subtle way, this is a question of generation and historical moment in which class has become slightly less significant. It is notable, though, that at the same time Bernie is strongly invested in the idea of Hepburn as 'classy'. While Hepburn could be understood as 'modern, new and different', appealing to girls growing up out of the frilly feminine 1950s and into 1960s youth culture, at the same time she was 'smart, innocent, and good'. This latter aspect of her image could both be used strategically by these women when necessary (for instance, at a family celebration), while it was also the ideal for those women who identified more closely with the 1950s, and for whom there was more at stake socially in being 'smart' or 'ladylike' – this is rather a case of 'tactics' in de Certeau's sense (1984). Often social status is at stake in such investments – there is a question about who could afford to negotiate over femininity in the way that Liz, Bernie and Rosie relate. In Chapter 5, then, I look at the resonance of Hepburn's Cinderella transformations for young women aspiring to and negotiating new social environments.

Notes

1 French designer André Courrèges, considered to be the father of the miniskirt, showcased his futuristic 'Moon Girl' look in 1964, with the emphasis on white, silver and geometric shapes. His introduction of the trouser suit into his collection in the same year brought it squarely into the mainstream.

2 See Jones (1994) for a discussion of the restoration of *My Fair Lady*, and Julia Roberts as 'an Audrey Hepburn for the nineties' in *Pretty Woman* and *I Love Trouble* (Charles Shyer, 1994), wrongly costumed in high heels.

3 Similarly, in 1959 Shirley MacLaine was quoted as giving the following advice: 'A woman's most valuable asset is simply being a woman. And too many girls are forgetting this fact by trying to be like men . . . be

feminine, learn what the boys are interested in, but don't try to better them' (MacLaine 1959).

4 *Georgy Girl* (Silvio Narizzano, 1966) – a 'Swinging London' film focusing on youth culture, 'determined to shock', 'a censorship milestone' (Halliwell 1992) with James Mason, Lynn Redgrave and Charlotte Rampling.

5 Pat: Oh, it was a lovely big shop – you used to go in the main entrance of Marshall and Snellgrove ... and if I remember right – in the middle of the ground floor there was this gorgeous staircase – red carpet – it used to go up both sides into the second floor – fabulous shop. [. . .] fabulous shop though – you used to feel as though you were somebody when you went in there, you know, it was that nice – not like Rackhams today – Rackhams is very impersonal, I always find, but Marshall and Snellgrove was a fantastic shop.

RM: When you say it made you feel like you were somebody – do you think that's because of the kind of treatment you got from the –

Pat: Probably – because the staff always used to speak to you when you went in – regardless of whether they knew you or not – 'Good morning, madam,' or, you know – you used to feel – 'Ooh – this is it' – yes, lovely.

6 Martine McCutcheon has presented herself as an Audrey Hepburn fan, describing the star as, like her, 'a girl from a not very rich family who wanted to be someone'. It is interesting in the light of these comments that Martine appeared on British chat show *TFI Friday* to talk about her forthcoming singing debut at the Royal Albert Hall in London, in an outfit clearly based on Hepburn's 'before' look in *My Fair Lady*.

7 Furthermore, Hepburn's 'class' also appears problematic in relation to her sexuality: 'If you want to be a duchess, be a duchess,' says Mark to Joanna in a knowing reference to Hepburn's image, in *Two for the Road*; 'If you want to make love, hats off!'

8 T.R. Fyvel (1963), *The Insecure Offenders: Rebellious Youth in the Welfare State* (Pelican, 1963) quoted in Hebdige 1988: 75.

Chapter 5

Audrey's Cinderellas: dress and status in the 1950s and 1960s

I mean that was a completely unknown world, completely unknown world, and that was, I think . . . finding how to look that was appropriate, that wasn't, yeah, that didn't sort of, give me away, really.

(Liz)

Dress and adornment become tangible means of gaining some control over the social situation.

(Roach and Eicher 1965: 187)

Clearly, clothes and lack of money to buy them are only part of the story. Giving a country girl a new and fashionable wardrobe would be like giving a poor flower girl an aristocratic English accent – both too much and too little.

(Wax and Wax 'The matter of clothing', in Roach and Eicher 1965: 264)

It is evident from the accounts and self-narrations discussed in Chapter 4, that the 'Hepburn look' was central to the appeal this star held for the group of women who spoke to me about growing up female in the 1950s and 1960s. This is apparent in their understandings of its social meanings and in their accounts of producing that look through shopping, dressmaking, hairdressing and making-up and of mobilising it at specific moments and in particular social settings. Furthermore, a profound relationship between dress and subjectivity is evident in these discussions, and in Chapter 3 I explored the inscription of the same discourse across Hepburn's major films. This relationship between clothing and an increased sense of self seems to be an especially resonant aspect of her persona, particularly if we understand her as a star who offers an address to a feminine audience.

This chapter picks up and elaborates a key strand of this discourse: the 'Cinderella motif' which marks Hepburn as an image-text. This motif can be understood as a historically specific articulation of a discourse about the acquisition of certain kinds of femininity and the potential for upward mobility through work, education and/or marriage. It is a discourse which is also highly visible in women's and film-fan magazines of the mid-1950s to mid-1960s, both in the form of 'Cinderella' fiction and also in the form of advice offered therein on personal style which understands the relationship between dress, self and status to be significant.

Furthermore, the narrative trajectory of what I have described as the Cinderella motif also structured a number of accounts of growing up female offered to me by women who admired Hepburn at that moment. I consider these 'Cinderellas' in this chapter, asking how the relationship between the motif around Hepburn and the telling of these often very personal stories might be characterised. By juxtaposing material generated in discussions with textual analysis of Hepburn's films, I do not intend to suggest a simple relationship of influence or effect between these films and the small segment of the audience I am working with here. Rather, as I discuss in Chapter 3, I want to suggest the terms 'resonance and recognition' as a way of understanding the relationship between text and subjectivity, and thus as a way of thinking about the articulation of the discourse I have been describing as the 'Cinderella motif'– a way of talking about the acquisition of certain kinds of femininity and social mobility – in these three sites: the film text, magazines and audience accounts. As I discuss in Chapter 3, 'resonance' hints at a more nebulous relation of suggestion and recognition, something akin to Williams's notion of 'structure of feeling' (1977), a flexible formulation privileging feeling over more formal concepts like ideology which is concerned with 'meanings and values as they are actively lived and felt' (132), and which describes 'a particular quality of social experience and relationship, historically distinct from other particular qualities, which gives the sense of a generation or of a period' (131). Furthermore, it remains outside the psychoanalytically informed approaches associated with the term 'identification' which has been hegemonic in film theory, whilst still allowing for the role played by unconscious processes in understanding the relationship between text and audience. Psychoanalytically informed approaches, whilst useful tools for thinking theoretically about spectator–text relations, are problematic when faced with 'real' people who have given freely of their time, memories and

hospitality, and the power relations involved in introducing psychoanalytic methodologies in the interpretation of audience accounts
are difficult to justify. Bringing the notion of resonance to bear on
the relationship between text and audience is a useful way of thinking about how discourses circulate and are articulated across different sites: films, print journalism and personal histories.

Furthermore, I argue that it is possible to discern across Hepburn's film work a difficulty around her image in which modern
femininity, social status and the domestic are conjoined in a quite
particular and increasingly complicated relation. Within this discourse, the anxiety of 'passing' in terms of class and gender, the
potential for social mobility and the tensions between public, urban
and domestic femininities are dramatised around dress. Richard
Dyer, who also notes the predominance of transformation scenarios
in her films, has suggested of Hepburn that '[s]he's a displaced
person, and yet suffers no anguish from this' (Dyer 1993: 59). While
it may be the case that Hepburn's 'serene misfit' image works to
negotiate the social difficulties that the characters she portrays face,
I will argue here that the key films of her career are permeated with
an uneasiness in relation to selfhood, class and the domestic which
is particularly interesting in the light of her enormous popularity
with women and the resonance her image had for those women
growing up in the late 1950s and early 1960s. As the epigraphs
which open this chapter suggest, it is imperative not to underesti-
mate the role played by dress in a creating a sense of self for some
women, and for women growing up working-class the sense of selfhood acquired through dress is often explicitly linked to the possibility of a shift in social status. Nevertheless, I will argue that such
stylish transformations as those undergone by Sabrina Fairchild in
Sabrina, Holly Golightly in *Breakfast at Tiffany's* and Eliza Doolittle in *My Fair Lady* do not *guarantee* social mobility. Stella Bruzzi,
discussing the similarity between *Sabrina* and *Pretty Woman*, rightly
remarks that in changing their clothes, the women in these films
change their sexual and economic status (Bruzzi 1997: 15). However, I hope to explore the complexities and contradictions discernible in *Sabrina* and *My Fair Lady* in particular with regard to
dress and social mobility, but also across Hepburn's film career generally. Moreover, the key films of Hepburn's career display a distinct
dis-ease around this acquisition of the '*signs*' of class, which appear
to significantly complicate the relation of the characters she portrays

to socially acceptable femininity, the public and the domestic. This chapter is in part then also an exploration of the ways in which this uneasy discourse is manifested textually in Hepburn's films, in related discourses circulating in British women's and film magazines in the late 1950s and early 1960s in Britain, and in audience accounts of growing up with Audrey Hepburn.

You *shall* go to the ball . . .

Hepburn's film work is marked by a number of Cinderella-type narratives and scenarios; this familiar story of transformation is a significant way in which as a star she can be understood to address a feminine audience. *Roman Holiday*, her first Hollywood film, began this with a 'Cinderella in reverse' narrative in which a young European princess escapes for a day, transforms herself into a modern young woman and is granted three wishes by newspaper man Joe Bradley (Gregory Peck). The day ends with dancing on a moored barge on the Tiber at which she had gazed longingly from her stifling room in the embassy – where she had just reluctantly attended a more conventional ball. *Sabrina* opens with credits rolling over a moonlit sky, with stars and wispy clouds, followed by a narrated introduction: 'Once upon a time, on the North shore of Long Island, some 30 miles from New York, there lived a small girl on a large estate . . . ', through which devices the film is clearly marked as 'fairy tale' from the beginning. Sabrina Fairchild dreams of going to the ball (the Larrabee party – 'As close to heaven as one could get on Long Island'), is transformed into a beautiful and sophisticated young woman during her two-year *Cordon Bleu* course in Paris, and returns to attend the ball in a beautiful dress and dance with the prince (David and Linus Larrabee). *My Fair Lady*, although based upon George Bernard Shaw's *Pygmalion*, is clearly also a Cinderella tale, centred as it is around the transformation of flower girl Eliza Doolittle into an elegant lady who dances with the prince of Transylvania at the embassy ball.

As a discursive formulation, 'Audrey Hepburn' was well suited to such Cinderella roles. Perrault's 1697 version of the tale, 'Cinderella, or The Little Glass Slipper', the basis for the most popular versions including the Disney film of 1950 (Warner 1986: 12), emphasises that hidden beneath her rags, Cinderella has basic beauty and 'fitness', excellent taste in clothes, and is thus naturally deserving of the happy ending (Perrault 1697 in Dundes 1988: 16). The transformation she undergoes simply reveals what is already present and merely hidden: Sabrina is already 'Fairchild'. As I discussed in Chapter 2, Hepburn's role in *Roman Holiday* initially established the 'princess' element in her image, and her poised, *couture* look, 'authenticity' and sweetness secure the appropriateness of such transformations throughout her film career. As I explore in Chapter 4, Hepburn's is always already a profoundly 'classed' image. As Jane Yolen points out, the Perrault version of Cinderella popularised in America is a tale of rags to riches, while the story in its other versions was explicitly a tale of 'riches recovered' (Yolen 1977: 296). Elizabeth Panttaja (1993) also notes that the Grimm brothers' version of the tale is one of 'intra-class conflict' (95) in which 'clothes are an important means by which class identity is both hidden and revealed' (98). Hepburn's beautiful clothes are both 'natural' as a result of her image, yet inscribed within the film as a possible means to upward mobility. It is possible, then, to see the way in which Hepburn's placing at the centre of the Cinderella narratives which mark her career manages to reconcile both the earlier European and the Americanised versions of the story, for while these films have a clear rags to riches thematic (circumscribed as this in fact may be), her image is a guarantee of the meetness of the transformation, allowing a message about the possibility of mobility to shine through. Furthermore, Perrault's tale points to Cinderella's lack of vanity and narcissism, and modesty has been seen to be a key element in Hepburn's appeal, established, once again, in *Roman Holiday* in the expression of wonder and disbelief we see pass across the princess's face when confronted with her new image (the 'Hepburn look'). The magical transformation of everyday things into articles of perfection in Perrault's tale – the mice which 'made a very fine set of six horses of a beautiful mouse-coloured dapple gray' (Dundes 1988: 18) – is equally a part of Hepburn's image – her repeated ability to make the basic and non-glamorous look perfect – men's pyjamas and a robe in *Roman Holiday* ('You should always wear my clothes,' says Joe Bradley), a robe, a bed sheet, a towel, a man's shirt – even brushing her teeth – in *Breakfast at Tiffany's*. While Hepburn's image is entirely appropriate to her Cinderella transformations, then, it also modulates these narratives in quite particular ways: for instance her rejection of traditional 'frilly' femininities which are typically the ideal in this scenario is made explicit and as the material offered in Chapter 4 bears witness, has been key to her popularity with some women.

The prominence of male characters as agents of change in Hepburn's Cinderella narratives has led Lisa Starks (1997), while acknowledging the Cinderella intertext, to characterise both *My Fair Lady* (rightly, of course) and *Sabrina*, along with the remake *Sabrina* (Sydney Pollack, 1995) and *Pretty Woman* as 'Pygmalion' films. In contrast, I would argue that placing emphasis on the Cinderella element of these films is particularly useful for the way in which it highlights upward mobility as an issue over the 'patriarchal plot' of the transformation narrative which is Starks's concern; furthermore, there is also a very precise way in which Hepburn's films modulate the Cinderella theme. It is undeniable that the role of the fairy godmother in Hepburn's Cinderella films is fulfilled partly by an older man, through Joe Bradley in *Roman Holiday*, the Baron (and Givenchy) in *Sabrina*, Dick Avery (but also Maggie Prescott) in *Funny Face*, O. J. Berman in *Breakfast at Tiffany's* and Henry Higgins in *My Fair Lady*. Furthermore, this role is no longer magical (although magic is still inscribed around the transformations with regard to dress – surely part of their continuing appeal), but becomes a process of acculturation, of *learning* – a process which is shown to be increasingly difficult as these films progress – and in this sense Starks's emphasis on patriarchal capitalism as a context is appropriate. However, there is a further point to be made about these films: their visual registers often emphasise something quite different. For instance, it is frequently the role and presence of Paris (or in the case of *Breakfast at Tiffany's*, a combination of New York and an idea of 'Frenchness'), as *the* romantic and modern city of the moment, which is the source of the magic and is central to the transformation, visually and emotionally. *Sabrina* is exemplary in this respect: as Sabrina writes home to her father of her growing sense of self, she sits before a window through which Paris is clearly visible – indeed she moves to open the window and let in 'La vie en rose'. While this certainly does not mitigate the 'male helper' discourse in these films, and in fact might be understood as precisely demonstrating the way women are encouraged to produce themselves in terms of desirable femininity, as a clear address to a feminine audience through the trope of the 'magical self-transformation' it is also an enormous source of pleasure. Furthermore, Starks's approach to these films is contemptuous, and she disregards the important role played by dress in securing a sense of self for many women, in, as Sabrina puts it, learning 'how to be *in* the world and *of* the world'.

Female characters in fact, while displaced from the role of fairy godmother to Hepburn's Cinderellas, fulfil a new function. Marina Warner has argued that Cinderella 'only secures her own exaltation when she excites the desire of the Prince, and is chosen by him. She needs the mirror of the Prince's approval to find her new self. Only in the glass of his love does she come into her own' (Warner 1986: 14). While initially Sabrina sees herself as 'nobody' because David Larrabee doesn't know she exists, her sense of self comes, as the scene described above demonstrates, in Paris, way before she returns to Long Island and David screams to a halt on seeing her at the station. In addition to the admiring gazes and whispers Sabrina and Eliza elicit from women at their moments of 'coming out', the emotional centres of these films suggest that it is in the eyes of women that Hepburn's Cinderellas look for support, judgement and approval (and it is perhaps significant in this respect that Hepburn's Cinderellas do not have female rivals – the 'ugly sisters' of the fairy tale. In *Sabrina*, it is the female cook who exclaims on Sabrina's return 'Look at you – you're such a lady, you've come home such a beautiful lady!' The final judgement, however, in class terms, rests with David's mother, who watches Sabrina at the party with her female friend: 'Who is that girl?' ... 'I don't know,' replies Mrs Larrabee, peering through her eyeglasses. 'Have I changed, have I really changed?' Sabrina asks her. Her reply is affirmative: 'You certainly have. You look lovely Sabrina.' That, however, is not the end of the story, as we shall see. In *My Fair Lady* it is Henry's mother and Mrs Pearce the housekeeper who support Eliza, and although she dances with the prince at the embassy ball, I argue that it is the previous moment where she is singled out by the queen of Transylvania which is the emotional centre of the film. As Eliza curtseys, the queen raises her gently, her hand beneath Eliza's chin, and looks into her face: 'Charming, quite charming.' I suggest that it is *these* resonant moments of recognition and validation, rather than the attempts to determine Eliza's identity by the Hungarian imposterologist (who significantly gets it entirely wrong), or the dances with the 'princes', that move and matter: 'recognition is a significant moment in the construction of subjectivity' (Skeggs 1997: 98). This specific conjunction of male and female gazes around Hepburn's Cinderellas at their moments of passing is key to her appeal and to the modulation around her persona of the most widely disseminated versions of the Cinderella story. As the material I discuss here illustrates, in the lived

'Cinderella' experiences of a number of the women I did research with, significant other women – friends, mothers and other female relatives, mothers of prospective partners – play an important role (as well as men) as bearers of a critical and influential gaze.

Even those films which do not have an explicit narrative relation to Cinderella – *War and Peace* and *Breakfast at Tiffany's*, for instance – have a key moment at a ball or a party. This moment of increased visibility, of 'coming out', is an enduring rite of passage for young women. Dances and dancing hold an important place in feminine culture, and are often seen as marking the shift from girlhood to womanhood; the continued importance of the high-school prom in the USA illustrates this precisely.[1] The elaboration of the occasion of Natasha's (Audrey Hepburn) first ball in *War and Peace* and her memory of the event plays out these resonances in a particularly touching way. As she ascends the staircase to the ball with her brother and his fiancée, the camera ascends in front of her, keeps pace with her, and catches every detail of her demeanour and expression. She asks her brother, 'Nicolas, the expression on my face . . . do I look disdainful?' Her aim, we discover, is to conceal the fact that this is her very first ball: 'Nicolas, is everybody looking at me?' she asks. 'Can't you see for yourself?' 'Not without changing the expression on my face,' she replies earnestly. At the ball, Natasha is shown in a long close-up, and we are privy to her thoughts through an internal monologue. She waits, she hopes, she checks the details of her dress and tries to maintain the expression on her face, and eventually her waiting is rewarded, her 'Cinderella' moment arrives. Prince Andrei appears, and asks her to dance. Later, as I discuss in Chapter 3, the dress she wore to this first ball prompts memory, music and emotion and the replaying of this important moment in Natasha's growing up. Significantly, Hepburn's Cinderellas seem not to marry the princes with whom they dance, and the resolutions to the fairytale scenarios of her films, as I will suggest, are anything but easy.

The first dance, the ball, often marks the moment of entry into the social; and in Hepburn's films, perhaps even more so than in Cinderella, the ball or dance – often the site of a very specific desire which motivates the transformation – is the point at which the female protagonist's identity is called into question, investigated as in *My Fair Lady*, or discovered. In *Roman Holiday* the dance on the moored barge (a significantly precarious space) is the scene of the discovery of the princess by her country's secret service and the end of her day of freedom. In *Breakfast at Tiffany's* Holly Golightly's cocktail party is the scene of repeated discussions by the men around her about her identity, of attempts to determine her authenticity. The following exchange between Holly's agent O. J. Berman and Paul Varjak (George Peppard) is particularly significant, especially in the light of the particular 'authenticity' of Hepburn's image discussed in Chapters 2 and 3:

O. J.: Is she or isn't she?
Paul: Is she or isn't she what?
O. J.: A phoney.
Paul: I don't know. I don't think so.
O. J.: You're wrong. She is. But on the other hand, you're right. Because she's a *real* phoney.

These anxious moments, however, are not simply a question of passing the test of elegance and sophistication, for this kind of idealised femininity is inextricably tied to class, a fact which is emphasised in those films which include a 'rags to riches' transformation such as *Sabrina*, *My Fair Lady* and even *Breakfast at Tiffany's*.[2] While it is made clear that Holly always 'had a lot of style, a lot of class', it was impossible to tell whether she was 'a Hillbilly or an Okie': they had to 'smooth out that accent' with, rather significantly, French lessons. Hepburn's particular association with continental Europe is key to her 'classiness'.

Feminist criticism of 'Cinderella' – for instance Dika (1987) – has emphasised the ideological problematics of the story, which Dika describes as 'an allegory of feminine success in a capitalist, patriarchal society' (32) – Cinderella's transformation of herself into a commodity. Elizabeth Panttaja notes the way in which feminist critics have written criticism on this narrative which focuses solely on the personal and psychosexual as a result of the 'psychologized notion of gender' which is their dominant analytical category. The result of this, as she rightly points out, is that questions of the social are either marginalised or excluded entirely (Panttaja 1993: 86). What readings such as Dika's fail to recognise is the ways in which films such as *Pretty in Pink* (the main focus of her critique), *Working Girl* (Mike Nichols, 1988) and certainly *Sabrina* and *My Fair Lady*, speak to a very precise feminine experience around status and clothing. They dramatise the difficulty of negotiating social position with a sense of self which remains true: what Beverley Skeggs describes as the way in which '[t]rying to pass as middle-class, to be accepted into another group, generates considerable anxiety for those who hope to pass' (Skeggs 1997: 87).

Recent work in cultural studies has begun to explore the significance of the conjunction of class and gender (Skeggs 1997; Walkerdine 1997). Valerie Walkerdine's autobiographical account of aspiration and class mobility in *Schoolgirl Fictions* (1990) uncovers the centrality of the intersection of class and gender in the constitution of subjectivity through her memories of growing up working-class in the 1950s and the painful process of being 'educated out' of that class. Aspiring to shift class meant one of two possibilities – marriage or work – of which she chose the latter. In *Daddy's Girl* (1997), Walkerdine notes the historically specific practices and discourses which constituted her subjectivity (1997: 24), pointing to the abundance of stories of affluent workers, and of workers becoming bourgeois, in the period when she was growing up: 'watching the possibility of Hollywood heroines change their life through education, as in *My Fair Lady*, spoke to me of the glamorous life that lay ahead of me if I too learned the lessons of school' (25). She goes on to discuss the anxiety of 'passing' in terms of class and gender, and the significance of the scene of the ball or dance (40).

For Valerie Walkerdine growing up in the 1950s and 1960s, the Cinderella narrative at the heart of Hepburn's image offered at that historical moment the possibility of social mobility through education: 'a whole post-war narrative about girls growing up into upward mobility' (94). This narrative of educational and class transition is historically and culturally specific and is common to many women academics who shared the experience of growing up working-class in Britain in the post-war period. Carolyn Steedman has described this story as following 'the educational progress of a girl born into a working class family and her success in making a journey of educational transition, by entry to a grammar school and then some form of higher education during the 1950s and 1960s' (Steedman 1997; see also Heron 1985: 2, and Kuhn 1995).[3] *My Fair Lady* has repeatedly either been offered to me in interviews as the favourite Audrey Hepburn film of women of this generation, or has emerged as a film which is pivotal in the accounts they give of growing up in this period; many of them share a similar educational and/or class trajectory. This was an entirely unanticipated finding, and is clearly key to an understanding of Hepburn's appeal for the young women who spoke to me about growing up with Audrey Hepburn in the 1950s and 1960s.

My Fair Lady was central to the accounts of all but one of the women I interviewed. It was often an interviewee's first point of contact with Hepburn, or the site of their most powerful memory of her. While it was sometimes offered as the favourite Hepburn film (Caroline, Barbara) this was not exclusively the case – indeed Rosie used the film as an illustration of a particular kind of femininity which alienates her.

> Well, I mean . . . I think she does it quite well, and I think there are some quite good characters in the film, I even quite like some of the musical numbers, but . . . it's not . . . an Audrey Hepburn film, to me. Well it's strange actually, 'cos I think all the women in my family like that best. They always have to watch My Fair Lady whereas I often choose not to.

Here, Rosie constructs herself as different from the other women in her family through her relationship to this film. When I asked Liz if this was her favourite Hepburn film as well as her strongest memory, she remembered going to see it, with West Side Story and The Sound of Music, with her mum, buying the LP and getting to know the songs, as did Caroline.

In three of the accounts about this period My Fair Lady was pivotal; discussion of this film was the starting point for a cluster of stories about growing up and moving upwards: about aspirations and dreams, expectations, education, work and marriage – about femininity, visibility and discovery – both positive and negative. These extremely moving stories, historically specific social and yet also highly personal narratives about the acquisition of both femininity and status, were often articulated through talk about visibility, dress and social conduct. At the beginning of our discussion, I asked Liz if she could remember the first time she saw or heard about Audrey Hepburn; she locates this around My Fair Lady, although she was aware of Hepburn before:

> Liz: I have a very clear memory of her in My Fair Lady, which was wonderful.
> RM: Tell me about that.
> Liz: Well, she looked so . . . *gorgeous*, you know, just *so* beautiful, but so inn – kind of wide-eyed and innocent, and of course, it's wonderful . . . kind of story of transformation, and I just thought she was

brilliant in it, I loved it, and the costumes and everything – wonderful. So I do remember that very clearly. But she was also in another film, called *Sabrina Fair* – I don't know if you – and that was very important, because at – I guess I was about, probably about eighteen, and I was very keen on amateur dramatics, it was when I was working as a secretary, or er – well a shorthand typist then, and my one, sort of, great hobby was . . . acting [laughs], so and I belonged at that time to a sort of small amateur group, *village*, where my parents lived then, 'cos they'd moved out of Leeds, and I got involved in that, and they cast me in this, they decided to do *Sabrina Fair*, because they thought that I had the, sort of, I could *do* the [laughs] do the part. So, of course, there was this incredible, and – I don't even know whether I'd actually seen the film at that stage . . . when I . . . but I – I certainly saw it after I was, *after* I'd been in the play, and I remember – you'd be interested in this – I – for the actual *play*, my mum and I *made* all my costumes for this [laughs] for this, for my part, because, you know, there were no, it was a sort of contemporary setting, kind of contemporary . . . United States, supposedly, and it's the story of, erm, the chauffeur's daughter, it's a sort of rich family, and it's the story – she's the chauffeur's daughter and she goes away, and then comes back, and sort of, sweeps the two sons off their feet, it's rather, romantic, and [laughs] yeah, I remember having to make all these very *smart outfits* . . . that my mum and I did . . . together.

Although I ask Liz here to tell me about her memory of Audrey in *My Fair Lady*, she shifts almost immediately to a personal story located around another Hepburn film with a similar narrative: the transformation of a gauche girl into a beautiful young woman. The story Liz tells of being chosen to play the Hepburn role – partly because she 'had the look' but also because she was right for the part – in the play of *Sabrina Fair* places her securely at the centre of this narrative of transformation. Indeed, this marks the beginning of Liz's own story of growing up and moving on through work, romance and education which is woven around and through our discussion of Audrey Hepburn, and, furthermore, clothes immediately emerge here as central to this process. The significance of the 'smart outfits' made for that production becomes clear, as this and the other stories unfold. Liz goes on to tell of how she won an award for most promising actress in a youthclub drama production:

and the guy who was the, sort of, instigator behind the village drama group came along to that, and saw, saw me, and decided that they should, have a, put on a play that, erm, had a part for me, so in fact there was that connection, which is very strange, and it's only since I've been thinking more closely about Audrey Hepburn that I've actually made that connection, it's quite strange.

The experience of being chosen for and starring in the role of Sabrina is discussed here in the context of and in contrast to Liz's work as a shorthand typist; somewhat uncomfortably, she recognises the resonance between the fictional narrative and the story she tells of her own experience.

> Liz: I suppose the narratives of both those films have got this . . . young woman being discovered, and then, sort of, suddenly, you know, the whole kind of – world turns around and looks at her, and I think that's actually quite a powerful . . . feminine dream, and I think it's probably particularly strong if you work in a typing pool! [laughs]
>
> RM: I'm sure!
>
> Liz: And what – I think that – working in a typing pool you had the sort of . . . you were in a very feminine world, you know, absolutely surrounded by other women, and again, I was the youngest there – I was the youngest there for years, and I think that – you know – the whole idea that you might actually – somebody might see you, or *discover* you [laughs] and take you away on, or at least see you in a different way, was actually quite, quite a strong, erm, *desire*.

This discourse of discovery and visibility is at the heart not only of Hepburn's roles, but also of the personal stories I was told in discussions about her; these scenarios are often articulated through a mode of talk about clothes which demonstrates their centrality in the lived experiences of the women I talked to. Barbara, for instance, describes a dress she made to go on holiday which she remembers as being like Hepburn's style in *Breakfast at Tiffany's*: 'nice little shoes to match, I think I even had a bag to match as well! [RM: Did you?] Yeah – because it was a big thing then, when you went on the aeroplane you dressed up . . . you didn't go in your jeans, or whatever, you actually dressed up when you went on a plane, 'cos it was such an important thing, you know.'

Janet remembered how she 'enjoyed the glamour of going to Drury Lane' to see *My Fair Lady* (with Julie Andrews), and also to the Odeon Leicester Square in London. I asked her what she enjoyed particularly about the film:

Janet: Well, I think you always try to . . . change places with somebody, don't you, in things like that, it's like – that's what you go to the films for!

RM: Do you think so?

Janet: Course it is! To escape real life, isn't it, to . . .

RM: So did that story appeal to you?

Janet: Course it did, yeah!

RM: Well, can you say anything about that – why it appealed to you?

Janet: Not really . . . I just enjoyed it.

RM: She changes from [Janet: Mmm] being a dirty little guttersnipe, to –

Janet: Well she wasn't a guttersnipe [indignantly] I mean, she was a very poor person – that doesn't make you a guttersnipe.

RM: No – it doesn't.

Janet: It was nice – I enjoyed it.

As I discuss in Chapter 3, this was a rather difficult interview in some ways. At this point, while Janet begins by acknowledging her identification with the character and her trajectory in this film, when I pick up on this, she retreats, unwilling to elaborate – a result, perhaps, of bad interview technique. When I use the word 'guttersnipe' of Eliza, however – a word offered to me by a previous interviewee who shared this woman's class origins – Janet responds indignantly in a way which perhaps indicates a greater investment than she consciously acknowledges. Janet also worked as a secretary, and later recalled being taken to London to see *My Fair Lady* at Drury Lane by her new boss:

And, I didn't really have to dress up for work, but I did start to become more clothes conscious when I worked there, because I used to go out with my boss a lot, and he used to take me to places like I'd never been taken to in my life before, very posh places, so I suppose, really, it was probably down to him, that changed my way of thinking on – he must have manipulated me without me knowing it, by suggesting things that I could buy to wear, I mean, I didn't realise it at the time . . . he would take me to places, and I'd obviously got the intelligence to look around me and think to myself 'I'm not really dressed suitably to come to a place like this' so the next time he took me, I would make sure that I was.

There is a clear indication here of the way in which clothing can produce a sense of self. The need to be 'suitably dressed' Janet talks about here is tied to a feeling of being out of her depth in new environments – 'places like I'd never been taken to in my life before, very posh places' – a fear of being 'found out' – and is a profoundly classed experience. What she precisely articulates here is the anxiety of the moment of realising that you need to 'pass', that is, to appear to have 'naturally' the signs of a particular (middle-)classed and gendered identity to get on, and of learning how to do it. She continued:

> And I can remember buying, and I thought I was the bees knees – I bought what they called – now I don't know what they used to call it – it was a straight edge-to-edge coat, and it was reversible, it was beige on one side – [RM: Sounds expensive –] it was – it was beige on one side, and it was cream on the other side, so you could wear it either way, and I bought new cream shoes and a cream handbag, and the shoes were a bit tight, and I made the mistake of taking them off while I was in the theatre, and I couldn't get them back on again! [shudders and laughs at the memory] Oh, God I was crippled! I was *crippled*, I, I don't think I've ever felt so miserable in all my life – as I tried to *hobble* back to the station [laughs] – oh, dear God!

Coming through clearly in this account is an acute sense of the importance of clothes and conduct at moments of increased visibility such as this visit to Drury Lane; at the same time, Janet expresses both her pleasure in the expensive new clothes she bought for this event, but also the labour and anxiety that producing an appropriate femininity for occasions such as this can generate. The way in which Janet offers this kind of story around going to see *My Fair Lady* is, I think, particularly resonant, not least for the way in which it produces her, like Eliza, as 'visible' in a highly public way, whilst articulating the pressures and pleasures of this type of experience. Similarly, Barbara continued her memory of going abroad on holiday:

> We went to Corfu, yeah, and I remember coming back off that holiday, and er, we got rained in, the runway was washed out, so we were actually stuck there for twenty-four hours, and they put us up in – I remember sitting in the airport, trying to be comfortable in this dress [laughing] and the belt was – oh! And I'd actually – I was actually pregnant, I'd – well I was only just pregnant, I didn't know I was pregnant until I was on holiday, and the second week, I started getting morning sickness, so, and I felt so uncomfortable, I remember this great big belt, and trying to be – sitting nicely in the airport, you know, and in the end they took us to a hotel, and put us up for the night! [both laugh]

While she took great pleasure in remembering and describing in detail the 'Audrey Hepburn' dress she made to go away on this holiday,

Barbara's recollection is tempered instantaneously with the memory of having to 'sit nicely' in it despite her discomfort.

Janet went on to offer a number of wonderful, detailed descriptions of outfits borrowed, or desired and saved for, around her story of learning how to manage herself appropriately in these new public spaces, which included formal dances and posh hotels. Furthermore, she described the way in which her (male) boss educated her in table etiquette 'although I'd obviously got ordinary family table manners'. She remembered later how she went out with a man from a radically different social circle, and how the things she learned in this previous relationship got her through:

> Janet: He invited me to London for the weekend, sent me my train ticket, met me at Kings Cross in an MGB GT with the top down, pale blue, took me to stay at the guest suite of his parents' flat, which was in Dolphin Square, and if you've ever seen Dolphin Square . . . Dolphin Square is like a self-contained village – it's got everything, it's got its own bank, it's got its own shops – I couldn't believe it – silver service in the morning – tray of tea, with a maid actually dressed as maids dress.
>
> RM: How intimidating.
>
> Janet: It was. It's a good job I'd got the background training from this other relationship, 'cos otherwise, I wouldn't have handled it.

Liz remembered a similar experience but in her case the person who undertook the educative role was another woman:

> Liz: It was very much learning as you went, really, [RM: Was it?] yeah, and I remember . . . the person who was most influential, not in dress, or anything like that, but in terms of *how to behave*, was my – she became my mother-in-law, that was my boyfriend's mother, and she – was very . . . *careful* – she did it very *carefully* – she did it rather *subtly*. [RM laughs] She taught me . . . how to, how to . . . *behave*.
>
> RM: Did she?
>
> Liz: Mmm.
>
> RM: What kinds of things?
>
> Liz: Well how to – you know – how to sort of, ask for things at the table, how to eat – I mean, that's not to say that my family didn't have manners, or anything, [RM: No, I know] but there was a certain, there were certain kinds of . . . etiquette, that . . . go beyond just, kind of, good manners [RM: There are . . .] and things, and I remember learning a lot from her.
>
> RM: Was she kind about it?

Liz: She was really – I don't – I'm not even sure that she knew she was doing it, but I certainly was . . . I was *receptive*. And I learned, I learned how to be . . . I learned how to behave in that kind of way . . . very . . . very interesting. But I think, I mean I do think a lot of young women in that position have got the ability to adapt to their surroundings [laughs].

Both of these women had an acute sense of the way in which ordinary family 'manners' are in certain situations not quite 'enough' – it's not enough, as Eliza repeatedly says, to be 'a good girl' and the difficulty of this discovery comes across clearly in both of these women's accounts. Liz's description of the learning process as one of adaptation is particularly interesting as it perhaps suggests that this kind of acquired behaviour, while partially naturalised, always also necessarily remains performative. We went on in this interview to talk about the common experience of elocution, deportment and ballroom dancing lessons which were part of both of our education at school, although twenty years apart:

Liz: Yes, I did, when I went to this – again it was a private school, but it was because I didn't – I failed my 11+, and my parents didn't want me to go to the 'secondary modern' school, because they thought it was too . . . rough [laughs].

RM: That was exactly my parents' reason . . .

Liz: So they paid for me to go to this school which was very poor, I mean, I only did – from the age of eleven I only had 'education' in the mornings, and every afternoon was given over to 'commercial' subjects.

RM: What – like –?

Liz: Shorthand, typing, book-keeping, so that was what I, so I learned Pitman shorthand, and, so between, for, between eleven and fifteen, that was what I learned, and those were my qualifications when I came out of it. But there was also – they offered elocution – because all of this was considered to be appropriate for office work, which is where we were destined, really – ballroom dancing.

RM: I did that, yep. [both laugh]

Liz: [laughing] Dancing backwards! [both laugh] And – now what else . . . keep fit, which was, you know, Eileen whatshername – Eileen Fowler – Health and Beauty [RM: Oh right!] – it wasn't keep fit, it was Health and Beauty! So we had – you know – we did exercises with Indian clubs, and things like that. [RM: Did you?] Yeah – nothing like 'gym'!

RM: No – much more 'elegant'!

Liz: Yes, yes. Erm, and that was – those were . . . the subjects – there
was nothing – they didn't teach us cooking, home economics, or anything like that, not sewing, but all to do with, I guess, performance.
RM: And being out in public.
Liz: Yes, yes. And elocution was, was very . . . interesting, 'cos I *must*
have had a Yorkshire accent – my parents do. And I learned how to
speak like – you did, without an accent –
RM: [at the same time] – without an accent. You see mine was Birm-
ingham, 'cos I'd been at first school, and [Liz: Right . . .] I had to
unlearn it. [Liz: Yes]
[. . .]
Liz: Yeah – and how to just, behave . . . like a . . . female, really.
RM: Like a lady –
Liz: *Like a lady*. Yes – in fact, it was called 'The Northcote College for
Young Ladies'.

This imperative to produce an appropriate public femininity is
clearly discernible in advice addressed to young women going out to
work and starting out on the road to upward mobility. Indeed, to
coincide with the release of *My Fair Lady*, *Honey* the 'Young, gay
and get-ahead' British magazine for young women published a
three-part 'Fair Lady' course in June, July and August of 1965:

Part 1. *A Voice to be Heard* – It starts today . . . our own 'Fair Lady'
course – to cut out and keep. Maybe, unlike Eliza, you don't want to
be 'a lady in a flower shop'. Maybe, like us, you don't think 'talking
proper' is the beginning and end of everything. But we'd all like the
things we say to rivet attention, wouldn't we? Those penetrating
observations that will show our discernment, those gems of wit we've
polished with such care mustn't be wasted with breathy squeaks, muddled mumbles and sickening slurs. This month we're all how-now-
brown-cowing with the help of Cicely Berry from The Central School
of Speech and Drama . . . next month we're polishing up our manners
for mods . . . then there's the low-down on poise and capability. So,
you see, you *could* go to finishing school if you like, but it costs more
than Honey's two bob.

(*Honey*, June 1965, p. 61)

Janet remembered the period when she began to be interested in
clothes:

RM: Did you try and be smart?
Janet: I did. Yeah, I mean, the age of about . . . until I was probably . . .
how old would I be . . . until I was about – terrible really – until I

was about nineteen, I never thought about smartness at all – never entered my head [laughs].

She 'smartened up' when her new boss took her under his wing and began to advise her. Like Janet, Liz remembered becoming interested in clothes when she started work. When she was fifteen, her parents moved out of Leeds to a more rural, small town area, and she started work in an office in the city. This, she recalled, was perceived to be rather grown up by her peer group, who were largely still at school.

Liz: I had access to some money, and I also had to dress for work, so it'd – you know, already for me it'd become something of an issue [laughs] – something to be thought about.

RM: Of course . . . what would you have worn for work, what kind of thing?

Liz: Erm . . . straight skirts, never trousers – trousers weren't acceptable – I wouldn't have, it wouldn't have occurred to me, actually, to wear trousers. Probably a blouse, and a jacket, or . . . my mum used to knit me sweaters. So I would have sweaters, and always kind of, the colour combinations were always good, and bright – always *smart*. I used to wear gloves.

RM: Did you?

Liz: Yes.

RM: Always?

Liz: White gloves in the summer! [laughs] And then summer dresses in the – yep – for summer wear. But it always had to be very – er . . .
. . . quite conventional, nothing . . . *showy*.

The notion in Liz's story of growing up and going to work that a girl's clothes had to be 'smart' and 'not showy' is echoed in advice offered to young working women in magazines of the time. Gillian Gilles's weekly women's fashion and beauty back page in the British film magazine *Picture Show and TV Mirror* had Lana Turner (*Imitation of Life*) advise the working girl 'Don't overdo the glamour': 'I still assert that business girls should set out to look glamorous, but they should bear in mind that in this instance discretion is the better part of glamour' (16 May 1959). The 'wardrobe of a working girl' should 'strike a happy medium' – neither 'silly siren' nor 'anonymity': the page showed examples of 'smart and simple clothes which any ambitious working girl might favour' (*Picture Show and Film Pictorial*, 23 November 1957). Similarly, the repeated warning to young women not to do their hair like Brigitte Bardot emphasised that Bardot's hairstyle is 'deceptive' – in fact she visits the hairdresser twice a week: 'though it looks beguiling on holiday and in the dance hall, it is not a style likely to win approval from your working boss; and it would certainly be forbidden in a factory. So keep your ponytail for work, you longhaired youngsters, and only "let your hair down" like Brigitte's for gay times' (*Picture Show and Film Pictorial*, 29 November 1958). Clearly, this can be related to the material constructing Hepburn as 'classy' and 'not sexy' in relation to stars like Bardot and Monroe discussed in Chapter 4. In 1960 Joan Crawford advised on this page against Beat styles for young women, as I discuss in more detail in Chapter 2. 'Good taste is NEVER old-fashioned':

> You'll never be a success at work if you are sloppy in dress . . . there is one code, and that should prevail year after year. It is downright foolish to go around looking untidy (which so many girls are doing right now). You've got nothing to be proud of and you're nothing to look at! Every girl, with a wit of intelligence, be she secretary, shop girl, factory worker or what have you, should aim to look her best . . . you'll usually find that the girl who is sloppy in her appearance and in clothes is slovenly at her work, too.
>
> (*Picture Show and TV Mirror* 23 January 1960)[4]

Despite the disclaimer that 'proper' speech is not the beginning and end of everything, the presence of such discourses in magazines for 'modern' young women – also apparent in films like *My Fair Lady* and *Sabrina* and in accounts by women growing up in this period in Britain which dramatise anxieties around acquiring the signs of class – indicates the importance of appearing 'classy' even where this is not explicitly linked to social status. It appears as a means of improving oneself and one's social position as late as the mid-1960s.

Liz spoke very interestingly about the significance of clothing for young women in relation to social mobility through work in this period:

> I think, I think it's very important . . . I mean I think that, I think there was a sort of, there was almost a kind of uniform for young women who'd gone into office work, and we were all the same, really, we all looked the same, and certainly I think in class terms, we were all the same, but we would – we'd done *well* [laughs], in class terms, 'cos we were largely a working-class background but we'd got – we weren't in a shop, and we weren't in a factory, we were actually in offices – so an office job was a good job for a girl, and that's certainly how – what my

parents felt, so what was important then, was to dress – to look appropriate, and it was that sense in which you had to look smart, but not, I suppose, reveal anything, of your origins, really, so you had to actually look the part. . . . I do remember my mum – when we were, when I was in my last year at school, and at school I learned how to do shorthand typing, so I was fully expecting a job, and I remember having this conversation with my mum, when were washing up one afternoon, and I said 'What will I *wear* at work, mum?' – 'cos I'd worn a school uniform – and she said 'You'll wear nice skirts, and I'll knit you nice jumpers' [laughs], and she knew exactly what I would wear, you know, what would be appropriate.

As she had pointed out earlier, 'being fashionable' was not part of the picture at this point, rather it was 'what was *appropriate* and, you know, what was *fitting* to wear'. Liz concludes this part of her story: 'As long as you got it right, you know, as long as you didn't step over the boundaries or anything, you were OK.' She moves on at this point to explain how her family moved 'to a much more middle-class location' and to describe the major change which accompanied it:

I then encountered kids, you know, who were still at school doing 'A' levels, and well, 'O' levels at that time, but fully expecting to go to university, whose parents were . . . more . . . professional . . . and I did hit a sort of *confusing* time as to who I should be and what I should look like, and I remember that very clearly, and then it also really intensified when I got together with this boy who went to Cambridge, and that was a big – I mean that was a completely unknown world, completely unknown world, and that was, I think . . . finding how to look that was appropriate, that wasn't . . . that, yeah, that didn't sort of, give me away, really – of you know, just being able to look – 'cos I – I mean, it was also not having any kind of education, really, as well, so I was suddenly in this group, you know, that had completely different, different background, and different access to knowledge.

This shift would include, for instance, going to a garden party and the May ball at Cambridge. Liz described managing such occasions by being able to occupy a rather romanticised position offered by 1960s films portraying young working women, and which were interested in fashion; fashion, in this sense, functioned as a kind of protective clothing.

The idea of 'looking the part' articulated by Liz above in relation to that earlier moment before 'fashion' became a significant and useful discourse for her, is precisely that which was so evident in Janet's account of going to Drury Lane: she also remembered the uniform of jumpers and skirts that she wore when she started work in an office. Clearly this is also related to etiquette and elocution – and Liz articulates this here in terms of not 'revealing anything of your origins', finding a way to look that didn't 'give her away', thereby explicitly locating the notion of being dressed 'appropriately' within a discourse about social class which is also inextricably a discourse about femininity. It is imperative that these acquired signs appear 'natural' – precisely what Pierre Bourdieu means by 'habitus' (Bourdieu 1986). What these women reveal through the stories they tell about themselves, about growing up and moving up, is the way in which those signs of class and gender are always already constructed for them, remaining a kind of meta-discourse: precisely that which is discernible in Sabrina's calculatedly off-hand pose as she waits at the Glencove station.

These are stories, primarily, of young women moving up through work in the late 1950s and early 1960s, and through an education which is not necessarily the more formal 'scholarship girl' route I described above. While Janet went to grammar school, she declined a place at college in order to become engaged, and when this didn't work out subsequently got a good job as chief cashier for a large entertainments company which enabled her to leave home and get her own flat before she eventually married. Liz described what was the expected path upwards, and through it hints at the significance of *Sabrina* to her own story, interpreting it through its resonance for her own aspirations at that moment:

> There was a – an absolute, sort of, specified route through, which was to get engaged, and get married, and then you would get out, but, you know, that – and so I suppose really, the kind of desire was always channelled into that, rather than, doing anything *different* . . . but I think what Audrey Hepburn did, was to do something *different* [laughs] and in those two films, particularly *Sabrina Fair*, I think that she had gone off and er . . . found out about the world, and discovered how wonderful the world was.

'What I thought I should be doing,' she recalled, 'was to get a boyfriend.' Later in the interview, she describes how her own aspirations diverged from those her parents had for her – to work in an office. She was interested in journalism and drama, neither of which was deemed an appropriate choice – eventually, she would go to university as a mature student.

Janice Winship's discussion of dress, demeanour and the notion of the 'classed body' in relation to social mobility in the interwar period is germane here (Winship 1998). Winship uses the formulation 'nice and neat' to describe the way in which the transgression of women into new spaces and across cultural boundaries was made non-threatening (and significantly, in relation to the material discussed in Chapter 4, non-sexual) through the mobilisation of a body made small, made 'nice and neat' through particular modes of dress (1998: 15). In the discussions of dress and mobility by aspirational working-class women in these accounts of the later post-war moment, the same mode of self-presentation – 'nice and neat' – is evident, and is particularly interesting in relation to the question of femininity and sexuality: the accounts of both Liz and Janet simultaneously suggest and skirt around the question of 'going away' with men for weekends. Most of these stories I was told in relation to liking Audrey Hepburn are set just before the marriages of the women take place, at a precise moment of negotiation around femininity, class and romance.

Love, marriage and the domestic

In Chapter 4 I discuss the way in which wedding dresses and going-away outfits emerge as a key point of focus around which discussion of Hepburn's look takes place in these accounts, although paradoxically perhaps, weddings and marriage do not feature in Hepburn's image. A wedding day is often the greatest moment of public visibility of a woman's life – the ultimate moment when she is centre stage. Furthermore, it is a particularly rich site in that it brings together ideas of growing up, becoming a woman, and, particularly in the Cinderella scenario, moving up socially. Bernie's marriage, for instance, would eventually enable her to describe herself as 'very middle-class': 'I was never, never, never going to stop down there, I can assure you,' she told me. It is perhaps appropriate, then, that these and other such moments – going abroad on a plane (I can imagine Barbara standing at the top of the aeroplane steps, waiting to descend), sitting at the airport, going to a London show – should be discussed around a star so explicitly associated with moments of coming out, of increased visibility. These may also often be, as I have argued above, moments which involve the threat of discovery. Balls, dances and dancing, parties, as in Hepburn's films, feature in all of these accounts – as in Liz's experience of the Cambridge May ball and garden party. Similarly, in a way which also indicates the resonance of Hepburn's image for young women just venturing out in the world of romance, Caroline recalls the following in relation to *Breakfast at Tiffany's*:

> 'Cos did she sing 'Moon River?' [RM: Yeah –] Yes, now you see, that's another, big sort of romantic association – my very first dance, the last dance, was 'Moon River', [laughs] dancing with some pimply adolescent boy [both laugh] – he was just sort of, required to be there, standing – but I can still remember that, yes, yes, yes . . . So yes, I suppose it's just caught up with – I was perhaps the right age, and at the right stage.

Valerie Walkerdine's account of the appeal of Audrey Hepburn in *My Fair Lady* is particularly suggestive of the dependence of social mobility for poor women, even for those who are educated and competent in the signs of 'class', on marriage to a man of a higher status:

> these films signal a particular trajectory which incorporates education, respectability, glamour, romance, and *upward mobility through marriage* . . . *My Fair Lady* was a favourite of mine, because Audrey Hepburn was transformed from a rough-speaking poor girl into someone who can pass for a princess and *marry out of her class into wealth, glamour and romance.*
>
> (Walkerdine 1997: 95) [emphasis added]

I consider here the way in which the dramatisation of this trajectory of upward mobility is discussed through personal histories, inscribed in women's magazines and embedded textually in the key films of Hepburn's career, particularly in *Sabrina* and *My Fair Lady*, released ten years apart in 1954 and 1964 respectively, and precisely spanning this historical period of possibility. It is my contention that while at this social and historical moment these narratives functioned hegemonically as tales of the possibility of successful transformation and mobility, nevertheless discernible within them are significant tensions around other elements of Hepburn's image which evidence the difficulty of articulating femininity in its relation to upward mobility, work, marriage and the domestic. As working women begin to appear increasingly in the public sphere, and there are apparently greater possibilities for improvement and mobility, these narratives speak increasingly clearly of the contradictions and difficulties of upward mobility for women, even as these difficulties are negotiated as a result of Hepburn's 'serene misfit' image. The personal stories of aspiration and achievement I discuss above are offered around Hepburn, not simply or necessarily in relation to her image, but often more generally in response to a certain resonance around dress and mobility available through her. This is articulated through a complex conjunction of marriage, work and education in the same stories as possible ways to move up. Indeed, while Walkerdine's characterisation of the trajectory of Hepburn as Eliza Doolittle in *My Fair Lady* indicates the resonance of this type of story at that moment, it nevertheless suppresses a significant discourse in the film around just this difficulty of social mobility for women which I elaborate below.

The difficulty of the domestic

> Look – I admit I came to Paris to escape American Provincial, but that doesn't mean I'm ready for French Traditional![5]

Throughout *Sabrina*, Sabrina's father emphasises the importance of respect for working people from those around them: 'We were respected by everyone – that's as much as any one can want in this world. Don't reach for the moon, child.' Sabrina, however, wants more, and through her stylish transformation, on her return she is seen to have acquired the outward signs of 'class', her ticket, she feels, to better things: La vie en rose. In contrast, however, to Lisa Starks's impression that 'her transformation complete, Sabrina transgresses class boundaries and marries a millionaire … these skills are all our 1950s Sabrina needs to elevate her station in life' (1997: 51) the path to upward mobility is hardly so straightforward. While sartorial transformation and the concomitant acquisition of 'class' in *Sabrina* are central to the female protagonist's sense of self, the tensions in the film around class, and the difficulties the signs of this on Sabrina's body produce around the domestic, leave her, as I will go on to discuss, literally 'all dressed up with nowhere to go'.

'Everything has changed!' proclaims Sabrina on her return from Paris. Indeed, she has acquired all the bodily and sartorial signs of class; she is clearly 'classy': 'Look at you – you're such a lady – you've come home such a beautiful lady!' exclaims the cook. Later, Charles the butler reports back to the staff downstairs on Sabrina's success at the party: 'You should see her – the prettiest dress, the prettiest girl, the best dancer, the belle of the ball. And such poise – as if she belonged up there.' *As if* she belonged up there, however, it becomes apparent, is inadequate to produce actual upward mobility: there is a significant distinction between having 'class', being 'classy', and social status. 'Have I changed, have I really changed?' Sabrina asks David's mother. Despite her reply in the affirmative, when David reminds her Sabrina has been to Paris, her response is telling: 'Yes, I know. You must come over sometime and cook something very special, Sabrina. I want to see what you've learned.' In one sentence, Mrs Larrabee tries to restore Sabrina to the domestic realm, attempting to nullify the effects of the transformation she has undergone: she puts her back in her place. The mise-en-scène subtly reinforces this refusal of Sabrina's access to the family and upward mobility through a textual articulation of the tensions at work around class in this film. At this moment, they are standing on the terrace where the dancing is going on; it is bounded on one side by the garden, and on the other by the ultimate sign of the Larrabees' social status – the family home. They stand before the glass doors which are leaded in a grid pattern, and through which are visible the drawing room, chandeliers and the family portrait (figure 5.1). At the end of this exchange, Mrs Larrabee opens one of these doors and goes in, closing it behind her and thus emphasising the impossibility of Sabrina's entry to this space.

Our access to this space as viewers at this point is aligned with Sabrina's; we see Mrs Larrabee go inside and reveal David's relationship with Sabrina, but we see this only through the barred windows, and hear only a brief snatch of conversation as the door opens, and then silence. To further reinforce the point, Linus and his parents stand before these windows watching David and Sabrina dance, blocking the open door. Elizabeth, David's rightful fiancée, opens the door and passes through. Even the reconciliation of Sabrina with Linus at the close of the film offers only an uneasy resolution. Their reunion takes place on board ship, out at sea and safely off American soil. While David's marriage to Elizabeth will go ahead, assuring the future of the business and the family status, there is little suggestion of a marriage between Linus and Sabrina, who are heading for Paris, the city of lovers. If Sabrina's upward mobility is dependent on marriage, then her future and respectability are less than certain: her social position, despite her apparent 'class', is difficult to change.

5.1 Upward mobility denied in *Sabrina* (1954)

Mrs Larrabee may have successfully prevented Sabrina's entry into the family, but her attempt to replace Sabrina in the domestic sphere appears less triumphal. At Linus's office, improperly dressed for dinner in the city, Sabrina offers to cook for them. The kitchen is highly undomestic; it is modern, urban, minimal (much like Hepburn's image) and is stocked only with tomato juice, puffed rice and crackers. Preparing to cook for Linus, her apron is improvised from a tea-towel, and she puts this on in such a way that it is almost as if she has slipped on a piece of expensive jewellery or a silk scarf. The shadow she casts across the kitchen is disjointed, the top separated from the bottom; she is literally a 'displaced person'. As her father describes her earlier in the film, 'She doesn't belong in a mansion, but then again she doesn't belong in the garage, either.' She certainly doesn't belong in the kitchen. Her domesticity is the result of a less than easy education, and it is not assumed that she will naturally become a cook as her mother was before her. The lady she has become could work for her living neither in the city nor as a domestic servant, and yet despite her 'classiness' she appears to remain unmarriageable: 'Sorry I can't stay to do the dishes,' she tells Linus when she realises his intention to trick her. Within this film there is a spatial economy which relates in precise and complex ways to Sabrina's disjunctive identity, a topography relating to her indeterminacy of identity which accompanies Hepburn throughout her films. Her quarters above the garage, at the top of a spiral staircase (also evident in *Roman Holiday*), precisely expresses her 'in-betweenness' with regard to class and the precariousness of her social position. The terrace where she dances with David is not truly part of the Larrabee home, but then again, neither is it part of the garden where the downstairs staff wave to her from behind the hedge separating it from the terrace.

Hepburn is endlessly caught in liminal, transitional spaces – on moored barges, balconies, staircases, in halls, on fire escapes, in doorways and windows – neither in nor out, nor free, in every film. This trope is an eloquent expression of her 'in-between' status, both as a star and as a character, in each of these films – not just with regard to class, but also in relation to age and national identity (see Chapters 2 and 4). Furthermore as Linus goes out onto the balcony of his office, Sabrina in the kitchen is separated from him by a gauzy screen. She comes towards him, and hovers in the doorway in her apron-which-is-not-an-apron, neither on the balcony looking out over the modern city and the *Liberté* bound for Paris, nor in the kitchen-which-is-not-a-kitchen. While she thinks that Linus is taking her to Paris, there appears to be no question of marriage. The difficulty of her position with regard to class and marriage, work, domesticity and her urbanite self is perfectly expressed in this moment;[6] she may hover around the boundaries, but it is unclear whether she can ever settle fully on either side (figure 5.2).

In Chapter 4, I explored the construction of Hepburn as 'modern' in Bernie's account, and the way in which Hepburn's modernity is intrinsically linked to her 'newness' in terms of style. 'Modern' means new, different, and with 'the modern' comes cultural capital: status amongst her peer group. Despite the fact that, as I suggest above, part of Hepburn's appeal for this woman lies precisely in her *difference* from the American culture in which Bernie invested strongly as a young teenager, nevertheless 'America' looms large in her description of the delight she felt at seeing *Breakfast at Tiffany's* for the first time:

RM: So, I mean, *Breakfast at Tiffany's* –
Bernie: Brilliant!
RM: What – so, I mean, why? Why was it brilliant? I mean I know because she was –
Bernie: (a) because it was set in *modern day New York*. Which you didn't see.
RM: Oh!
Bernie: Well, you didn't! You saw . . . Al Capone-type New York, and all you saw was the cars, you didn't see any of the big buildings, you didn't see any of *that* – or the views, or anything like that – so it was a great way of seeing the fabul – I mean, Amer – anything *American* – [RM: Yeah –] was like – you'd break your neck for it! You would, you know . . . I mean, American, if it was American, it was [sharp intake] the *best*.

5.2 Hepburn hovers in between the city and kitchen in *Sabrina* (1954)

We go on to discuss the views of New York in the film, and importantly, the shops:

> Bernie: Yes, yeah! And I mean, you heard of these, of Goodmann, and Gildorf – or whatever it was called – [RM: Yeah –] You would *hear* of these, or you'd read about them, actually, wouldn't you, you didn't hear about it, you read about it, so you got these, you know . . . this *vision* – and then you saw it! *Not* somebody's impression of it, or if you went to a thea– , and you know, you'd say *Broadway*, and it'd show you a picture, and it wasn't *really* Broadway, it was a stage set of Broadway.
> RM: Yes, of course.
> Bernie: But this was – *New York*.
> RM: Real –
> Bernie: Real – with the traffic and the whole schmoddle. And the fashion.

What is notable here, I think, is the way in which the America which captures her imagination, and which she associates with Hepburn, is not the 'beachy' West Coast America she associates with Sandra Dee, but is a modern, urban East Coast America which, crucially, is understood to be more real, and in some way, as I discuss, both more 'classy' *and* thus more accessible or appropriate. Earlier, Bernie had remembered going to the cinema with girlfriends to see romantic, modern films, primarily to see what female stars were wearing. In contrast, 'blokes always wanted to see, like, *cowboys* films [both laugh]'. This is a vision of New York she has not been offered before at the movies – it's a New York of fashion, shopping, *style* – rather than of gangsters and cars. When I continue by asking what appealed particularly about Holly Golightly, Bernie responds by talking about *Roman Holiday*:

Bernie: There was one where she was a *princess* [laughs] [RM: Yeah –]
and she *escaped* . . . that's it, so she was, again, she was escaping
from this, you know, fantastic life, to what she really wanted to be –
which is really her, isn't it? So, you know, that was fabulous. Another
one, was there one set during the war, when she was . . .
RM: Yeah . . . *The Nun's Story.*
Bernie: [very quietly] Yes – oh, that was *won*derful.

She connects these three films through a characterisation of Hepburn's roles as 'escapes', and as searches for self. *Breakfast at
Tiffany's* expressly inscribes Holly's search for self from the outset
through predominant devices such as reflections (amongst the crys-
tal chandeliers in the window of Tiffany's the jewellers, as in the
window of the barber shop in *Roman Holiday*) and mirrors. However, this search becomes increasingly defined through a complex
relationship to marriage and the domestic which also can be dis-
cerned in other of her films. Raymond Durgnat suggested in his
'little dictionary of poetic motifs' that

> [p]hotographed as reflected in the shop window, your character is
> transparent to what he is gazing at – his desires and obsessions are
> more solid and real than he [*sic*] himself . . . Shop windows are the
> realm of the coveted, the fairyland of desire . . . Audrey Hepburn has
> *Breakfast at Tiffany's.*
>
> (Durgnat 1967: 233)

Holly may have Tiffany's as the scene of her desire and search for
self, but despite her distinctly urban and indeed public mode of
femininity, Tiffany's becomes increasingly aligned with complexities
around the domestic and marriage throughout the film. She's looking for 'a place where me and things go together. I'm not sure where
that is, but I know what it's like – it's like Tiffany's!' This is a safe
place: 'The quietness and the proud look of it – nothing very bad
could happen to you there.' She finally declares that when she finds
a real-life place that could make her feel like Tiffany's then she'll
'buy some furniture and give the cat a name!' This statement takes
place against the domestic chaos, or rather, 'domesticity as urban
chic', of Holly's minimal, 'on edge' New York apartment, where the
sofa is half a bath tub, upholstered, the phone lives in a suitcase,
shoes live in the fridge and she drinks milk from a champagne glass.
Holly, it transpires, has escaped one domestic arrangement as wife to
Doc Golightly and step-mother to his numerous children in Tulip,

Texas. As New York playgirl Holly, she still yearns for the domestic, and in preparation for her move to Brazil with José she attempts to domesticate her flat and find herself through it. There is proper furniture, flowers on the table, and she is knitting, although as she points out, the pattern has become muddled with some plans and 'It's perfectly possible that [she's] knitting a ranch-house!' She stresses that finally she's really happy, she has 'found herself', but when Paul asks her, 'You *are* getting married then?' she replies, 'Well, he hasn't really *asked* me, not in so many words . . .' and soon after the pressure cooker explodes, scattering chicken in chocolate sauce around the flat. Holly fails at domesticity and her rather *too* public urban femininity is inappropriate for José – she is unmarriageable for a man of his status. He has discovered in a 'brutal and public manner how different [she is] from the kind of woman a man of [his] position could hope to make his wife'. 'Proper' femininity is tied to domesticity, and in the last analysis, Holly's relationship to the domestic is, like Tiffany's, just so much urban chic – a stylistic choice – and they head out into the city for dinner. 'Oh I love New York!' she exclaims, smoking a cigarette and looking at the skyscrapers.

As Bernie's description of her delight in this film suggested, *Breakfast at Tiffany's* offered an appealing vision of Hepburn as the modern girl in *the* modern city – a vision which Bernie constructs explicitly as 'for girls'. She will *not* bring her 'nine Brazilian brats' to see this – the indication is that she will remain here with Paul in the somewhat unconventional domestic arrangements they share. The ring which, in the final scenes of the film, she slips onto her wedding finger, even if it was engraved at Tiffany's, came from a box of crackerjack.

While Holly Golightly is clearly a figure who anticipates the 'new woman' of the mid-1960s, at this point her urban, literally 'working girl' identity must, it seems, be contained within some kind of domestic arrangement, although, as I have tried to show, her relationship to this is anything but simple. As Yvonne Tasker reminds us, the term 'working girl' has both an 'innocent literal sense and . . . [an] acquired sense that women who worked outside the home were morally suspect' (Tasker 1998: 6; see also Skeggs 1997: 46), eventually coming to mean 'prostitute', which Holly, although less explicitly than in Truman Capote's (1958) novella, is. In *Roman Holiday*, while Hepburn as the princess manages to hold in tension selfhood, 'proper' femininity and work, public identity and visibility, this is at the expense of love, marriage and her yearning for the domestic – these feminine roles appear incompatible. The princess clearly yearns for the domestic; 'Shall I cook something?' she asks Joe in the brief interlude in his flat where they 'play house'. This room, again, doesn't have a kitchen, however. She continues: 'I'm sorry I can't cook us some dinner . . . I'm a good cook: I could earn my living at it. I can sew too, and clean a house, and iron. I learned all those things – I just haven't had the chance to do it for anyone.' It is articulated quite clearly in this film that her work in the 'public sphere', as it were, locates her outside the domestic, and moreover her class status means she will not perform this role either in a relationship or as paid work. At the same time, however, her 'work' and her decision to return to it are not choices: being a princess is shown to be a 'natural' duty to her *family* and her people, and in this sense, can perhaps still be understood as 'women's work'. The princess's struggle at the end of *Roman Holiday* is to satisfactorily hold together her sense of herself with her public identity – the changes in her dress dramatise this visually – and in the end something must be sacrificed. In this case, it is the possibility of domestic bliss with Gregory Peck. While it appears, then, that she sacrifices love and domesticity for her work outside the home, nevertheless her work is figured in such a way that it remains within an appropriately feminine sphere. As we have seen in *Sabrina* and *Breakfast at Tiffany's*, these relationships become increasingly strained.[7] Sabrina Fairchild's acquisition of 'class' in the form of chic, urban style significantly alters and complicates her relationship to the domestic, and fails to guarantee her upward mobility through marriage. Urbanite Holly is continually restless in relation to the city and the domestic, at which she continually fails, although the film, in an ending which is significantly different from Capote's novella,[8] attempts to bring her into line through the suggestion of a marriage of some sort to Paul.[9]

While Hepburn's characters have the signs of class, they are unmarriageable and in her films it is precisely the desire and difficulty around social mobility which is so apparent.

'I'm a respectable girl, so I am . . .'

The 'frilly' femininity which is central to *My Fair Lady* is, as Penny Sparke has pointed out, intrinsically linked to the domestic ideal (Sparke 1995: 3, 15); Eliza's relation to the conjugal and domestic, however, is in this film once again complicated as she acquires 'class'.

My Fair Lady explicitly addresses the difficult (and at times in this film quite *literally* painful) process of acquiring class for women through the figure of Eliza Doolittle, in stark contrast to the ease with which her father Alfred becomes 'middle-class'. While he quite literally 'does nothing' for his new status, and is bequeathed the money which guarantees his shift, Eliza must learn the outward signs of class – clothing and appropriate speech (and the loss of her working-class, regional accent) – in order to pass as a lady. 'Passing' in this way, however, is not quite the same as upward mobility; in contrast, for men, it would seem that this is merely a matter of economics and the 'gift of the gab'.

As Eliza achieves the desire to be 'inside' which she expressed through 'Wouldn't it be luverly?', and acquires the signs of class, her respectability is increasingly called into question, as Mrs Pearce and Henry's mother repeatedly point out. Her position in Higgins's house and her relation to the domestic is problematic – she is neither a servant, nor his wife. By the end of *My Fair Lady*, Eliza is once again figured as a 'displaced person', she has literally nowhere to go. She is out of place at the flower market: flowers are now a symbol of her femininity rather than her means of supporting herself. The film makes this distinction very clear in its opening images which juxtapose in close-up the beautiful floral displays on the staircase at the opera with the jewel-like fabrics of the women's dresses, subsequently cutting to Eliza's despair at her 'two bunches of violets trod in the mud'. The only way she can support herself now that she has 'class' is through marriage, the guarantee of her upward mobility; as she points out, however, this is tantamount to prostitution: 'We were above that at Covent Garden. I sold flowers, I didn't sell myself. Now you've made a lady of me, I'm not fit to sell anything else.' Although Eliza claims, 'I can stand on my own without you . . .', in explicit contrast to the end of Shaw's *Pygmalion* upon which the film is based, she *does not* leave Higgins, or, as the epilogue suggests, marry Freddy Eynsford-Hill and achieve her dream of being a respectable (married) lady in a flower shop. Eliza returns to Higgins's house at Wimpole Street, where, as in *Sabrina*, there is no explicit suggestion of marriage and her position remains uncertain both in terms of her social status and her respectability. She will organise his diary, 'pick up [his] slippers and put up with [his] tempers and fetch and carry for [him]' but as neither his wife nor his housekeeper. 'What am I fit for – what have you left me fit for? Where am I to go, what am I to do, what's to become of me?' she asks. The film suggests the impossibility of reconciling 'class' (in terms of style rather than social status) with mobility outside marriage, and in the process leaves Eliza with no way to support herself. Her new 'self' cannot respectably work outside the home, and her relationship to domestic femininity within it is less than certain. The tension around femininity, work and marriage I have drawn out in Hepburn's films is fascinating, for it is suggestive of the circumscribed possibilities for young women in this period. Liz recalls her parents' aspirations for her, which did not accommodate her own aspirations – journalism and drama, which were deemed inappropriate careers:

> Although they aspired in certain ways, it was a really kind of, quite limited set of aspirations for me, which were much more . . . traditionally female [. . .] And – and it's just very interesting, and it's very difficult to explain it to someone who hasn't had some sense of what was going on, you know, [RM: Yes, I'm sure] that kind of, and just how little choice, really, there was at the time.

Liz would marry first, and *then* go to university as a mature student.

These tensions around women's roles in the domestic, private and public realms are clearly discernible in the predominance of 'Cinderella' stories in magazines addressed to girls and young women in the late 1950s and early 1960s. *Woman's Weekly*, despite its clear address to women at home with children, commonly featured stories such as 'Cinderella Smith': 'Yesterday's story . . . today's story . . . tomorrow's story! Because there is always a little Cinderella among us waiting for a glimpse of romance that could be hers'(16–23 September 1961). In this story the Linda has to stay at home doing domestic work while her step-mother and step-sisters go out to work and lead more glamorous lives, although they are represented as both well-educated and unfeminine. Linda, by contrast, wants to be a model (a conventionally feminine career). As she tells her fairy godmother Ada Golightly, 'I want some training, I want a career.' 'Why?' asks her godmother. 'Well, everyone has one, nowadays.' 'Isn't marriage one?' the godmother returns. 'Yes,' replies Linda, 'but I feel rather young for marriage.' Despite this, her transformation for the ball sends her into the arms of her husband to be, and all mention of work magically disappears. This story in a traditional woman's magazine, at a time when the number of women in the workplace was increasing, may have operated to reassure women at home that their labour was as romantic and fulfilling as the lives of those women who went out to work. Similarly, in *Mirabelle and Glamour*, 'Cinderella Jones' (4 January 1964, pp. 21, 22, 24) is an office girl looked down upon by the 'more important' secretaries and who gets to go the Christmas ball and meet the man of her dreams.

The ideological work of these and other similar stories, their suggestion of romance and marriage as the proper ways for women to 'get ahead', is more straightforward than that either of the accounts of the women I spoke with or the narratives in Hepburn's films in which her 'classy', non-domestic, 'uptown' femininity complicates her relation to marriage to a considerable degree. In contrast, this discourse in the 'Young, gay and get-ahead' girls' magazine *Honey* was addressed at precisely a new kind of modern young woman who is presumed to work, and mobilises this 'Cinderella' discourse of self-improvement, as I discuss above, in relation to this.

Marjorie Rosen in *Popcorn Venus* (1973) contrasted Hepburn and other 'waifs' of the 1950s physically with 'the parallel sexual ideal, the Mammary Woman . . . a succulent conquest – but no man's notion of a mother to his children. . . . The paperthin gamine – all that was wholesome, clean and domestic incarnate, was her polar opposite' (285). I would take issue with this characterisation of Hepburn as 'domestic incarnate', as I argue above. Molly Haskell, however, like the women who spoke to me, also identified her in contrast to stars such as Marilyn Monroe, particularly in terms of her body shape, as representative of a moment 'before the body has sprouted those features designed so explicitly to imprison her in her role as woman and mother' (Haskell 1987: 265), later suggesting that this body was particularly appealing to 'an embryonic feminist' (Haskell 1991: 10): a body of possibility. Further, she argues that '[i]n her person more than what she does, she represents a defiant subversion of the suburban family ideal of nesting and proliferating' (12). Hepburn's relation to the domestic is part of a more complex process of negotiation, I think, than this characterisation suggests. It is in her body, though, as Haskell intimates, that this trouble is located; not simply, however, because her body is non-maternal and in contrast to the sexual ideal of the time – as Rosen points out, the 'Mammary Woman' was neither domestic nor maternal. It is also then, I suggest, because Hepburn's body can be understood as profoundly *classed*, that her relation to the domestic, maternal ideal of the 1950s is problematised. Indeed she *yearns* for this domesticity in her film roles, but it is never to be fulfilled. Beverley Skeggs points out that while historically the cult of the domestic was central to definitions of middle-class femininity, the labour involved in producing the domestic ideal was invisible due to the presence of downstairs servants (1997: 5). Hepburn's pared-down, 'uptown' style is profoundly outside the 'frilly femininity' of traditional domesticity (Sparke 1995: 15), and her characters' complicated relation to it – their yearning and/or competence in it – in conjunction with the fact that they never quite *do* it, seems paradoxically to produce them as quite specifically classed. It is perhaps then the coincidence of the 'classedness' of Hepburn's body and look, guaranteeing her Cinderella transformations in terms of class and style, *with* the tensions I have indicated around social mobility, work and marriage that makes her such a resonant figure for those women, growing up female and moving up socially at that first moment of her stardom, whose stories I have offered here.

The archival and empirical research I have conducted around Audrey Hepburn reveals the centrality of discourses around femininity, dress and status; and the importance of such discourses in film, film magazines and extra-cinematic material such as women's magazines, and in the constitution of the subjectivities of young women growing up in the 1950s and 1960s, should not be underestimated. Hepburn's young women characters are usually women transformed, often women hoping to move onwards and upwards. In their complicated negotiation of the contradictions between competing definitions of femininity in the private and the public spheres at a key historical juncture in the history of women and femininity, Audrey Hepburn's 'Cinderella' films dramatise the anxieties of being '*in* the world and *of* the world', indeed, of being 'worldly'. I have suggested that certain key motifs such as the relationship between dress and subjectivity and the Cinderella motif can be understood as structuring both 'Audrey Hepburn' and audience accounts of her, through the juxtaposition of textual analysis of film and extra-cinematic material with a discussion of those accounts.

Two kinds of relationship are brought into focus through this methodological approach. First, there is the question of the relationship between text and audience, and second, the relationship between the textual analyses I offer here and the audience accounts I discuss. As a way of understanding the first, I have suggested the notion of 'resonance and recognition' to describe both the constitution and gendering of subjectivity and texts, the idea of address, and the movement between the two – for instance around the 'Cinderella motif'. Both my textual analysis and the audience accounts I discuss in this chapter privilege particular motifs, moments and discourses: public visibility and discovery in both positive and negative aspects – for instance around fear of discovery; around romance, marriage and the anxieties for upwardly mobile working-class women concerning social status and 'being in the world and of the world' which are dramatised through dress. Equally, I would argue that it is impossible to satisfactorily separate my textual analysis of Hepburn from my understanding of the accounts of her I discuss in the book: the experience of interviewing and transcribing the accounts has necessarily inflected my textual analysis. Similarly, how can I be certain that my understanding of the texts has not then informed my understanding and perception of the accounts? My own subjectivity is surely constituted in relation to the same discourses I have identified – have I then privileged those discourses in my own account of the project? It is essential that these complexities and resonances around subjectivity and textuality be acknowledged.

My textual analyses and the accounts are nevertheless in some ways distinct; there is not an absolute correspondence. Through my analysis of both 'Audrey Hepburn' and contemporary magazines I have identified, for instance, a contemporary discourse around marriage and domesticity in relation to Hepburn which does not appear explicitly in the accounts I discuss here, which focus primarily on the moment just before the shift into this different life stage. It does, however, make Audrey Hepburn available to the young women growing up with her in the 1980s and 1990s, whose accounts I discuss in the final chapter.

Notes

1 Valerie Walkerdine (1997: 139–154) offers a nice discussion of the importance of dances and dancing in relation to social class in feminine culture. See also Pat Kirkham (1995: 207–208).

2 Beverley Skeggs points out in relation to Mary Poovey's (1984) study of the evolution of the concept of the 'proper lady' that femininity was established by the end of the nineteenth century as 'a (middle) classed sign' (Skeggs 1997: 99).

3 This is not to suggest, however, that narratives dramatising these social shifts are no longer so powerfully resonant; this has also been the

trajectory of many women growing up in the 1970s and 1980s, of which I am one.

4 Writing in 1953, Vera Brittain in *Lady into Woman: A History of Women from Victoria to Elizabeth II* proposed the following: 'Even in the posts which ranked as professions, the "typical" governess or teacher, like the lady's maid, wore a virtual uniform in neutral tints which suggested subservience. No one understood in 1901 that the woman who earns her living cannot afford the dead-weight of an inferiority-complex. Women still had to learn that self-confidence is the keynote of success, and that to be beautiful is less important than to feel beautiful' (Brittain 1953: 23).

5 Audrey Hepburn as Regina Lambert relates her life to domestic style in *Charade*.

6 George Axelrod, screenwriter on *Breakfast at Tiffany's*, points out that producer Martin Jurow's 'idea of "uptown" was Audrey Hepburn, not Jayne Mansfield' (McGilligan 1995: 20). 'Uptown' seems to bring together rather nicely the combination of the urban and the profoundly classed which is integral both to Hepburn's image as a star and to the majority of her best-known film characters.

7 In *Charade* her eyes, the indication of her subjectivity, have become the sign of her subjection and fear, and her domestic space has become alien and terrifying. While she marries and has a daughter in *Two for the Road* the non-linear narrative, in conjunction with the representation of her 'mothering' exclusively in makeshift circumstances – hotel rooms and on the road – destabilises it profoundly. By *Wait Until Dark* (1967) domestic space is explicitly threatening and her character is blind. Interestingly, Hepburn's off-screen domesticity and committed role as a mother was well documented and available in the press, but was never part of her image (see 'Audrey: everybody's mother' in *Photoplay* (March 1964, p. 7)); somehow, the publication of Audrey's recipe for 'Baked Alaska' on *Picture Show and Film Pictorial*'s weekly women's page (29 December 1956) didn't seem quite right!

8 In Capote's novella *Breakfast at Tiffany's* there is no romance, and Holly is last heard of trekking through Africa as her calling card in the story indicates: 'Miss Holiday Golightly: Travelling'.

9 Similarly, *The Children's Hour* explicitly addresses the issue of single, working women's appropriateness as guardians of children. Karen (Hepburn) and Martha (Shirley MacLaine) are accused of having a lesbian relationship, which results in the loss of the school for girls they have established and run together. Martha tells Karen over the washing up, in a clear reference to Hepburn's image generally which also marks her as an 'uptown' girl, that compared to her (a 'blouse and skirt girl . . . we're always in fashion') Karen needs clothes: 'You're Fifth Avenue,

Rue de la Paix . . . you need to be kept up.' Significantly, after Martha's suicide at the end of the film, Karen does not return to her fiancé, but walks on alone. It seems impossible for 'uptown' girl Hepburn to have a conventional relationship, domesticity, work *and* her identity.

Chapter 6

Audrey Hepburn, nostalgia and postfeminism in the 1990s

A strong independent woman with a man   (Mel)

People are constantly struggling, not merely to figure out what a text means, but to make it mean something that connects to their own lives, experiences, needs and desires . . . A text can only mean something in the context of the experience and situation of its particular audience.

(Grossberg 1992: 52–53)

I want finally to turn to a set of discussions I had with young women who have grown up with Audrey Hepburn in the 1980s and 1990s. In beginning this chapter with words from Lawrence Grossberg's essay 'Is there a fan in the house? The affective sensibility of fandom', I want not only to suggest the very different relationship of those young women to Hepburn, but also to signal once again what has been a central, structuring concern. In the process of conducting and writing about this research, the complexity of the relationships between the text 'Audrey Hepburn', my reading of that text, the readings of those women who spoke to me, and indeed my reading of their readings – in short, the issue of where 'meaning' is located – has been a problematic to which I have continually returned. Can 'Audrey Hepburn' be understood to 'mean' outside of this collection of specific readings? And indeed, how do those readings stand in relation to each other?

Grossberg's emphasis is on meaning as situated, as produced exclusively in relation to 'lives, experiences, needs and desires': the suggestion is that a text has no meaning outside of these readings. I want to hold onto Grossberg's sense that texts are made to mean in relation to context and situation of the reader, but I want to complicate the picture a little. Grounded in this research, my argument is that we can understand a text – here 'Audrey Hepburn' – to offer certain structures and concerns: in this case, the narrative of transformation, for instance, and a concern with the production of femininity through dress and behaviour. These structures and concerns may be 'preferred' or *resonant* to an audience whose habitus produces those structures and concerns as especially significant. We can argue, as I have in Chapter 2, that narrative structure and aesthetic organisation may offer a point of entry to the text, an address to an audience whose subjectivities are constituted in relation to a particular discursive formation such as femininity. As a concrete instance, then, I share with all the women I spoke to the experience of growing up female. While we may each have different levels and kinds of investment in them according to class, generation, education, race, ethnicity, sexuality, we share an understanding, for example, that certain codes and rules exist in relation to femininity, and that the narrative of transformation is a familiar structure in relation to this. We can and do identify them in the text. In this sense, it could be said that our habitus is shared around gender. To what degree these tropes matter to us, however, and how this is manifested in the way we talk, depends on how we share that habitus in relation to those other factors within which gender is embedded. John Fiske points out that Bourdieu's notion of habitus is particularly useful for the way in which it 'refuses the traditional distinction between the social and the individual', suggesting how 'cultural tastes and habits are produced by social rather than individual differences' (Fiske 1992: 33, 37). I would argue that the advantage of Bourdieu's formulation is that it can be taken up as a way of placing emphasis squarely on the role of shared *social* rather than simply shared *psychic* structures, whilst keeping in play a sense of the way in which the specificity of one's personal history and indeed unconscious processes significantly determine the way a text is made to mean.

One factor may play a more significant role – class, say, or, as in this chapter, generation. These structures allow situated, skilled readings to be made. For instance, while I offered a skilled symptomatic film studies reading of the relationship between Audrey Hepburn, the urban and the domestic in Chapter 5, finding trouble in the text and insisting on the lack of resolution in these narratives, as the material considered in this chapter will show, the young women I spoke to who have come to Hepburn in the 1980s and 1990s pick up the same set of concerns, but offer a series of skilled postfeminist readings which produce Audrey as a girl who manages to 'have it all'.

Thinking about the different ways in which these structures and concerns around Hepburn were discussed by the two generationally distinct groups of women I worked with is a useful way of illustrating the point. Furthermore, this in itself is impossible without a consideration of the ways in which I was able to read their readings. Looking at the interviews I conducted with the group of women who grew up in the 1950s and 1960s, it is clearly the case that I have been able to read the narrative of transformation which is central to the text 'Audrey Hepburn' through the way it is embedded in those women's memories of growing up, their personal stories and experiences. Their retelling and reordering of their own trajectories around discussion of *My Fair Lady* resonates with this structure concerned with growing up, coming to a new kind of femininity and shifting in social status. Their relationship to that structure is manifest in the way in which it is profoundly embedded in memory and personal experience; this is often shared along lines of social class. These stories of personal development and history are interested particularly in narrating the self; in another way, they are also stories about becoming modern.

In contrast, the interviews with young women growing up in the 1980s and 1990s produced quite different kinds of knowledge. Necessarily they are not about memory; they are less about personal experience and personal history – in a very important way they are much less about a coherent understanding of 'the self' and more about the contradictory nature of identity. These interviews are quite self-consciously about questions of representation, and are thus particularly useful for what they can suggest about the nature of the relationship between these young women and Audrey Hepburn in the contemporary. They are suffused with a sense of the experience of growing up with postmodernity; the quality of the talk is significantly different – it is highly media-aware and often deconstructive and analytical in approach. Femininity, for instance, is here understood quite precisely as a construct and as performative. Where this kind of critical repertoire was available to some women I spoke to in the pilot interviews and in the first group through higher education, for these girls it is rather a consequence of the historical moment in which they have grown up. So, whereas in a number of the 1950s and 1960s interviews the significance of the transformation narrative was apparent through the way in which the women structured their personal narratives in memory and in talking about Hepburn, the approach of the younger women is analytical, deconstructive of the film narratives and Hepburn's image, and their relation to the

Hepburn look is generally profoundly performative. Despite the fact that the younger women appear to have an increased sense of intimacy and connection with Hepburn, their talk was largely characterised by a critical distance which made this set of interviews in some ways more difficult to deal with analytically, as at times they almost seemed, in a rather postmodern way, to contain their own analysis.

Lawrence Grossberg usefully suggests that 'we can call the particular relationship that holds any context together, that binds cultural forms and audiences, a "sensibility". A sensibility is a particular form of engagement or mode of operation' (1992: 54). Grossberg's notion of sensibility here is surely something akin to Williams's 'structure of feeling' (1977). While a number of understandings of Hepburn are shared across divisions of generation, the particular kinds of meanings which are made are nuanced in ways suggestive of both the historical situatedness of reading, and the particular sensibility or structure of feeling which characterises them. This indicates how reading formations – the relations between audiences and cultural forms – are structured in relation to historical specificity, and at the same time how they are also about more nebulous attachments – affect, feelings and investments: resonance and recognition. The young women in this second group of interviews describe themselves as having grown up in the 1980s and 1990s;[1] it became evident, however, that the youngest women, who saw themselves as having grown up in the 1990s, revealed a quite distinctive sensibility in relation to Hepburn and her films.

I had difficulty in describing the first group of interviewees as 'fans' of Audrey Hepburn; many of the questionnaires I received as a result of my original advertisement in *Sewing with Butterick* were either already unsigned or requested anonymity if I used material from them. The relationship between these young women and Audrey Hepburn was quite different – there was a significant degree of what might be described as 'fandom'. Cally, Anna and Lucy all showed me pictures of Audrey, on bedroom walls or in books. All the women had videos – a commemorative box set which included *Roman Holiday*, *Sabrina*, *Funny Face* and *Breakfast at Tiffany's* was available at the time of the interviews and was either owned or desired by most of the interviewees. Jayne, the only interviewee in this group to have the responsibilities of a family, did not have a video collection, but was eager to start one which would include the films of both Audrey Hepburn and Doris Day. She told me, though, that she had never been able to do this because 'many a time you say these things and then never get round to it – or the money's never there – and you think, Oh, God, I've got to get this, so I'll get that next month, I mean you know, but you're never going to get it – there's always more – there's always other things that money's got to be spent on', for instance the house which she and her husband were in the process of redecorating, and the children. Her own 'fan' interests were at the bottom of her list of priorities.

Everyone who had seen the remake of *Sabrina* with Julia Ormond and Harrison Ford hated it, and those who hadn't hated the *idea* of it. The women in this group had particular kinds of 'expert' knowledge about Hepburn and her films which generally was not in evidence in the first group. Cally, for instance, described herself as 'a real film buff', and Chloë, who had a really detailed knowledge of a number of Hepburn's films, said 'I feel like such an anorak – it's *so* bad –' at a point in the interview where I admitted sharing her level of invest-ment, clearly demonstrating an awareness of the way in which 'fandom' is often considered to be problematic. They sometimes knew things about her life, but the group was divided between those who had read biographies and sought out information (Cally, Anna, Jayne) and those who were adamant that reading about Hepburn's off-screen life would 'spoil' it for them (Chloë, Mel). Lucy had only read a little about Hepburn's life and shared this feeling, but interestingly, had read lots of other film-star and celebrity biographies.

What united the group, though, was a common love of 'old movies', often 'old black and white movies', particularly those of Audrey Hepburn. Where the women in the 1950s/1960s group often came to Hepburn through women's and film-fan magazines and were less invested in the films (which may, of course, be an issue related to memory), these young women were all very invested in the movies as well as the style, and had come to Hepburn through them, going on to search out more films, pictures or information. In the light of the way in which Hepburn's image had circulated in the 1990s, it was perhaps to be expected that the film around which most of the discussions were focused was *Breakfast at Tiffany's*. The women's particular interests in Hepburn varied, but were split broadly in a very interesting way which I will discuss in more detail in the second part of this chapter. Briefly, where the slightly older women (Cally, Anna, Lucy, Verity, Jayne) were interested primarily in Hepburn's look – often in a quite performative and sometimes specifically 'retro' way – and in the lifestyle offered in *Breakfast at Tiffany's*, Chloë and Mel, the two youngest women, while obviously interested in Hepburn's look, seemed more interested in her character and behaviour in the films, and were invested in a highly nostalgic way in the innocence and romance of the era represented in the films and by Hepburn's stardom.

Mothers and daughters

Before I elaborate on those issues which are related to the generational specificity of this group, I want to begin with a discussion of some features of this set of interviews which were to a degree shared with the first group across the generational division, going on to look at the ways in which even those shared readings can also be understood as generationally specific. This seems to be a useful strategy, because it offers a way of looking at the double 'preferred/skilled reading' structure I suggest above.

As I suggest in the introduction, the literal and metaphorical mother–daughter relationship – actual mothers and influential older female figures, the absence of mothers for Hepburn's characters – figures in this research as a particularly significant formation. While Lucy is actually Shirley's daughter, it is useful to think about the way in which the girls in this group are, in generational terms, the metaphorical daughters of the women in the first group.[2] As in the first set of discussions with 1950s/1960s women, mothers and indeed the idea of 'mothering' featured in each of these interviews to varying degrees.

The majority of the young women had come to Audrey through the same activity – watching old films on television with their mothers in their pre-teenage years. A number of their mothers had been Audrey fans themselves. Indeed, my own introduction to and fascination with Audrey was initiated in exactly the same way. Lucy, for instance, had acquired her appreciation of stars like Hepburn and Doris Day from her mother Shirley (see Moseley 2001). Jayne would watch old films on TV with her mum and through this had developed a love of 'old stars', and Mel and Chloë both remembered first discovering Audrey in this way:

> RM: Can you remember how you first saw Audrey Hepburn, or where, or heard about her?

Mel: I don't know really, I just, . . . my mum sort of introduced me . . . she sort of, watches all the old films, and listens to all the old music and I sort of just got into it through just being brought up in that environment, I don't know – probably the first film I saw was *Roman Holiday*. [RM: With your mum?] Yeah – just sort of, in front of the television – she's sort of got the same sort of opinion of her as me. [. . .]

Chloë: 'Cos like when I was – my mum and I used to watch loads of old films. [RM: Did you?] Yeah, but then – I was thinking about this, actually, I can't, I can't – I remember things like – was she in *The Nun's Story*? [RM: Yeah] And watching ones like that, not things like *Breakfast at Tiffany's*, but more along the lines of – because if it was with my mum it would be things like, *Funny Face* and *Sabrina* – that kind of thing. Watching them with her, and then I didn't really, I don't think, think 'Oh that's Audrey Hepburn' – and all the stuff that goes on there – just kind of, just sort of, like, knowing about her in the back of my mind, and then it was kind of like – *re-finding* . . . her in a different way when I got older – when I was in later teenage years, got – found a lot more, in her, than I had done then – it was just something we did . . .

While a number of the women in the first set of interviews had enjoyed musical films like *My Fair Lady* with their mothers, their primary access to Hepburn, as I have said, had been through women's and film-fan magazines; for all of the 1990s girls, films on television and subsequently on video had been their primary contact. These were often described as 'classic' films and stars – 'They're all Saturday afternoon classics, or Sunday afternoon classics' (Lucy) – and a number of the young women told me things about the way they watch the films now. There was a degree of solo viewing: Chloë and Cally both talked about watching films alone, and both self-consciously described this as 'anorak' activity. Chloë was quite detailed about her reasons for watching her collection of Hepburn films in this way:

I tend to – I tend to watch them on my own, because they have like – most – a lot of the films I've got – some of them I've got just because they're good films, and some of the films I've got . . . I've got because they really suit certain, kind of, well – what you want at a certain time – if you want to watch such and such a film – because you're in such and such a mood, then you choose that one, and they're the kind of films I would generally watch on my own.

Articulated here is the way in which films can be understood as meaningful in relation to affect and feeling – 'what you want at a certain time'. Chloë watches films to both fit in with and also to create particular moods for herself, as well as because they are in some way 'good'. Cally also preferred to watch alone sometimes:

> I do like to sit and watch a film by myself, but I also like, you know, a nice girlie Saturday afternoon sort of film – I've watched films – we've watched *Funny Face* – Anna and I have watched *Funny Face* together – and we've watched *Breakfast at Tiffany's* and things like that – but I do tend to watch a lot of stuff by myself, but I like – it's also quite good – I tend to find though that if you're watching something, or if you go round to a mate's house and it's a social evening, you don't tend to watch the film anyway, after a while – you all start talking and it's just on in the background, sort of thing, so you know – I do like to watch them on my own really, I suppose.

Cally also enjoyed watching these films in a group of girls. What she describes here are quite different kinds of 'fan' activity; solo viewing enables concentration and attention to detail and as we will see, Chloë and Mel, who both preferred to watch alone, were extremely knowledgeable about the details of mise-en-scène and dialogue in Audrey films. Communal viewing is something quite different, and was often described as a 'girlie Saturday afternoon' activity. Again this emerges as about creating 'mood', but here for a group – in Cally's description the film is in the background. It's also about consensus: 'I think the general impression is . . . Audrey's all right! [laughs] We all like our Aud!' Anna talked about her favourite film, *Breakfast at Tiffany's*, in a way suggestive of both of these types of viewing:

> I was always going on about it, and I taped it when it was on – and it's just one of those films that you – I always had on – every weekend – like you know when you wake up on Sunday and you'd be really hung-over, and you'd be like – cup of coffee and some orange juice – and stick *Breakfast at Tiffany's* on, and one of my friends actually said to me once, that – she actually sat down and watched it once, when it was on the TV and she said – I knew I'd seen this, she said 'I've seen it round your house every morning, haven't I?' [laughter] It's on every Sunday – and it's just like one of those things – like, I know all the dialogue off by heart, 'cos it's sort of, in the back of my head.

I think Audrey begins to emerge, here, as 'one of the girls'; this is a form of intimacy which is perceptible throughout this set of interviews, and which is related to the ways in which Audrey is understood as 'not sexy' and as 'natural'. As I discuss in Chapters 3 and 4, these are discourses which were apparent in the interviews with women who liked Hepburn in the 1950s and 1960s; in this chapter I will discuss the ways in which they can be understood to have become historically and generationally specific, and thereby illustrative of the way in which while structures and discourses can be seen as shared, say, in relation to gender, they also become meaningful in relation to the specificities of context – the particular ways in which audiences relate to those structures and discourses describes a 'sensibility' (Grossberg 1992) or 'structure of feeling' (Williams 1977). I will argue that the specific understandings of Hepburn offered by these young women should be understood within the contexts of both postfeminism and postmodernism.

Hepburn was often perceived in a positive way by women who liked her in the 1950s and 1960s as 'not sexy'; in relation to this, she was repeatedly constructed in their talk through discussion of Marilyn Monroe and Brigitte Bardot. The notion that Hepburn was 'not sexy' frequently emerged as part of the formation 'classy, not sexy'. This understanding of Hepburn, which is generationally shared, must nonetheless be understood as historically specific. For those women growing up in the 1950s and 1960s the appeal of a star who wasn't sexy may be understood in relation to social imperatives and notions of appropriate femininity. The 1990s girls I spoke to discussed her in a similar way – although quite often they described her more precisely as 'not about sex': 'You see I think she was sexy, and I'd love to look like her, but – she's sexy without being about sex. Whereas Marilyn is sexy, pin-up, chest, everything' (Mel). In the distinctions made between Hepburn and Monroe, 'sex' is always located in the body. As we will see, this construction of Hepburn in the second set of interviews is clearly formed through a peculiarly 1990s inflection of a feminist sensibility which can be described as 'postfeminist'.

Hepburn appealed to Verity, as to a number of the women I spoke to about liking Hepburn in the 1950s and 1960s, because she could be skinny and still be a star, but also because she is not a 'caricature of a woman' – in other words, not excessively gendered. In relation to a picture she had on her wall (figure I.1), I asked Anna why she thought Hepburn is still seen as the world's most alluring woman:

I think it's because she's got like a really timeless sort of, like – well, she's graceful for a start, you know – you look at the way she carries herself, sort of thing, I mean even if you look at the one where she's sort of like, pulling a little face with the cigarette holder, if it had been like Marilyn Monroe that would have been like, a dead sexy shot – with her it just looks a bit sort of, like somebody's given a child a fag – and like, you know – to play around with it – you know [laughter] it's not – it's sort of like, it's not overtly sexy, do you know what I mean?

She goes on to talk about the casting of Hepburn instead of Monroe (Capote's choice) in *Breakfast at Tiffany's* – she can't imagine Monroe in this role because there would be 'too many curves for a start!' I think Anna's contrast between the two stars is very significant: her identification here of Hepburn as 'graceful' is key. Monroe is indeed too sexy to be graceful – this is a question of poise, as well as the relation of the body to clothing. This is a distinction between the movement of the body which emphasises secondary sexual characteristics (Monroe), or that which emphasises the line of the dress (Hepburn). When Marilyn moves, what is most significant is her body in her clothes – the clothes are only important in so far as they relate to and reveal her body. In Hepburn's performance, the body displays the clothes, rather than the clothes displaying the body. It is not necessarily a question of body shape, then; rather it is one of movement and behaviour. Later in our conversation, Anna talked about the difference between sexiness and 'allure':

I like the way they do actually use the word alluring – because alluring is a sort of like *drawing in*, you know – it's not like saying who is the most sexiest woman and the most attractive woman, because that's a very sort of . . . *detached* way of looking at it, you know, you're looking at someone and going – oh, you're pretty, or you're this, or you're that, but alluring is – it's like you're inviting, and you're welcoming, you know.

Anna's use of words like 'drawing in', 'inviting' and 'welcoming' is important: it is suggestive of a potential for intimacy which is apparent in almost all of this set of interviews about Audrey's appeal for other women, and of the argument I made in Chapter 2 about the nature of the 'attraction' of clothes in Hepburn's films. Similarly, she felt that in contrast to Audrey, '[Grace Kelly's] got no warmth, though – I mean that's what I always think about her when you look at any of the photos – I always think – she just looks very warm, and she's just got like that sort of personality whereas someone like you know – Grace Kelly . . .'. This is not a relationship of detachment (as exhibited in the critical work on Hepburn I discuss in Chapter 2); it is rather one of closeness. It is also significant that it is precisely because Hepburn is *not* sexy that many of these young women felt they could be close to her. Anna feels from reading about her that she was felt to be 'very very nice', and says that this is partly why she likes her: sexy girls are not 'nice', are not your friend. When I asked Lucy why she thinks so many women like Audrey, she told me:

> Lucy: A safe rival, isn't she? A bit less than like, Marilyn Monroe wouldn't be a safe rival, you know – you don't think *sexy* when you see Audrey Hepburn, do you? [RM: No, I don't think so] You think *sweet* [laughs].
>
> RM: Do you think she was sexy though?
>
> Lucy: She must have been – I'm assuming she must have been – I mean you can see it more obviously in Brigitte Bardot . . . she's got to be, hasn't she?
>
> RM: I wonder how appealing she actually was to men?
>
> Lucy: Oh the men I know like her, they all like her, but I don't know from when they liked her. But then all the women I know like her, so she must be like a safer – a bit like Doris Day – safe. The girl-next-door type.

Audrey is 'safe' to like here because she is not a sexual rival – there's little likelihood that she will steal away your boyfriend – she is potential-friend material. This is partly because she is sexually non-threatening, and partly because of the potential and desire for intimacy she inspires.[3] This is also linked to the fact that she is understood to be authentic, genuine and sincere; Audrey is 'real':

> RM: If I ask you what you particularly like about her, what would it be?
>
> Anna: Her warmth and spontaneity. Because I think that's what – I mean you're talking about someone you don't actually know personally, but [laughs] – just from the way that she comes across in the films, I think that sort of, you know, there's like a genuine, sort of, affection and generosity of spirit, sort of thing that you get from the roles that she plays anyway. You'd want to be friends with her, basically. You'd hate her guts at the same time – but you'd want to be her friend [laughs], so er . . .
>
> RM: Especially in *Breakfast at Tiffany's*, maybe?
>
> Anna: Yeah – especially – I mean – I don't know what it is about that more than any of the other films – maybe because of the – you could

actually imagine that whole scenario happening in your life – you can't actually imagine *My Fair Lady* happening in your life, or something like that, but you can with *Breakfast at Tiffany's* – a lot of that sort of – ties in with various bits of my life, so –

RM: Yeah – 'cos in fact – do you remember that day when we bumped into each other in town – when I first asked you about this – P—— had said, 'Oh, talk to Anna' [Anna: Oh right – yeah] and you said to me, 'Oh, I live my life like *Breakfast at Tiffany's*'. [Anna laughs] I just thought that was *brilliant* – I mean, maybe it was a flippant comment – but what did you mean? 'Cos I thought that was wonderful.

Anna: Erm – probably because my life's quite scatty [laughs] at the best of times to be quite honest – and I tend to sort of, wing things and expect them to turn out OK, and I'll do something like, you know, like have a massive party in your house, sort of thing, have the police turn up and just run up the fire escape to someone else's flat and leave someone else to deal with it, you know – there's that whole sort of, acting . . . irresponsibly, sort of thing . . . [RM: And sort of knowing, or hoping, that it'll turn out all right] It's all all right, you know, and sort of, fingers crossed – but that sort of optimism, which is generally what I sort of do – it always reminds me of being basically like a kid, you know – you just run around with actually not knowing what the consequences of your actions are going to be, but sort of, you carry on doing it anyway – and I don't think I've grown out of that, to be quite honest [laughs], so . . . .

Here, Anna describes how she is able to understand her favourite star in relation to her perception of herself and the way she conducts her own life. She made a number of comments of this kind throughout the interview, usually in relation to *Breakfast at Tiffany's*, her favourite film, which repeatedly constructed Audrey as accessible and real in relation to her own experience, and in indeed in contrast to other stars:

'Cos all of my – most of the women I really look out – is from that period sort of thing – but it's because she wasn't . . . I don't know how to describe it – she wasn't standoffish, she wasn't like someone that you had up on a pedestal, it was like, you know, you see her running around getting ready because she's ten minutes late, sort of thing, and you're thinking – that could be me – if I looked like Audrey Hepburn – unfortunately I don't [laughs] – and just the fact that she had a really great sense of humour, all the way through it. [. . .] I mean I think what you get with someone like Audrey Hepburn is basically you project your own self onto her a bit, you know, it's sort of – it's like that.

RM: Do you think she's particularly accessible in that way?

Anna: Yeah – oh definitely, yeah. I mean – she doesn't – it's like Ingrid Bergman – you couldn't imagine sort of like – 'Come on Ingrid – let's go down the pub' or something like that – but you could imagine taking Audrey Hepburn out, you know – like the bit where they get drunk in *Breakfast at Tiffany's* – you're just thinking – this could be you – you now, like you're sort of in a bar with Audrey sort of thing – you know.

RM: Yeah – definitely – so I suppose in some ways maybe she is a bit of a girl next door, as well as –

Anna: Yeah – yeah – I mean it's like – I think what it is – even though she looks like drop dead gorgeous, *it could be you* sort of thing – do you know what I mean? It's like you know – whereas I don't think . . . someone like Grace Kelly, you don't think – oh I could actually like you know – *be* like Grace Kelly, d'you know what I mean?

Breakfast at Tiffany's has such purchase for Anna because it seems to say something about her own experience of life in the 1990s. She describes this as 'empathy' and attributes it to the fact that Audrey is 'real'; she is simply 'herself':

> It's just like – and also a lot of what she's – when she's talking to George Peppard in the car, and you know that she really likes him, but she can't deal with the whole idea of a relationship, when she talks about love being like a cage, or whatever, and like, people don't own people – and when I first saw it, that was exactly what I thought – I was like yes! You know. . . . I mean I can objectively say I think Grace Kelly is very attractive – but I would never want to be her, you know, whereas like Audrey Hepburn is someone you can actually sort of think – I mean if you look through most of her films, she's like always, like, herself.

If Anna looked like Audrey, 'it could be her'. It would be facile to suggest the impossibility Anna expresses here of 'looking like Audrey' is attributable solely to Hepburn's whiteness – although that is not to deny that this factor may be in play; most of the young white women in this group felt similarly. In contrast to Grace Kelly, however, whom Anna describes as 'Aryan' and 'too perfect . . . it's like they've got some little clones', Hepburn's naturalness, as well as the individuality of her beauty, makes her a figure that she might aspire to. Hepburn's behaviour, however, is both resonant and appropriable. Audrey is someone you might like to go to the pub with, and indeed someone you could *imagine* going to the pub with.

She offers the potential for intimacy: she's the kind of girl you'd like to know. 'Ice queens' Kelly and Bergman are not accessible in this way – neither of them is 'one of the girls'.

'She's a real phoney'

As in the first set of interviews, here Audrey is always understood to be 'herself':

> I mean, she seems to be *her* in all of her films. Although she's sort of different characters, so there seems to be, this kind of thing, this kind of, thing that you can't define is present in all her films, in her, and she is, kind of, her in all her films – but not in a *bad* way, not like Winona Ryder is, or like how she plays herself in every film – I don't mean that, I mean it was in a *good* way.
>
> (Chloë)

Chloë seems to be pointing here to a sense of how highly defined Hepburn's persona is ('this kind of, thing that you can't define is present in all her films'). At several points in the interview Chloë told me how she always thinks of Audrey as living 'through the films, and that's the only life she has – and they like get her out of a box, and like – she lives in a box, and then they let her out, she does a film, and that's how she lives, and then they put her back in'. Clearly she is aware of the constructedness or unreality of the star Audrey Hepburn. At the same time, what she is also trying to articulate is her feeling that Hepburn is rather more 'self' than persona. The contrast with Winona Ryder is telling; while Ryder is always the same in her films in a 'bad way' – i.e. she always plays the same character – Audrey is just herself in a natural, and therefore good way. Similarly, Cally described Audrey as coming across 'quite naturally, you know, which is – and it's quite unusual in a lot of ways – quite kookie I suppose', and as 'ingenuous', suggesting a certain frankness and artlessness – she is 'up front', she's not hiding anything – what you see is what you get. It is interesting how 'kookie' here is used to mean 'natural'; as I discuss in Chapter 2, the expression 'kookie' was used in the late 1950s and early 1960s to denote a 'different', more unusual kind of (exclusively female) star. This is suggestive then of the way in which other stars are considered 'artificial', not just in terms of the constructedness of their persona, but also in relation to beauty. Indeed the article on 'kookie beauty' from *Mirabelle and*

Glamour was focused on creating a 'natural' look. Jayne also commented on this aspect of Hepburn's appeal in the context of a discussion of the imperative for women to be slim and the current crop of super-thin models. She described how even un-made-up – natural – Hepburn looked wonderful, despite the fact that you could see the shadows under her eyes, unlike those girls who would look awful without make-up. She expertly points out that there are 'touches of blusher' in this image, but that's all: 'There's no make-up to hide it, is there?' Particularly interesting in this respect is the way in which in contrast to current examples of the slim feminine ideal like Kate Moss and Jodie Kidd, Hepburn's extreme thinness is acceptable precisely because it is understood to be 'natural': just how she is. Jayne uses Twiggy as a comparison, around whom she considers there was an attempt to glamorise and impose thinness as an ideal; Audrey 'was just thin'. Twiggy's rise to fame coincides with Jayne's pre-teen years – perhaps a particularly influential time for young girls in terms of feminine role models. Audrey in some respects already represented a time which was past at this moment, and the potential for idealising the recent past should not be ignored. Cally discussed why she likes Hepburn's thinness, and can accept it, in a similar way:

> So it's not for any kind of . . . more unhealthy, sort of, anorexic reasons, or anything like that, it's just that I think she embodies a certain type . . . and I think a lot of women, if they're honest, do like that type – even if they're nothing like it themselves. They've got to see the attractiveness of it, providing it's sort of, natural, and not, sort of, someone trying to starve themselves to death.

Equally, while Anna felt that usually, 'from a feminist point of view' she would find such thinness problematic, in Hepburn's case 'for some reason it doesn't bother me about her at all'.

Audrey is seen to be entirely genuine – this is perhaps the reason why the 'Moon River' moment from *Breakfast at Tiffany's* and the 'mouth of truth' incident in *Roman Holiday* were frequently cited as 'favourite Audrey moments' across both sets of interviews. Similarly, a number of women mentioned Hepburn's UNICEF work, and talked about how they felt that her caring and compassion were genuine; for those women who knew about her experiences as a child in occupied Holland, this was felt to be the result of personal experience – the ultimate authentication.

I found Anna's comments on her understanding of Hepburn as 'real' particularly interesting. In this excerpt she talks about Hepburn's appeal in relation to other actresses:

> I mean if you look at most sort of actresses – they've got like you know one particular look – like you know – with Marilyn Monroe it's oh – she's you know, overtly very sexual or whatever, Ingrid Bergman was like very aloof, and that was it – I mean if you see Ingrid Bergman in – what was I watching the other day . . . oh, it was *Indiscreet* with Cary Grant – and it's quite a good film, but she can't actually sort of do comedy very well – because she's still being Ingrid Bergman, yeah – and she's still very detached from the whole thing . . . whereas I – you see she probably – she's got all of those elements, but in one person – which is what most people are like, you know.

Audrey is 'real' because like 'real' people, there is more than one side to her – she's three-dimensional:

> I mean it's like – the bit in – in *My Fair Lady* where they take her to Ascot and you know and she's being perfectly, perfectly serene and you're just like thinking 'Oh God', you know, complete ice queen, and then she's like cheering on this horse and everything [laughter] like that, and you think, well that's like both sides of her personality that most people have got, you know, you've got that bit where you want to be sort of dead detached, but underneath you're like dead excited, like you know, sort of. I think she probably seems more real. You know – it's like admitting that you have got all these characteristics, and you have got all these faults, but that's like what you are, rather than – I mean if you do look at a lot of people like Ingrid Bergman which is probably heresy to P—— to say this, but she's very like two-dimensional, you know, but I mean somebody like Audrey Hepburn's like – you know – all-rounded, you know.

Audrey is human – she has flaws – and this makes her real. She isn't perfect, which makes her an accessible star in contrast, for instance, to Ingrid Bergman in this account. I want to argue that the particular understandings of Audrey as 'real' and 'authentic' which emerge from these interviews with 1990s girls can be seen as an historically specific inflection of the same formation which produced Hepburn as 'natural' in the 1950s/1960s group. It will become apparent that in part, what is understood as Hepburn's 'realism' and authenticity in the sense that Anna describes it above – 'two sides of the same coin' – is rather an expression of the way in which Hepburn's ability to be a number of things at once, thereby managing some key contradictions of gendered identity, embodies the possibility of utopian resolution.

In the summer of 1996 Chanel launched their first fragrance in many years, 'Allure', which coincided precisely with a revival of lounge and easy listening music and a renewed interest in Hepburn's image. *Harper's and Queen* of June 1996 was one of a number of magazines at this moment to feature Hepburn on the cover (figure I.1) as still 'The world's most alluring woman', often tied in to features on Chanel's newest perfume and articles which attempted to define the essence of feminine allure. Chanel's campaign for 'Allure' featured eight 'different' women, different not only from each other but also from conventional standards of beauty. The emphasis was on warmth, realism and individuality (shared also by the campaign surrounding Calvin Klein's fragrance 'CKBE', and suggested in the title of a short-lived British magazine for women, *Frank*). This key discourse of difference and individuality in relation to feminine allure was carried through in a number of articles at the same moment which featured new young models predicted to take over from current supermodels. Features such as 'The new individuality' (*Cosmopolitan*, July 1996, pp. 200–203) and 'Pretty cool: wonderful today, weird tomorrow? The new supermodels have looks which challenge conventional ideals' (*Vogue*, July 1996, p. 26) described a 'beauty revolution': new values of difference, individuality, naturalness and realism as central to female beauty, 'unvarnished reality' rather than 'glitz and glamour' (*Cosmopolitan*, July 1996). Clearly, this is not a new discourse in relation to standards of female beauty; it is an ideological sleight of hand which was equally evident in material from earlier beauty pages, which I discuss in Chapter 2, and as Wendy Chapkis points out, feminist claims about every woman's 'natural' beauty have been incorporated into widely circulating discourses about femininity, in turn encouraging attempts to produce this 'naturalness' through the purchase and use of cosmetics (Chapkis quoted in Coppock, Haydon and Richter 1995: 24). 'Naturalness' was also key to Hepburn's star image – the construction of her look as natural, different, real and therefore democratic was key to its perceived achievability.

While Audrey Hepburn is then still appropriate to the primary discourse of selfhood and beauty circulating in the mid- to late 1990s, the 1990s girls, while strongly invested in this, at the same time recognise the sleight of hand – indeed there is a powerful sense in these interviews of the impossibility of 'being like Audrey'. One might be able simply to take up elements of her style in a performative way. The imperative to be natural, to 'be yourself', operates across both periods around both beauty and personality and is offered as key to female attractiveness. What is interesting is the historical specificity of this discourse. In the late 1950s and early 1960s it is 'tasteless' to be artificial – heavily made-up and self-consciously posturing – and this could perhaps be explained in terms of contemporary social mores. In the mid- to late 1990s the imperative to be natural is couched in terms of democracy and 'realism' – it is about authenticity and individuality, although Chanel's 'Allure' is also interestingly discussed in relation to a return to 'good taste'. The discourse of naturalness in female beauty remains a powerful one, even as the highly media-aware young women I spoke to were able to deconstruct it almost automatically. Alongside an understanding of Hepburn as 'natural' and real, the ideological sleight of hand was picked out quite precisely by these young women in their discussions. Audrey, for all her naturalness, is extremely well-groomed: 'She's *very* turned out,' as Chloë put it. Through Audrey, being 'natural' seems to offer the possibility of 'being oneself' as well as being attractive and presented in the right way, and therefore of being successful. She manages to reconcile contradictions which are recognised to be impossible. As I discuss below there was often a keen feminist sensibility at work in these interviews through which these young women were able to deconstruct the complexity of Hepburn's image. In response to a comment she had made, I asked Anna why it was that women like female stars who are not overtly sexy:

> Because – it's probably because of what you'd want to have for yourself – you know, at the end of the day Audrey Hepburn does exist in a little idealised world where you know it's not like she walks out the house and people are wolf whistling at her, or going, 'You're a woman, you can't do this,' or you know, or 'How are you dressing for your interview? How are you dressing for work?, you know, and it *is* in an ideal world, you should be able to look like that all the time, and be judged on your – I mean, OK she does get judged on the way she looks, but you get like people look at her and her personality, whereas like, you know, in an ideal world that would happen but in the real world [laughs] as we all know, it doesn't happen, and so it's probably something like that.

Such a problematisation of the myths of postfeminism is offered alongside an understanding of Hepburn as 'more real' than other stars. While Anna for instance recognises really that Hepburn's world is an idealised one, she appeals to her precisely because through her 'realness' she offers the possibility of a world where women are not judged just on their looks. She looks great – she has wonderful clothes, hair and make-up, and she has the perfect life. At the same time, she is not punished for it. Surely, the emphasis in this set of interviews on the appeal of Audrey as a star who is 'not about sex' is related to this; in 'Audrey-land' a woman can be attractive, well-dressed, successful and herself without being continually reduced to her sexuality. She offers the possibility of 'having it all'.

Nostalgia and escape from the postmodern

At the same time, there is a discourse about authenticity in a number of these interviews which describes a dis-ease with an 'artificial' and self-conscious contemporary world which is recognised to be interested primarily in the ironic. In these instances the 'real' is the authentic and concomitantly the valuable, and is precisely located, through Hepburn, in the past. Chloë and I talked about the current vogue for 1950s fashion, furniture and lounge music, and Chloë commented that the bare 'loft-living-style' interior design of *Breakfast at Tiffany's* was currently popular. She thought 'kookie' a horrible word to use, even though it summed up the mood of the film, and she went on to talk about this in relation to Hepburn's behaviour, in which she is particularly interested, at a later point:

> The small, little things, like how she climbs up to get her whiskey while putting her foot in the drawer, and then she sits with her feet in the other drawer, and she's drinking, and *little* things like *that* – just kind of, things that you think God – you know – like I say – it's just so cool – but you couldn't – and you – but you just wouldn't – I mean, you can't say, you would think to do that, because she doesn't think to do that, if you see what I mean – it's just, kind of, *done*, and if you thought to do that, it wouldn't be the same thing at all.

Chloë feels one could not be like Audrey Hepburn precisely because she is authentic and unique; for this woman this is a key part of Audrey's appeal. Although she accepts the possibility of doing the Hepburn look in a performative way, nevertheless at the same time the self-conscious mimicking of behaviour and style is rejected in favour of an authenticity of behaviour and effect. Hepburn appeals

> because she – it's so un-self-conscious, it's just – seems to be, every-thing she does is kind of like . . . like a natural reflex thing to do, it's not done in a self-conscious way. And in the way that kooky things are done today, in a really self-conscious, you know, to be kind of . . . What she's doing, she totally seems natural, and that she's doing all the things she would be doing in something like *Breakfast at Tiffany's* – not in the earlier ones, because they're much more, sort of, staged, in a way – apart from the little bits you get, the little gem bits, where she's kind of . . .

Chloë looks for these 'little gem bits' which are her favourite in Audrey Hepburn films – the language is indicative of the worth of the genuine in this account – 'gem' signifies rarity, value and authen-ticity. The way she talks about Audrey in relation to contemporary female stars is revealing, as in the example of Winona Ryder above; in the same vein she told me, 'Say you just saw one of her films, maybe you couldn't tell, but I think you'd still get . . . insight – a lot more insight into her, and how she was, how I *think* she was, through watching that, than you would say through watching Gwyneth Paltrow in whatever she was in.' There is a clear sense here of the authenticity, the 'realness' of Audrey in comparison to the stars of the 1990s. As we will see in the rest of this chapter, for these two youngest women who grew up in the 1990s there is a clear desire to retreat from the pressures and complexities of the self-con-sciousness, irony and confusing gender roles of the 1990s and into a period which is seen to embody innocence and idealised hetero-sexual romance.[4] Before considering the ways in which Audrey emerges as a distinctly postfeminist figure in this set of interviews, I want to set this up through a short discussion of the emphasis in them on 'mothering'.

The capacity of Audrey Hepburn to inspire intimacy which I dis-cuss above also produces a discourse about mothering. Hepburn char-acters are usually motherless, producing the familiar father–daughter configuration which is either articulated in a family relationship and/or in her pairing with an older man in the formation of the romantic couple. In this way Hepburn is usually doubly fathered, pointing even more strongly to the lack of a mother for her charac-ters. In the interviews, a mother–daughter relationship is formed and often privileged in personal stories almost by way of compensation for the lack in the narratives. On a simple level, these young women very often spoke about their mothers, as I discuss above and below, in relation to the idea of nostalgia. On another there is a very particular discourse about 'mothering' Hepburn, and, by proxy, *being* mothered. Indeed, in these interviews I continually found myself 'feeling sorry for Audrey' and relating the story of how, after months of vocal training and practice, Hepburn was dubbed, without being consulted, by Marni Nixon on the soundtrack for *My Fair Lady*.

This discourse is articulated in a number of ways. First, there are frequent comments which simply suggest Hepburn's child-like qualities:

> I think there's something quite child-like about her, something quite ethereal, you know, she's not a normal – well, I say normal . . . she's not our average kind of – she seems quite vulnerable in comparison to other people – she's so slight – it's a physical thing – it's those big eyes – and her sort of – she's got some very sort of . . . *sweet*, endearing mannerisms, that . . . I don't know . . . I think she's got that star quality thing, whatever that is – that elusive quality, and it *is* the fact that she is this slight – she's got a very clearly defined image, as well . . . what else can I say . . . but I personally like her because she's got that very sort of wide-eyed, easily affronted, easily offended, kind of [both laugh] demeanour, and it's very endearing.
>
> (Cally)

In this case it is clearly acknowledged that 'it's a physical thing', Hepburn's frailty, which makes her endearing, inspires care. Words like 'sweet' and 'cute' were quite often used of Hepburn in this set of interviews, but were absent from the 1950s/1960s group.[5] Lucy told me:

> She's just like the sweetest looking person you've ever seen, and that's what it is – probably because she looks like a cat! You know – and she's so *little* – well, she's not, she's probably very tall isn't she, but she looks like she needs looking after, and she's really sweet, isn't she? [laughs].

During my interview with Lucy, who loves cats, her own cat came into the room asking to be fed. It had been in a road accident, and consequently required long-term care – just as Hepburn, whom Lucy likens to a cat physically, 'needs looking after'.[6] Similarly, Chloë responded to my comment that Hepburn looks very small against the New York skyline in *Breakfast at Tiffany's* in a way that focuses on her physical frailty and yet, simultaneously, her ability to cope:

> Yeah – and *so* – she looks so vulnerable, and so kind of, susceptible to all these things, and you really do worry for her in a lot of, and a lot of it – and I mean, physically, she's so small as well, and everything seems to be falling apart at the seams, and you know, and it's all going pear-shaped, and yet, on the other hand she's like holding it together, nonetheless. Erm, so you, and I think it's that maybe you don't want to – I mean you'd *like* to, but you don't want to be her, but you'd kind of, you know, you'd like to sort of, I don't know.
>
> RM: Be like that? Or, have that ability, maybe, to – I don't know – is it appealing, to be – to appear vulnerable?
>
> Chloë: No – I don't mean – to, kind of, I think it would be nicer to know her, than to kind of, be like that, really, or to kind of – if she was vulnerable, to kind of, to know her, and to kind of, you know – you just want to wrap her up, I think.

Again, evident here is the appeal of Hepburn's ability to be successfully two contradictory things at once: here physically frail or vulnerable and yet psychologically strong. Both Chloë and Mel, the two youngest women, point to this element in Hepburn's appeal, suggestive perhaps of the increasing pressure on women in the 'postfeminist' 1990s to both conform to and transcend traditional gender expectations.

While she perceived it as impossible because her frame is so different to Hepburn's, Mel aspired to the kind of fragile femininity she perceived Hepburn to embody: 'I don't know, I suppose she was just . . . something that I wanted to be. Something, almost sort of, fluttery, or something, just so small, and delicate, and just sort of like a butterfly, or something.' Mel spoke very interestingly about her relationship to this form of femininity. Towards the end of the interview she came back to this, saying that Audrey could get away with wearing a kimono: 'And you can imagine her – just like the little Japanese women, like walking really slowly, and doing that little – feminine steps – 'cos they are so feminine, they've got that whole look, but she's got the western face.' Comments of this kind throughout the interviews are full of repetitions of words like 'tiny' and 'little'. What is particularly interesting about Mel's comments is that she relates her aspiration to this fragile femininity explicitly to her mother. Here, we are talking about the possibility of finding 'original' Audrey-style garments in charity shops:

RM: Have you found any, sort of, original . . . garments?

Mel: None that fit me! [laughs] 'Cos they always seem to be a size eight, that Audrey would have got away with. I think, as well, the appeal of her is the fact that she reminds me of my mum. When I would look at old pictures of my mum – I mean, my mum's five foot two, she weighed about six stone thirteen at the time, and she could have been Audrey really. At work, she was – one of her friends actually referred to her as 'her little Audrey', because she really reminded her of Audrey Hepburn – she's got the same sort of hair – a similar look – I mean, she doesn't look exactly like her, but she had the same sort of, shape, and everything. And I think that's sort of some of it as well. She's sort of like, she's my mum but in the big screen.

RM: But isn't that interesting – so she reminds you of your mum in some ways –

Mel: Yeah – she does. But I mean, I've got so many old pictures of my mum, I've got a sort of little album, and I keep them all in there, and I love that – just the fact that she was so – I mean, she's still attractive now, but just the fact that she was this person that I sort of, want to be, almost.

The next time we met, Mel showed me her photo album with the pictures of her mother. In one way, her desire to be like her mother is linked to her general nostalgia for the period when her mother was a young woman like herself. It is interesting, though, that her mother is representative of the mode of femininity she most desires for herself, suggesting a very complex relationship between mothering and being mothered.

Mel's mother was like Audrey, and thus embodied the femininity that she now desires herself. This is a mode of femininity, however, which, as I discuss in Chapter 2, has been considered emblematic of the non-maternal. Mel's desire to be as her mother was would enable her to be physically fragile (child-like/non-maternal) and yet at the same time to be like the person who became her mother and cared for her ('She's sort of like, she's my mum but in the big screen'). In a convoluted way, her wish is perhaps to be able to care for herself like her mother does – to be both mother and child. In a way, this might be seen as a particular form of the postfeminist imperative to 'have it all'. Similarly, Jayne – the only one of these young women to actually be a mother – recalled how at school it was always the petite girls who got the attention:

I think it's because in a way, like when I was younger I was never like the *tiny little* – I went to school – I can always remember that there was someone around at school who looked very much like her – tiny, pretty – all the boys liked her – I mean it's different as you get older – you suddenly become a teenager and you change – I don't know if I'd want to be little and petite now, but I think in the earlier days it's because she always looked so . . . you can imagine *she was the type people would fall for, people would want to do things for,* and I think when you're younger, particularly early teens and that, and perhaps if you're not having such a good time yourself, you know – everyone else has got a boyfriend and you haven't, and you suddenly start seeing someone like her, and you think – 'Oh, I wish I was like her, because if I was like that it would be completely different' – but it's not, though, is it? [emphasis added]

As I suggested above, the first group of women whose memories I consider in Chapters 3, 4 and 5, can be understood as the metaphorical mothers of these young women. As in Mel's more literal model, these metaphorical mothers represent Audrey in generational terms. Audrey might then be seen as the 'mother' who teaches her daughters how to reproduce themselves as feminine – in terms not only of personal style but also of both the need to be mothered and to mother.

Verity, Chloë and Mel all talked to me in quite an extended way about their mothers, all of whom had also admired Audrey Hepburn as young women. The idea of the accoutrements of femininity being metaphorically 'handed down' from mother to daughter is intriguing – suggestive of the ways in which femininity is reproduced, whether within the actual relation between mother and daughter or indeed in the relationship between young women and a female star. In this case the star and the young women who admire her are two or more generations apart and so the modes of femininity in question are necessarily 'old-fashioned' in one way or another. What does it mean when young women in the 1990s hark back nostalgically through Audrey Hepburn to femininities associated with the period when their mothers were young? What, precisely, is at stake in the terms 'classic' and 'timeless' by which they repeatedly refer to those styles?

Dressing up

Perhaps predictably, given the 'retro-chic' context for the renewed interest in Hepburn's image in the 1990s, one of the main sources of interest for these young women was the period look and feel of

Audrey Hepburn films, particularly *Breakfast at Tiffany's*, in relation to both femininity and lifestyle. This was often articulated quite simply in relation to iconic 'moments' (cf. Stacey 1994) and Audrey as a 'style icon' – for instance, the image of Holly looking in at the windows of Tiffany's, the cat, the cigarette holder. Lucy recalled 'the glamour parts of it', but never remembered what happened in the film: 'I think the images at the beginning of *Breakfast at Tiffany's* is what does it, isn't it? The idea of just having this great life where you don't work and you know – you go to parties all night and eat breakfast at six in the morning and then go to bed – tripping alongside Tiffany's.' Similarly, Cally told me, 'I also like *Breakfast at Tiffany's*, just because she looks so cool – it's got nothing to do with the film, particularly – it's not my favourite film by a long stretch.' Common to Cally, Anna and Lucy's and accounts was an investment in the kinds of femininity typically associated with this period, in the idea of 'dressing up'. This was associated with particular kinds of music and was accompanied by a performativity often associated with liking 'retro' styles. All of these women referred at some point to the retro styles of the late 1980s which had focused particularly on the 'Beat' look of the late 1940s and early 1950s.

Cally told me that she enjoys dressing up and going out and buying 'real glad-rag clothes'. I asked her which was her favourite Audrey outfit, and she told me about the black dress, pearls and cigarette holder from *Breakfast at Tiffany's*:

> Well, I think I'm a bit of a sixties freak, actually. I think that's what it is – and it's just – it is real early sixties *haute couture* and it's just – it's a real classy look that people could wear – say if you were going to a wedding or something – and you wore that everyone would say 'Oh, that's a fab Audrey Hepburn outfit' or something like that, and it's – it's 'cos it's a classic outfit – it's timeless and you know – it's glamorous, it's elegant – it's all this thing about a bygone age when people used to wear hats and gloves and matching bags and all the rest of it, and now everyone's really slapdash, and doesn't really bother half the time, whereas it would be great to wander round looking like that all the time – it would be just excellent!

This short extract is rich in a number of ways. First, there is the nostalgic desire articulated here to be able to 'do' a style of femininity from this historical moment. The 'matching hats, gloves, and bags' look which was particularly important in relation to class and aspiration to certain women in the first set of interviews is now a kind of subcultural retro style. However, Cally points out that today, this kind of feminine style is really only appropriate on special occasions like weddings – putting on these kinds of clothes is understood explicitly as a performance. Similarly, Lucy told me about her own Audrey dress which her mum made for a party she held: 'I've worn it a couple of times, but you know what it's like, you – when do you find occasions to, unless you're Audrey Hepburn!' This is not to suggest, however, that the contemporary performance of this kind of femininity divorces it from its social meanings. Later on in the discussion Cally returns to this point: 'I've always been the type of person who liked to wear hats – I've always been the sort of person who liked to dress up' and bemoans the loss of opportunity in modern life to 'mak[e] an effort, and you know, mak[e] a big occasion of dressing up – and I love getting ready to go out – it's usually the best part of the night', articulating this as 'glamour'.

Cally goes on to describe the idea she shares with Anna of opening a 1950s-style supper club where there would be easy listening music – 'the sort of stuff my dad was playing when I was a kid, and it's sort of stuck in my mind – things like Jack Jones and Andy Williams, all that sort of – Matt Monroe, Frank Sinatra'. This delight in the contemporary retro mood is clearly in some ways performative in a 'postmodern pastiche' sort of way, and indeed is offered as evidence of 'individuality' in the face of a mainstream take-up of the vogue for easy listening: 'I'm not just saying it because it's trendy, I've always liked his records.' Mel, too, took pride in being the only one in her group of friends to be into this period of films and music. However, I would argue that even though Cally herself later dismisses this as 'just a superficial thing' there is equally a genuine investment in 'dressing up' not just as a pure performance, but also as pleasure in doing the labour of femininity and thereby conforming to the contours of conventional femininity. While in an ironic way Cally likes the idea of 'getting really dressed up on a Friday night and going to a club, and swanning around looking glamorous and making social chit-chat, and generally being very effervescent and charming! [laughs]', she also articulates this in terms of 'loss'.

The use of words like 'classy', 'classic' and 'timeless' is always interesting; what exactly do these terms mean in relation to femininity? While 'classy' and 'lady-like' are words which were used primarily in the first set of interviews, they were occasionally used by younger women too. New girl band 'Hepburn' described Audrey in one of their first television appearances as the inspiration for their name and 'a classy chick' (*This Morning*, Granada, UK, 1988–2001). Cally described herself as having grown up working-class, but as 'classless' now – i.e. she was associated with a class, but no longer exhibits the signs of that class; nevertheless she uses the word 'classy' to describe Hepburn's style, a word which indicates that something carries the signs of a particular class (middle). Similarly, the term 'classic' usually refers to a hegemonic style of dress which is acceptably neutral – inoffensive because free of the signs of working-class femininity or other unacceptable forms – a little black dress, for instance.[7] Class, as usual in the 1990s, is a structuring absence in fashion as in the wider culture. Anna remarked that her preference for wearing black and liquid eyeliner was was much related to her teenage 'Goth' identity as to her admiration of Audrey Hepburn – a particularly clear example of the way in which Hepburn's hegemonically 'classic' image is flexible enough to accommodate unacceptable 'otherness' and make it safe – in the same way in the 1990s as with 'Beat' style in the late 1950s. A 'classic' look, she points out, is what you come to as you get older, and is something that can 'carry you through'. 'Timeless', in the same way, suggests that something seems to transcend the specificities of historical period – the postmodern, for example, is often referred to as timeless, as lacking historicity – but it should be borne in mind nevertheless that Audrey's 'classic', 'timeless' style is inherently rooted in the late 1950s and early 1960s, and equally is structured by precisely that which it effaces – the signs of class. While for most of these young women, their interest lay primarily in a nostalgic appreciation of the 'cool' fashionable look and lifestyle associated with Audrey Hepburn films, the two youngest women who had grown up in the 1990s placed a greater emphasis on the romantic appeal of the era embodied in Hepburn's films, concentrating on the narrative of the films and the behaviour of the star rather than on style.

Chloë and Mel were invested in very particular ways in the period and style of their mothers' youthful femininity. Chloë talked about her mother as having been cool and glamorous:

Chloë: Because it's funny – because, like, to see her now, she's like a real, like, *mum*. But then, I've got, like, photos of her – she was *such* a – she was *so cool* – she had like, 'cos she used to – she trained at L'Oréal – [RM: Did she?!] – in London, and Dad was like an engineer on the *Queen Mary*, he was first engineer on the *Queen Mary* – and they were really glamorous, I mean – they're nothing like it now.

RM: When was this – sixties?

Chloë: Sixties, yeah. And, all kind of, you know, sunglasses – and the kind of little Chanel, sort of, you know – those – where you have the little dress, and the little jacket over the top, and a kind of really – and Dad was all kind of, like, pinstripe suits – a real bachelor kind of, sports car man, but they're really different people now.

This era of glamour and sophistication is clearly articulated as a moment which is 'lost' in this account – its only reality is in photographs. Chloë's account of Audrey is suffused with a nostalgia for the romance and perfection of this historical moment which coincides with the period of her parents' youth and courtship. Similarly, as I discuss above, Mel talked in detail about her mother as a young woman, her photograph album, and throughout our discussion she repeatedly referred to what she perceived as the 'innocence' of that period:

> The stories she tells, and what she got up to, and it's all – even though she did get up to a lot, it's still really innocent, and the way she thought about things was completely innocent, and doing something bad, was sort of, buying a few cigarettes, or, you know, and that sort of thing, and it's, you know, it's just nice, and I, I want to be able to be in that time, but it's just impossible really, so this is the closest I'm going to get, is clinging on to these people, the idols.

Across this set of interviews a range of readings are produced around Hepburn's image in which feminist sensibilities sit in negotiation with a nostalgic retreat from the contemporary. Uniting these apparently contradictory readings is a set of anxieties which might be described as 'postfeminist': the desire for and simultaneous acknowledgement of the impossibility of 'having it all' – here, in relation to femininity, to be both good/innocent but also naughty and modern. Hepburn emerges as a figure who is particularly appealing because she manages to reconcile these contradictions and, indeed, manages to 'have it all'. How is it that a star largely associated with the 'pre-feminist' 1950s and 1960s can be understood to address and reconcile contemporary 'postfeminist' tensions so satisfactorily? The remainder of this final chapter is devoted to an exploration of this complex interweaving of reading positions.

Having it all

I want to consider a set of reading positions identifiable across these interviews which can best be described as 'postfeminist'; this is true both of the way in which they engage with the anxieties of 'post-feminism' and of the kinds of desires articulated through this. Furthermore, the understandings of Audrey Hepburn constructed from those positions produce her as a utopian postfeminist figure. Ann Brooks (1997) makes a helpful distinction between postfeminism as a stage in the evolution of feminism which sees its intersection with 'a number of other anti-foundationalist movements including postmodernism, post-structuralism and post-colonialism' (1), and popular notions of postfeminism in the media, commonly identified with a 'backlash' against second-wave feminism by writers such as Susan Faludi. Linked to this is the occurrence of terms like 'the man shortage', 'the biological clock' and the 'career mother' in the media and the blaming of feminism for the pressures faced by women in the 1980s and 1990s. Carried within this is the idea that feminism undermines romantic heterosexual relationships, and in relation to this Brooks refers to research carried out by Susan Bolotin in 1982 which revealed how young women are keen to return to old values, rigidly segregated roles and 'institutionalised notions of heterosexuality, marriage and the family' (Brooks 1997: 4). In Chapter 4 I discussed the repeated association of Hepburn with weddings and wedding gowns in the first set of interviews, and her perceived appropriateness in this respect as a model of sophistication, innocence and 'taste'. For young women of the 1990s, Hepburn continues to be associated with weddings; *Hair and Beauty* magazine (October 1998; figure 6.1) carried a feature on Audrey-style wedding dresses based on Givenchy dresses from her film career. Similarly, Cally told me that her mother had made an Audrey-style ball dress for her sister in shantung silk, for which she used a wedding-dress pattern (similar to her own wedding gown). In answer to my question about wearing Audrey-inspired styles, Cally, who as I have indicated was particularly invested in the loss of opportunity to 'dress up', told me:

> I mean, I must admit, if I was to get married, I always say, 'Ooh, I'll have an Audrey Hepburn style dress', sort of straight – very simple [RM: What would you go for –] – er, I don't know – probably something with a sort of scoop neck, and an Empire line lacy top – short sleeves, and then like a plain skirt, and – and I'd have, sort of, bridesmaids wearing similar sort of outfits, in a different colour – oh, I've got it all planned out – it's never going to happen, but you know [laughs].

Similar comments are made by celebrity Audrey fans Darcy Bussell and Jayne Middlemiss: 'If I ever get married, I would love to dress like Audrey in *My Fair Lady* on my wedding day' (*OK!*, January 1998, p. 56).

Particularly significant here is the way in which young women who are clearly the inheritors of the discourses of second-wave feminism around issues such as equal rights and sexual liberation and who often described themselves as feminist, are nevertheless highly invested, as Brooks suggests, in ideal heterosexual romance in its institutionalised forms. It is this conjunction of feminism (strength, independence, equality) and the pleasures of traditional femininity, both in terms of 'dressing up' and here also 'every little girl's dream' – the white wedding – which I would argue are the particular markers of post-feminism. In important ways, it is this postfeminist discourse which organises the interviews discussed in this chapter.

In *Screen Tastes*, Charlotte Brunsdon (1997) is interested in the way films such as *Working Girl* and *Pretty Woman* both depend on and disavow second-wave feminism, and argues that they 'share an address to, and representation of, a new kind of figure, the post-feminist girly . . . a persona best understood as offering some kind of embodiment of, and engagement with, the changing status of women' (4). Brunsdon points to historical, discursive shifts within feminism in relation to consumption and femininity, suggesting that the reconsideration of the pleasures of feminine consumption identifiable with postmodern feminism are also part of popular understandings of postfeminism (85). A postmodern, postfeminist girl can unproblematically wear a Wonderbra, lipstick *and* be a company director. As I have begun to suggest, what this set of interviews with women to whom this ideal might apply reveals is a simultaneous deconstruction of and yearning for precisely this kind of negotiation. Brunsdon offers a formulation of the relationship of this new figure to femininity which is particularly useful to my project here:

> she is neither trapped in femininity (pre-feminist), nor rejecting of it (feminist). She can use it. However, although this may mean apparently inhabiting a very similar terrain to the pre-feminist woman, who manipulates her appearance to get her man, the post-feminist woman also has ideas about her life and being in control which clearly come from feminism. She may manipulate her appearance, but she doesn't just do it to get a man on the old terms. She wants it all (1997: 86).

PRODUCED IN ASSOCIATION WITH WEDDING HAIR AND BEAUTY, THE ONLY HAIR AND BEAUTY MAGAZINE FOR BRIDES

Women in the 50s usually wore their hair short and that's great news for short-haired modern brides who want to wear a long, glamorous dress as 50s style gowns match 90s crops to perfection. This simple dress from Wizard of Gos works best with an understated style that's been slicked down using styling creme. Tiara by Basia Zarzycka; Gloves by Steinberg & Tolkein; Choker by Butler & Wilson; Shoes by Anello & Davide; Organza shawl by Christiana Couture.

Cine-*chic*

If you're looking for some style inspiration, look no further than your video collection. The films of Audrey Hepburn offer plenty of choice for weddings that are both romantic and oh-so-chic

A very tall hairstyle really should be combined with a long dress - but make sure it's a slim dress like this empire line style from Caroline Castigliano. The hair has been plaited and dressed up high - the strength of the plait helping to keep the look up in the air. You can use a hairpiece if you haven't enough hair of your own - that was a popular trick in the movies during the 60s and most women had a variety of hairpieces they could bring out for special occasions. Tiara and choker by Butler & Wilson; Wedding ring by Tiffany & Co; Shoes by Anello & Davide.

Early 60s dresses were simple with minimalist decoration and that look is ultra fashionable now. This vintage dress from Steinberg & Tolkein works beautifully with a tall style that has the concept of early 60s beehives without being too exaggerated. Shoes by Anello & Davide; Platinum and diamond wedding ring by Tiffany & Co; Earrings (used as hair accessory) by Butler & Wilson; Sunglasses by Cutler & Gross.

88

6.1 'Ciné-chic' — wedding dresses, Audrey-style, in *Hair and Beauty* (October 1998), pp. 88–89. Reproduction by permission of *Hair and Beauty* magazine

A simple shift dress from the 60s (from Steinberg & Tolkein) gives an authentically retro feel to this look which you could achieve just as well with one of the many simple shifts available in the shops now. Keep the hair look simple - a soft flick-up fits in well with the retro feel while also being totally modern. The Evita Peroni perspex hairbands further emphasise the modern feel. Alternatively, you could try a high impact hat (this one's by milliner extraordinaire, Stephen Jones) and this style works well as it won't be flattened. Shoes by Emma Hope; Gloves by Caroline Castigliano; Chiffon from Liberty; Platinum and diamond wedding ring by Tiffany & Co.

Some brides feel that short hair doesn't work with a long dress and veil but that couldn't be further from the truth. What you have to avoid is teaming a tomboy cut with a totally girlie, fairytale-style gown. Instead, take a tip from the movies and choose a slim ivory satin column with the kind of youthful, quirky style Audrey Hepburn made fashionable in the 50s. Dress it up further with an exquisite tiara and short veil that allows you to see the hair underneath. Dress, gloves and veil by Wizard of Gos; Earrings by Butler & Wilson; Tiara by Basia Zarzycka; Shoes by Emma Hope.

HAIR BY CHRISTOPHER & SONYA DOVE, ARLINGTON, TEXAS; PHOTOGRAPHS BY CHRIS BISHOP; MAKE-UP BY KAREN LOCKYER; STYLING BY GUY HIPWELL FOR MICHAELJOHN MANAGEMENT; ASSISTED BY VIN KEY; FASHION DIRECTION BY TIM FRISBY; WORDS BY SANDRA HALLIDAY.

PRODUCED IN ASSOCIATION WITH WEDDING HAIR AND BEAUTY, THE ONLY HAIR AND BEAUTY MAGAZINE FOR BRIDES

89

There is a way in which the generations of women I have interviewed in the course of this research precisely span the historical shifts in relation to feminism identified here by Brunsdon, and I would argue that this is particularly the case with regard to their relation to femininity and dress. What the postfeminist women whose understandings of Hepburn in relation to feminism and femininity I discuss below express is both a profound dis-ease with the notion that the goals of second-wave feminism have been achieved, a utopian longing for this, and, frequently, a nostalgic desire for a retreat to 'the way things were back then'.

For a number of these young women as with the 1950s/1960s group, it is the fact that Hepburn can be both boyish and conventionally feminine with equal success that makes her appealing, and importantly, 'real'. In the instance quoted below, Anna identifies this as a characteristic also shared by Doris Day (most of the women of both generations also admired Day):

> Well, you look at her sort of, like, you know, skipping about, wearing, you know, boys' clothing, or whatever and then you see her – you know when they're doing this scene where she's running down the stairs in that sort of it's flashed up red and green and everything like that – it's just like a completely different aspect of her – she gets to show all, like the different personalities that everyone is – 'cos you're not just like 'I'm dead glamorous' or you know 'I'm this' – there's everything and I think that sort of shows in the way that she's – that's what I like about her dressing is she can get away with looking like a bit of a bloke – like Doris Day always looked like Doris Day – whatever she was wearing, you know – even when you put her in a really nice cocktail frock you still thought 'It's Doris Day, isn't it?' [laughter] so . . .

Evidently, this might be read as suggesting a post-structuralist understanding of identity as multiple and contradictory; Audrey embodies this in her ability to be both boyish and conventionally feminine – 'glammed up in a fab frock' with ease and success, refuting any attempt to position her securely. Similarly, it is Hepburn's embodiment of key contradictions which forms the basis of her appeal for Chloë. The particular terms of contradiction she picks out are especially interesting as they focus on Hepburn's ability to combine, for example, innocence with insight, social and personal 'polish' with liberation:

> And the other thing is the dad, in that film, the chauffeur, he says something like . . . when he's driving Humphrey Bogart to work, he

says – 'She's like a displaced person, she doesn't belong in a mansion, but she doesn't belong above a garage either', and – you just
can't place her, because in some ways she seems so traditionally kind
of, *English*, even though, I mean, she wasn't – she seems like, and
her vocabulary, some of that is kind of, I mean it's odd, in some
ways, and that's one of the interesting things about her, or one of the
things I like about her, but she seems so, like . . . *polished*, and like
finishing school kind of with her *posture*, and she's so kind of, you
know in a way that people aren't, any more, I mean she really seems
. . . typically English like that, I suppose stereotypically – but then in
other ways she's messing about . . . and like I mean – *Breakfast at
Tiffany's* is a totally different thing, I think, anyway, I can't – I sit
there, and I think 'I can't, I can't *believe* this.'
RM: Why?
Chloë: Because like, like – you see her *bra*! [RM: I know!] And like,
you see her – she answers the door, and she's got like, a sheet around
her, and she turns round, and George Peppard's at the door, and she
says, 'Oh, well I'll turn around then', and like, all things like – and
she gets drunk, and she's smoking, and you just think 'Oh my God,
you know, what's going on?' It's really odd, but then, I mean, that –
she totally suits that *as well*.

It is the perception of Audrey managing to be both sexually liberated
and demure here which is so interesting, and so suggestive of the
way in which such imperatives and dichotomies remain pertinent
and resonant for young women growing up in the 1990s, despite the
popular understanding of the contemporary as 'postfeminist' in the
sense that such contradictions are no longer significant. Audrey is so
appealing in this woman's account precisely because she manages to
appear at one with feminist demands for sexual liberation (although,
interestingly, as we have seen she is *not* about sex) while remaining
within the bounds of what is considered appropriate feminine
behaviour and appearance. The précis on the jacket of Candace
Bushnell's New York-set *Sex and the City* (1996) precisely articulated the problematic of negotiating sexual liberation, glamour and
'niceness': young single women 'trying hard not to turn from the
Audrey Hepburn of *Breakfast at Tiffany's* into the Glenn Close of
Fatal Attraction'.[8]

It is perhaps suggestive of the power of Hepburn's persona that
Chloë brings together characteristics from film characters almost ten
years apart, Sabrina and Holly Golightly, in her figuring of Hepburn.
She 'speaks' to young women like Chloë; she is both real and utopian,

because she both expresses and reconciles such contradictions. It seems significant, though, that one of the most notable aspects of Chloë's account was her investment in the romance of the period and films with which she associates Audrey. She returns continually to the 'romance' of these films, seeing this as an 'intellectual escapism' from the 'gritty realism' portrayed in contemporary film, and like a number of the women I spoke to, has no desire to spoil her 'romantic notions' about Hepburn by reading biographical material. This, perhaps, is why she figures Hepburn as 'living in a box' and existing only through her films. Similarly, Lucy, who had read a number of film-star biographies, had resisted reading Audrey's:

> I think maybe it's like you like to keep the myth about somebody and what they're really like, and it ruins it a little bit, doesn't it? I mean I read a little bit about her – unhappy marriages and miscarriages and this sort of thing, and you know, you don't think of that when you think about Audrey Hepburn, do you – you think 'She's got a perfect life' – she must have a perfect life, 'cos she's beautiful [clearly tongue in cheek, laughs] and you know, you have this stereotype in your head, whereas you know, with someone like Marilyn Monroe, you knew that they had a tragic life as well as – you know, and looked like they did, as well.

This desire not to know about Audrey Hepburn the wife, mother, divorcee and sufferer of numerous miscarriages is common to all the women in this set of interviews. Sordid knowledge about Audrey's 'real' life would undermine the utopian possibilities she offers as a star in relation to postfeminist demands. I would argue that it is precisely in this refusal to know that the fragility of the postfeminist myth of 'having it all' is indicated.

While Lucy clearly signals the deliberate naivety of her comment here, her contrast of Hepburn's perfect life with the tragedy of Marilyn Monroe's is revealing. There is clearly a way in which Hepburn is perceived as managing their key combination of innocence and sophistication more successfully, and I suspect that this distinction is located, once again, in the fact that Monroe is perceived as 'about sex', while Hepburn is not. She is naughty, but most definitely still a 'nice girl':

> I don't know, I think she's just an endearing sort of star – she's not – she's not *gross*, or in your face – or – she's sort of reminiscent of a bygone age – she's quite innocent, she's quite charming and elegant [breathes in] you know, but there is the fact that she could be that

Holly Golightly sort of character, who's quite debauched in a way, and yet carries it off as though, you know – she's too nice – you can't actually imagine any seedy goings on happening with any of these people, but you know – it's just sort of hinted at, and she gets away with that – she just comes across as being a bit kookie, and a bit sort of – not altogether on the straight and narrow, whereas I suppose her earlier films, she's young, young, charming, vulnerable . . . I don't know.

In a similar way, Chloë pointed out Audrey's ability to make being drunk look charming in this film – precisely the same discourse which was discernible around Hepburn in the 1950s, if updated. As I discuss in Chapter 2, Audrey could make it OK to take off your shoes and spill tea in your saucer in polite company. It seems that in the face of the actual impossibility of managing contradictions like Audrey does, a nostalgic retreat into a past where 'stars were really stars' (Chloë) is the only solution.

The sense that the postfeminist utopia can only be discovered in the past is common across these interviews. Anna talked about why she likes female stars of the 1940s and 1950s:

I quite like . . . I like *High Society*, Grace Kelly – even though she's simply a spoilt little cow in it – but actually that's one of those films I just like, I think – see it goes back even further – it's people like Katharine Hepburn – is probably, like, another you know like massive sort of heroine – Ingrid Bergman, Lauren Bacall I really like – and also because how that mirrors in their personal lives, because all of them had, really good strong relationships with equal partners, you know, you look at Katharine Hepburn and Spencer Tracy and Lauren Bacall and Humphrey Bogart – they had . . . possibly like, you know, in your little romantic world – the sort of relationship you'd actually want to have, you know – with somebody who treated you like your equal, and not as a woman.

Anna located the possibility of equality between the sexes in a period of the cinematic past often discussed in terms of the strong female characters it offered. She also contextualised Hepburn's characters historically:

I mean at the end of the day, I always consider myself as a feminist, and you're talking about your heroine is a woman who basically sponges off men [laughs] and that was it, and like didn't get a job, sort of thing, but I think it's like the context of how you look at these things – you know, this was in the 1950s, you know, she was never going to go out and like have a fabulous job, and do this, you know – she made, she

sort of like lived by her own wits, but then still called the shots – I mean
she gets sort of, fifty dollars to go to the powder room, and then sort
of, disappears off – you know, up the fire escape, or something. So –
she doesn't really compromise her ideals, you know – I mean obviously, if that was happening now, in the nineties, you'd be like slapping
the woman round the head, 'C'mon – get a life!' [laughter] you know,
but because of like the time that it was in, it's very interesting. And a
lot of it is probably the sort of – I don't know – they always seem to
sort of, lead their men by the noses, basically. You know – the men at
the end of the day, I mean, I know that she's basically prostituting herself in the film, *but* the men are essentially all very weak and the
women all tend to be very very strong, you know, and they are just sort
of like – you know, the men are sort of like, you know, slobbering
about at their feet – basically 'Have me, have me!' sort of thing – and
they're just picking and choosing, you know.

Anna's account is clearly informed by second-wave feminism; in
Breakfast at Tiffany's Hepburn is perceived as a strong woman in control of her life, as well as a style icon, although by 1990s postfeminist
standards she doesn't quite measure up. Nevertheless, Anna offers a
skilled reading of *Breakfast at Tiffany's* which reclaims Hepburn for
feminism: she appears here as a proto-feminist figure. As I discuss
above, she also appears in this account as a figure who clearly manages the contradictory pressures Anna sees as experienced by women
in the 1990s. Anna uses the examples of a job interview and walking
down the street to explain that Audrey can wear the clothes she
wants, but be judged for her personality as well as her looks: 'in an
ideal world that would happen but in the real world [laughs] as we all
know, it doesn't happen.'

The sense that Audrey 'has it all' by managing contradictions
which are experienced as irreconcilable by these young women in
their own lives is key to her appeal for them. For instance, Audrey
was understood by both Lucy and Verity as conventionally feminine
in terms of dress, grooming and glamour, but importantly also as
non-domestic, particularly in *Breakfast at Tiffany's*.

Holly represents the pleasures of being a young, independent
woman with a chic urban apartment, free not to do the washing and
leave shoes under the bed. As Lucy put it, the opening of *Breakfast
at Tiffany's* offers '[t]he idea of just having this great life where you
don't work and you know – you go to parties all night and eat breakfast at six in the morning and then go to bed – tripping alongside

Tiffany's'. This is a look Lucy has 'performed' for a party; interestingly, she describes this look as both 'sweet' and 'glamorous'. As I discuss below, there is a significant way in which Hepburn can be figured in relation to two sets of terms in these interviews: she is both 'glamorous and strong' but also 'glamorous and good/sweet'. Where I offered a 'film studies' reading of Hepburn's problematic relation to marriage and the domestic in Chapter 5, symptomatically finding trouble in the text, the young women in this set of interviews offer what I argue can be understood as 'postfeminist' readings which identify the same formation – chic urban femininity in conjunction with romance (but not marriage), and lack of domesticity – *positively* in relation to their own experience and desires. At the same time Hepburn's image is flexible enough to enable her to remain, in other accounts, the ideal bride. In the context of postfeminism, these two readings may co-exist unproblematically. Mel, for example, figures Audrey as Holly as 'a strong independent woman with a man'; as we will see, however, this reading is not entirely comfortable.

Lucy also made very interesting distinctions between Hepburn's and Doris Day's respective relationships to domesticity. Whereas Doris Day is understood as distinctly 'homey' – 'she might rebel for a bit, but she'll settle down and be good', Audrey is a 'good-time girl rather than a woman at home'. Lucy offers a sophisticated reading of the trajectory of this relationship with the domestic across Hepburn's career, situating this historically from the 'pre-feminist' 1950s to the emergence of the women's movement – in the earlier films, for instance *Roman Holiday*, 'she's like good-time, and then does her duty – a bit more Doris Day . . . but yeah – she's definitely a good-time girl in the sixties films, isn't she?' In the 1960s Audrey is both 'glamorous' and 'strong' (non-domestic); 'feminine' and 'feminist' (see Read 2000).

For Lucy, this ideal combination of strength and glamour is not to be found in the contemporary, or even the recent past. She expertly deconstructs current ideals of femininity and postfeminist claims about the redundancy of feminist politics, locating this utopia in the 1960s in figures like Emma Peel as played by Honor Blackman and Diana Rigg. When I offer *Charlie's Angels* (USA, Spelling-Goldberg Productions, 1976–1981) as an example from the 1970s, Lucy argues that they 'didn't fight properly':

Lucy: You see – they were just insipid to me, in comparison to the six-
ties girls – they were great, and Emma Peel was great, wasn't she?
RM: It's funny though, isn't it – because I mean they're sort of – I mean
I agree – but they're sort of like, pre-feminist girls aren't they, as well
[Lucy: Mmm – yeah] whereas I suppose you know – the women we
had in the eighties and that are more –
Lucy: Theoretically – tell that to the Wonderbra campaign.
RM: I'm interested in why they still appeal to us . . .
Lucy: Even though they're not feminist women, they're very independent, I mean – none of them went home and cooked their husband's
tea at the end of an episode – they all lived on their own, and you
know – for the sixties – I think that was pretty right on for the sixties – I mean women didn't live on their own in gorgeous flats and
have glamorous, like or kick men around, so you know, I think they
were pretty good for the time.

She had read numerous biographies of 1960s celebrities including
Jean Shrimpton and Terence Stamp, and felt that more contemporary examples would not be as interesting: 'You get this idea that all
the best people are dead, and there aren't any film stars replacing
them, and you know, when someone dies now, like you know, when
Bob Hope goes, or when Frank Sinatra did, it's like – oh, that's it,
that's the end.' The past is figured as meaningful, authentic and a
time of hope, and despite Lucy's feminist deconstruction and criticism of the domesticity and traditional marriages and relationships
of the 1950s female stars she likes, there is still a yearning, as in the
accounts of a number of the young women in this set of interviews,
for some kind of romantic ideal. While she was disappointed that
Jean Shrimpton wanted 'a hotel and a husband and marriage', she
also wanted her to declare Terence Stamp 'the love of her life' and
'complete perfection', as he did her.

While such postfeminist readings of Audrey figure her as both
strong and glamorous, feminist and feminine, there is also a consen-
sual acknowledgement across these interviews that while strength
and glamour is the postfeminist ideal, there is also a concomitant
social imperative for women to be 'glamorous and good' (Lucy).
Princess Diana and Audrey are both seen as examples of this particular conjunction, with Audrey managing to be strong, glamorous
(able to attract a man) and at the same time good. Hepburn's
UNICEF work and the comparison with the princess were repeatedly mentioned in relation to this.

Mel's account of Audrey's appeal was especially interesting around the difficult negotiation of these three terms. I would argue that this difficulty is articulated in her confusion about the degree and kind of Audrey's strength and independence, and in her simultaneous and quite particular investment in innocence. Mel was very interested in old movies, musicals and music, and particularly in the 'innocence' she perceived as the key feature of the era these films represent. At the same time, she was invested in the romance (as opposed to sex) of these films, and in their leading men. The first Audrey Hepburn film she saw was *Roman Holiday*, which she described as the most innocent of her films, where 'it's very sunny – it always seems to be in the day'. In films of this period, she feels:

> It's so naive, and, and like they're all in this sort of bubble and they don't take into consideration all the bad things that are happening, that I mean, which are like you get in films today, which sort of, tackle those issues. But I prefer the ones where you don't have to think about that [laughs], and you know, it's just sort of, the colour is so synthetic, and it spells somewhere nice, and everything's so, sort of, it just – it's all *happy*, really.

While this extract indicates a nostalgic retreat into what is perceived as a simpler, more innocent, happier, sunnier past, it is nevertheless combined, a few minutes later, with a feminist valuing of Doris Day's 'feistiness'; at the same time, though, Mel's choice of the word 'gentlemen' to describe Day's sparring partners is significant, suggesting a rather polite kind of confrontation. Mel acknowledges that this perfect past is a construct in her point about the synthetic colour of these films, and like Chloë sees this as a way of escaping the 'bad things' and difficult issues in the contemporary which are almost 'too real'. She is often criticised by her friends for her 'old-fashioned' taste in films and music, but she reclaims this by talking about her expert knowledge of the films of this era as something which individuates her from her friends, as cultural capital: part of the reason she doesn't like *Breakfast at Tiffany's* is because everyone else does, although I will argue that there is more at stake in her account of this film. While she has no trouble in indicating the strength of Doris Day, she has more difficulty in thinking about this in relation to Audrey; this becomes most apparent in our discussion of *Breakfast at Tiffany's*, the film most frequently discussed in relation to these issues across this set of interviews.

Importantly, Mel understands the 'tomboy' aspect of Hepburn's persona as 'the real Audrey'. She explains to me why she doesn't like the end of *Roman Holiday*:

> Mel: I don't like her as much at the end.
> RM: Oh – you mean, the bit where she comes out?
> Mel: As the princess, yeah. [RM: Do you like the other –] I like the other bits, where she's pretending, yeah [obvious delight in voice] she's sort of – almost *tomboyish*, and more – how she wants to be, how I *imagine* she wants to be, and then at the end, and she's all – it's the same actually, as *My Fair Lady*, 'cos when she's, sort of, got all her jewellery and everything, and she comes out at the ball, she's not so Audrey Hepburn – she's not the real *person* – she sort of shines through when she's wearing a really simple outfit like in *Funny Face* and she's just walking around in little black leggings, and things – yeah – I think I prefer her looking like that. [RM: Do you?] Nice and simple.

Apparent here is a kind of feminist discourse which understands and prefers the 'natural', unconstructed and therefore authentic Audrey to the 'made-over' version. Accordingly, Mel argues against my characterisation of the films as transformation narratives, preferring to read them as stories of discovery in which the 'real' Audrey is recognised as beautiful, thus enabling her to negotiate the difficult question (in feminist terms) of Audrey being transformed by a man, and to restore both her authenticity and her control of the narrative. She reads *Funny Face*, for instance, in terms of 'the fact that no-one can see that she's wonderful, except this particular gentleman, and I am in this complete bubble of innocence [laughs] and I like it and I don't want to come out, so . . .'. She performs the same strategy in relation *My Fair Lady*, her favourite film:

> It's more a case of sort of seeing – 'cos she is the same person – like at the end she goes back and she visits and stuff though she feels a bit, sort of, like, on the other side now, you can tell that she's actually the same person, she just sounds different – and it's almost – it's more about someone else seeing . . . that she is beautiful, rather than making her beautiful . . . because I think in that film, I think people always mistake it for . . . them sort of, changing her, I think that's – you see I really hate him in that film – he's so horrible, because he – especially when they congratulate each other – it just makes me sick, because I – [RM: It's horrible, isn't it?] – it is, and I'm just completely, completely on her side the whole time, and you almost want her to slip up, just so that he'll have failed, but you know, she does her bit.

Mel wants to argue, in relation to Audrey as with Doris Day, that 'she's the one really doing it', and consequently offers a set of redemptive readings in relation to what I have characterised as narratives of transformation, which produce Audrey as *more* in control of the narrative, rather than Dick Avery (*Funny Face*) or Henry Higgins (*My Fair Lady*). The difficulty she has in reproducing this in relation to *Breakfast at Tiffany's*, though, reveals the problem. She told me she didn't like this film; one of the problems Mel has with characterising Audrey positively in *Breakfast at Tiffany's* relates to her investment in innocence; here Hepburn is

> I don't know – a bit more brazen than she is in anything else, and I don't like that. I don't like the fact that she's you know – the – her character isn't as innocent as the rest of the characters have been – she's got this thing about money, and marrying into it, and the whole – this is her plan, her master plan.

This 'brazenness' is much less of a problem in relation to Doris Day, whose sexuality is often contained within marriage either through the film or by implication at the end. Mel wants to read Audrey, as we have seen, in contrast to Marilyn, as about 'romance': 'There was some sort of innocence there, and though there was always romance, and stuff, it was romance, and it wasn't, you know, sort of hitching up her skirt.' Her initial analysis of the film suggests this, and also points precisely to the way in which Holly manipulates men through her appearance, as pointed out by Brunsdon above in relation to what she terms 'the postfeminist girly'. She wants it all, and this knowingness is unacceptable in Mel's schema of innocence and naivety. At the same time, though, she critiques the way the film finishes with Holly, who began as 'a strong independent woman', soaking wet in the arms of George Peppard. Mel nevertheless describes her as 'still a strong character', although less so than in other films, and likes the way she ends up 'a strong independent woman with a man'. She finally describes her as 'least dependent on a man' in this film, contradicting her initial position. In her ability to negotiate romance and independence, she is a postfeminist ideal, but the terms of the negotiation are uneasy; she repeated this later around Hepburn in relation to dress: 'I'm sort of aspiring to be fragile in my own way [RM: – yeah] so that I look fragile, without actually being so.' It is Mel's difficulty in articulating a coherent position on the issues of fragility/femininity and strength in *Breakfast at Tiffany's*, and her desire to retreat into a 'bubble of innocence' which point most clearly to the difficulty of this position. Ultimately, Mel, despite her desire to redeem the film and Hepburn's role in feminist terms, ends by returning to her desire for innocence – thus retreating from the difficulty of the position she is trying to articulate into a moment (more perfectly expressed in the romantic comedies of Doris Day and Rock Hudson) in which gender roles are more clearly defined, difficult issues are less explicitly addressed, and endings are less ambiguous. Feminist understanding, postfeminist desire and nostalgic retreat are simultaneously articulated throughout her account.

On the one hand in these readings there is a critical feminist engagement with what writers such as Coppock, Haydon and Richter (1995) have described as the 'myths' of post-feminism, in conjunction with a return to traditional modes of feminine dress and self-production as performative. On the other, and often simultaneously, there is nevertheless a yearning for the possibility of adequately managing the contradictory positions it holds up as ideal (e.g. traditional heterosexual relationship and motherhood combined with perfect career and independence) which is suggestive of the power of those myths even as they can be deconstructed. In the figure of Audrey Hepburn these positions, understood here as impossible and contradictory in 'real' life, are often perceived as successfully reconciled. Mel's account, however, reveals the tensions inherent in that negotiation, and a consequent nostalgic retreat into what can only be described as the pre-feminist in search of the postfeminist ideal.

While as Richard Dyer has pointed out, one key function of all stars is to reconcile contradictions, the particular kinds of difficulties Hepburn is seen to successfully negotiate are especially resonant for young women who have grown up into the postfeminist 1990s, and ensure her continuing appeal for this generation of young women. At the same time, Audrey represents hegemonic (and yet 'timelessly modern') feminine style, 'a bygone age', and a time of romance, innocence and clearly defined gender roles idealised by the two youngest women who spoke to me. In this way, as Dyer suggests, Hepburn embodies values which society perceives to be in crisis. It is the polysemic nature of 'Audrey Hepburn' which has secured the enduring appeal of this star: she can be understood simultaneously, in Raymond Williams's terms (1977), as a residual, dominant *and* emergent figure in relation to femininity and the history of feminism at both moments of her popularity in the late 1950s/early 1960s and the 1990s.

Notes

1 I use 'group' here to indicate a grouping according to generation, as with a couple of exceptions the women in each group were not known to each other and all were interviewed separately. See Appendix I for brief a biographical note on the interviewees.

2 Shirley was a pilot interviewee. See Moseley (2001).

3 A number of the women in this group commented, as in the first 1950s/1960s group, that there is no sexual scandal attached to Hepburn.

4 Jameson's discussion of pastiche and the nostalgia film, and his suggestion that this cultural tendency relates to an inability to bring the present into focus, are clearly significant here (Jameson 1983: 116).

5 Hepburn's enormous popularity in Japan is interesting in relation to 'cutie culture'. See Skov and Moeran (1995).

6 Hepburn is often likened to animals in popular rhetoric – she is often thought to resemble a faun. The key thing about the most famous cinema faun, Bambi, of course, apart from his large eyes, is the fact that he loses his mother.

7 Although as Anne Hollander remarks, today's' 'classic' little black dress is the shopgirl's uniform of a previous era (1978: 385).

8 *Sex and the City* is also now a major American TV series (USA, HBO, 1998 –).

Conclusion

When I began this research, I was interested in three kinds of question. The first was about Audrey Hepburn as a star: I wanted to investigate the construction, circulation and reception of her image, but I also wanted to find out something about her enduring popularity. I was interested in why her image had apparently re-emerged in the 1990s, and held such currency with young women across fifty years of social, political and economic change in many women's lives – across the women's movement in the 1970s, for example. I wanted to find out what Audrey Hepburn meant to women who cited her as an inspiration and influence. It emerged that those women who offered to participate in the research fell into two generationally distinct groups: one growing up in the 1950s and 1960s, and the other in the 1980s and 1990s, two periods which are held to represent a set of social and political changes in relation to feminism and the lived experience of women: from the pre-feminist to the postfeminist, perhaps. It seems significant, for instance, that only one woman (Jayne) whose 'growing up' was identifiable with

7.1 On the verge of becoming 'Audrey Hepburn' – the princess contemplates changing her look in *Roman Holiday* (1953)

the early and mid-1970s offered herself as a participant in the research. While it is clearly the case that Hepburn's screen career was really falling away at this time, it may also be significant that this is also the point at which political activism in relation to race and the women's movement was at its height. Hepburn can be a pre-feminist, a postfeminist, but not a feminist, figure. I wondered if the continuing currency of 'Audrey Hepburn' was no more than the iconic power of surface – a depthless pastiche represented by the perpetual return to the image of Hepburn as Holly Golightly in *Breakfast at Tiffany's*? Second, I wanted to explore the nature of the relationship between the women I talked with and Hepburn. How was the relationship between them and their favourite female star expressed? Through what kinds of practices did they articulate their fascination for and closeness with Audrey?

Third, there was a more theoretical question underlying and informing my research. I was concerned to explore whether the notion of 'identification' which has been hegemonic in film theory was the most appropriate way to characterise the relationship between female viewers and a female star. In this sense I had a quite an explicit research agenda – to try to work outside psychosexual film theoretical approaches to this relationship, and to maintain an historically, socially and culturally grounded approach to the project.

I approached these initial questions through a tripartite methodology which reflected my concern to address equally questions of text and audience. I carried out textual analysis of the 'star-text' Audrey Hepburn, including in this conceptualisation of the star a consideration of film texts but also press and publicity, gossip and the ways in which 'Audrey Hepburn' has circulated in more ephemeral sites such as women's magazines and film-fan magazines, to produce an idea of the specificity of the address of the star-text. I also conducted an audience research project which in its initial stages included letters and questionnaires, but which in the end focused on a pilot study and a main body of interviews; the final text has been limited to these latter for reasons both of space and parity of method. As a result of this methodology, the book has become as much a reflection on the process of conducting and writing about this approach, as about Audrey and the women who admire her. This meta-critical concern, which in some ways is the richest, if least conclusive, element of the book, emerged unexpectedly in the process of producing it, and was born of a desire to develop a method which accounted for both text and audience without privileging either. In an organic way, it is also this concern which has literally shaped the book: it became increasingly necessary in the process of writing to fashion a structure which reflected my desire to articulate text, address and audience together. At the end of this process, a key finding, perhaps, has in fact been the uselessness of attempting to separate an idea of 'text' from one of 'audience'.

The findings of this research can be characterised in relation to four key areas which overlap with but in many ways exceed the initial research questions: Audrey Hepburn as star; the social history of British femininity; the nature of the relationship between audience and star; and a rather more methodological question about the complexity of working with both text and audience. The book is necessarily, and as originally intended, about Audrey Hepburn as 'star-text', and about the significance of that star-text for the women I spoke with. A central finding has been in support of Richard Dyer's suggestion that stars can be understood to reconcile ideological contradictions, for instance in relation to gender (Dyer 1991). The research has shown the historical specificity of this operation in relation to Audrey Hepburn – and in this and other ways has something to tell, through the detailed talk of the women who participated, about the social history of femininity in Britain. At the same time it has suggested the significance of the flexibility of 'Audrey Hepburn', akin to Dyer's notion of structured polysemy (1979). Central to this flexibility is the way in which Hepburn has represented both modern, pared-down 'trousers' and fairy-tale 'tiara' modes of femininity, a flexibility which has been key to her appeal both within and across two historical moments: the 1950s and 1960s, and the 1990s.

For women growing up in the 1950s and 1960s, the modernity and/or social acceptability of Hepburn's look was key, and was enabling in relation to factors such as age, region and social class. Yet in this regard, and in the particular context of British society on the verge of women's liberation, it was essential that Audrey was 'boyish, but still a girl'. In the 1990s, while Hepburn clearly functions in an iconic way, what was earlier described as the modernity and/or acceptability of her image is now understood as 'timeless', but not simply in the sense of pastiche. It is rather in relation to a perceived loss of certain ways of being female, particular modes of femininity – dressing up and 'glamour' – that Hepburn appeals. At the same time, what was described as 'boyish, but still a girl' is rearticulated as 'fragile, yet strong' in an explicitly postfeminist way. In terms of lifestyle and appearance, in the accounts of the young women who have participated in this study, Audrey in the 1950s and 1960s – a 'pre-feminist' figure – represents the management and reconciliation of key contradictions in the lived experiences of these women in the 'postfeminist' 1990s, in a way which is quite explicitly outside domesticity but still invested in idealised, heterosexual romantic love and marriage. Nevertheless, the difficulty of this position is acknowledged in their accounts: 'It's never going to happen' (Cally). While the ways in which the 1990s girls in this study talk about Audrey are 'outside class' (and indeed they often described themselves as 'classless'), there is still a sense, through the powerful appeal of the now 'timeless' kind of feminine glamour Audrey represents, that the same hegemony is still in place, and to that extent, class remains a structuring absence in the final chapter of the book. There is still quite a narrow set of acceptable ways of being a woman – ways which are in fact essentially class-related, if not class-bound (cf. Skeggs 1997).

There are two main things to say about the nature of the relationship between the women in this study and the star, Audrey Hepburn. First of all, they cannot *broadly* be described as 'fans'. Although a number of the younger women I spoke to did describe themselves in this way, as I discuss in Chapter 6, and were highly conscious of how such fandom might be perceived, the women who grew up with Audrey in the 1950s and 1960s explicitly, and without cue, distanced themselves from this identity. Perhaps one thing which this generational distinction suggests is the contrast in the affective nature of the relationship articulated by those women in the study for whom Audrey represented something inherently related to them – something which is part of a particular (past) time in their lives – youthful femininity in a specific historical and sociocultural context – and those young 1990s women in the study for whom Audrey represents something past which they have never known, but which nevertheless speaks to their experience of the present.

Second, there is the question of 'identification'. Existing discussion of the relationship between viewers and stars is either broadly sociological in approach, working within a discourse of 'fandom', or it is within the realms of psychoanalytic theory, focusing on unconscious psychosexual structures and processes and notions of fantasy. The way I have tried to think the relationship between audience (not necessarily viewer or spectator in the specifically cinematic sense) and text attempts to recognise that unconscious processes do play a part in that relationship – for instance in the mirroring of textual structures and the structuring of audience accounts in relation to the Cinderella motif – although I do not find it useful or necessary to attempt to specify those processes.

What I am interested in as an 'object' is something akin to what Virginia Nightingale has suggested as the 'audience–text relation', which in her words 'operates along a continuum from impersonation to improvisation, where people find ways to enact the themes and discourses of the stories they experience . . . with the problematics of their lived everyday (particularities)' (Nightingale 1996: x–xi). Perhaps the notion of 'usable stories' (Mepham 1990) – the articulation of self through discursive forms which offer ways of producing and understanding that identity, in conjunction with an appreciation of the historicity of discourse – might potentially be a productive position from which to begin. I want to argue that the relationships between audience members and stars are more diverse and indeed nebulous than existing theories of identification, or indeed Nightingale's formulation, despite its insight that 'the self' is inseparable from 'everyday life', can suggest. Accordingly, I want to hold on to the notions of affect, resonance and recognition as useful starting points which enable an address to the specificity of personal history; questions of gender, class, race, sexuality, generation, education and national identity are key factors in determining the form and the nature of relationships between audience member and star-text.

'Resonance and recognition' is a formulation which, as I have suggested above, I intend to indicate the constitution of subjectivity and the coming together of subjectivity with textuality. In this way it is possible to retain a notion of the address of a text, which may or may not be engaged with in relation to the particular conjunction of these factors. 'Resonance and recognition' is a particularly useful formulation in connection with the material from the interviews discussed in Chapters 3, 4 and 5 with women who grew up with Audrey Hepburn in the 1950s and 1960s. It is perhaps the important role played by memory in those accounts, that makes the term 'resonance' and its suggestion of a perpetual, harmonic 'back and forth' so appropriate as a way of conceptualising their relationship with the star. Interestingly, there seems to be a slightly different sensibility at work in the ways in which the 1990s girls in this study related to Hepburn.

While resonance and recognition clearly work in some ways, for instance around Hepburn as a 'pre-feminist' star speaking to their experience of the 'postfeminist' 1990s, paradoxically perhaps in the light of their overwhelming sense of closeness to the star, there is also evidence in their accounts of a kind of performative distance. This distance is indicative of 'pastiche' as a 'structure of feeling', as an historically specific mode of relating to the past, but *at the same time* that distance is also suffused by nostalgia, a sense of the impossibility of capturing the utopian moment Hepburn signifies to them to which they, unlike the other women in this study, do not have access through *experience*.

This, then, brings me finally to what is perhaps the most complex and inconclusive issue of the research. While I have been able to suggest something about the nature of the relationship between text and audience emerging in this study, perhaps more problematic and indeed less attended to in existing scholarship is the intractability of the relationship between textual analysis and audience research when used in conjunction as methodological tools. It is no longer possible at this point in the process of conducting and writing about the research represented in this book, to retrieve something which is 'what I thought about Audrey Hepburn before I began'. It is no longer possible to watch the films or look at images without recalling other images, phrases and stories offered to me in relation to them. In the few scholarly works which do address both text and audience, the complexity of the relationship between the researcher-critic's textual analysis of the 'texts' proper (i.e. not the audience accounts) and their analysis of those accounts is rarely addressed.[1] While Janice Radway (1991) produces her readings of and choice of romance novel texts through her analysis of her readers' accounts of reading them and Helen Taylor (1989) uses audience accounts to variously 'support and question or demolish' her own critical readings of the text (19), Jacqueline Bobo (1995) chooses to separate out analyses of film and novel texts and audience accounts of them. The intractability of the relationship needs to be acknowledged – that in the process of conducting interviews and performing textual analyses one necessarily informs the other, just as the accounts of Audrey given by women remembering growing up in the 1950s and 1960s are necessarily inflected through the process of remembering and informed by their experience and understanding of the circulation of that image in the 1990s.

There is a way in which the three kinds of question which formed the research are emblematic of the interdisciplinary nature of the project, and thus are also representative of the methodological and theoretical difficulties which have both plagued and enriched the experience of conducting and writing about the research. The study of stars, now key to film studies, is essentially both semiotic and sociological in approach; this research project has attempted to address both text and audience, and in its interest in both star and audience essentially speaks to both film studies and the sociological concerns of cultural studies. Equally, it might be argued that historically film studies has been an interdisciplinary field. The theoretical question underlying the research addresses the interdisciplinary nature of the project directly: the attempt to conceptualise audience–star relations outside hegemonic notions of identification in film theory. I have wanted to do this without collapsing the complexities arising from such an investigation into purely sociological terms, retaining an idea of the subject and a sense of the importance of the part played by less than wholly conscious processes. However, it is perhaps the methodological questions arising from the concern with addressing both text and audience, which have most explicitly suggested the problematics and productivity of such an interdisciplinary approach.

I suggest that the conjunction of approaches employed in this research offers a particularly useful way of doing film history, which is perhaps best illustrated in Chapter 5 in tracing the articulation of the Cinderella motif in the three sites: film text, archival resources for investigating the sites of circulation of the image such as women's and film-fan magazines, and audience accounts. What I hope to have offered is an account of the process of bringing history to film, of attempting to get to grips with the moments of the construction, circulation and reception of a 'star-text' such as Audrey Hepburn. This process could be described as a kind of cultural studies of film, film history as personal history and *through* that, social history – a history which is as interested in 'ephemera' and the difficult but inextricable issue of personal experience as it is in other, more conventional kinds of evidence.

Notes

1   Morley and Brunsdon (1999) offer a careful account of the relationship between the text's 'preferred reading' and the decoding of that text by audience members, and are a key exception.

Appendix I: the main interviews

The interviews

The research took the form of open-ended, semi-structured, conversational interviews which usually lasted between one and two hours. The questions around which they were structured are reproduced below. I also asked the women to fill in a form 'About you'. Some interviews took place in my home or in the women's places of work (Barbara, Caroline, Rosie, Chloë, Mel, Verity); the others took place in the women's own homes. I already knew Barbara, Bernie, Janet, Rosie and Verity, who offered to take part in the study; Bernie introduced me to Pat. Other women were introduced to me by friends (Cally, Lucy, Caroline, Liz, Chloë) who then introduced me to Anna, Jayne and Mel. Cally, Anna and Lucy are all single, professional women in their late twenties and at the time of the interviews all were living in rented accommodation in the trendy leafy suburbs of Birmingham. Lucy was living alone; Cally and Anna were both sharing houses with friends. Cally and Anna are good friends, and they and Lucy to some degree share the same culture and were introduced to me through the same person. Jayne was a work colleague of Cally, who put us in touch. Despite her very interesting account of Audrey, I decided to largely exclude Verity from the discussion of the accounts because it emerged that her formative years had been spent in France. The interviews took place over the period which saw the deaths of both Princess Diana and Frank Sinatra.

Transcriptions

In the extracts and quotations from interviews, italics indicate particular emphasis in speech; . . . indicates that a sentence tails off or a pause; – indicates interruption or running together; [. . .] indicates an elision. Extraneous speech indicators have been removed.

The interviewees

1950s and 1960s

Barbara
Barbara grew up in the 1950s in the Midlands and described herself as white European and middle class. After leaving school she became a hairdresser. At the time of the interview she was working in an administrative position in higher education.

Bernie
Bernie grew up in Birmingham in the 1950s and 1960s. She described herself as white European and, while having grown up working class, now saw herself as 'very middle class'. On leaving school she trained as a pharmacist, but gave up this career to support her husband through university.

Caroline
Caroline grew up in Buckinghamshire in the 1960s, and described herself as white European, growing up middle-class but having become upper middle class through marriage. After leaving school she worked full-time in the home and at the time of the interview was studying part-time for a master's degree in women's studies.

Janet
Janet grew up in Coventry and Derby in the 1950s, and described herself as white European and working class. She went to grammar school and went into secretarial work after leaving school. At the time of the interview she was working as a PA. Janet was also a pilot interviewee.

Liz
Liz grew up in Yorkshire in the 1950s, and described herself as white European. Although she grew up working class, she described herself as 'professional' middle class, but with a working-class background. After leaving school she did full-time office work, and went to university in her thirties. She is now an academic. Liz was also a pilot interviewee.

Pat
Pat grew up in Birmingham in the 1940s and 1950s, and described herself as white European and having grown up working class. However, she saw herself as middle class now: 'You sort of work at it, don't you?' She went into full-time work in her father's garage after leaving school.

Rosie
Rosie grew up in Yorkshire in the 1960s. She described herself as white European, having grown up working class but having become middle class through

education. After travelling around Europe after leaving school, she did various causal jobs, going to university at the age of 29. At the time of the interview she was a senior lecturer in film studies at a college of higher education.

1990s

Anna
Anna grew up in Birmingham in the 1980s, and described herself as Asian and middle class. On leaving school she completed a degree in languages and politics, and at the time of the interview was working as an administrator.

Cally
Cally grew up in Solihull and described herself as white European. Although on her questionnaire she saw herself as having grown up in the 1970s, her points of reference suggested to me that she identified more closely, like Anna, with the 1980s. She described herself as having grown up working class, but as 'classless' now. She went to university after leaving school and at the time of the interview was working as a customer services representative.

Chloë
Chloë grew up in Middlesex and Devon in the 1990s, and described herself as white European and working class. At the time of the interview she was in the second year of a university degree in fine art.

Jayne
Jayne grew up in Birmingham and Solihull in the 1970s, and described herself as white European and working class. The only one of this group of women to have a family, she had to accommodate our interview in the short time between leaving work and picking her children up from school, and around a visit from the gas board. On leaving school she went into office and then library work, and at the time of the interview was working in administration.

Lucy
Lucy grew up in Birmingham in the 1980s, and described herself as white European and 'classless if possible!' After leaving school she went into higher education, and at the time of the interview was working as a secondary school teacher.

Mel
Mel grew up in Surrey in the 1980s, and described herself as white European and working class. At the time of the interview she was in the first year of a university degree in fine art. Mel was introduced to me by Chloë.

Verity
Verity grew up in Paris in the 1980s, and described herself as white European and middle class. At the time of the interview she was a film studies research student living alone in her own London flat.

Interview questions

1 Can you remember where you first saw or heard about Audrey Hepburn? What was your first impression of her?
2 Where have you seen or read about her most? (films/video/TV/mags/ papers). If cinema/video, who did/do you watch with?
3 Do you have a favourite Audrey Hepburn film? Why is this one your favourite?
4 What in particular did you/do you like about Audrey?
5 Is there an outfit she wore which particularly comes to mind? What did you like about it?
6 Did you ever/do you have a dress or outfit similar to one worn by Audrey Hepburn?
    What was it/is it like?
    Was it bought or made?
    Where did you/do you wear it?
    Can you think of any others?
7 Would you say that her style has affected/affects yours at all?
8 Why do you think she has remained such a popular star? What is the reason for her ongoing appeal?
9 Is there anything else you would like to add that we haven't talked about?

Appendix II: extended interview extracts (Chapter 4)

Liz

Liz: Absolutely love it. And I love these Capri pants.

RM: Do you?

Liz: Yep. And they're back, aren't they? [laughs]

RM: They are – they're absolutely everywhere! Although some of them are quite a lot shorter than that –

Liz: Yes – I like *this* length. And I *love* . . . the little flat shoes.

RM: Do you?

Liz: Yep.

RM: Do you still wear them?

Liz: Yep. Now what I was wearing at the time, which is very interesting, were high heels.

RM: Were you?

Liz: Because it – there was something about being feminine at that period where flat shoes just wouldn't – you know – I couldn't feel that I could get away with flat shoes – everybody in the typing pool wore stilettos.

RM: So you would have really stood out?

Liz: No – yes I would have done –

RM: *If* you'd –?

Liz: Yes – and I hobbled around on stiletto heels. Erm – and it was – it was *years* . . . actually, I didn't feel that I could wear flat shoes until I was – I can't remember when it was, it was in the seventies sometime.

RM: Really?

Liz: Yes.

RM: So you didn't – you didn't, sort of –

Liz: I didn't, no –

RM: [at the same time] – strike out?

Liz: I didn't. And I remember seeing another film star, Natalie Wood in *West Side Story* [1961] and that was . . . a *wonderful* film. That had a big impact on me as well.

RM: Did it?

Liz: But what was striking about *her* was that she was . . . she was *running* and *dancing*. And she had flat shoes on [laughs]. She always wore little flat shoes. And that – I thought that was *wonderful*, but even then, I couldn't feel that I could wear flat shoes like that.

RM: So who – I'm interested to know – in terms of *glamour* –

Liz: Ahh . . .

RM: – who would you . . . sort of . . . who would you put forward in opposition to Audrey Hepburn at that moment, and who would you put, sort of, *with* her, were there any other stars?

Liz: At the time?

RM: At that time?

Liz: Yes, well I *didn't* like . . . I didn't like Marilyn Monroe.

RM: Didn't you?

Liz: No.

RM: Why didn't you like her?

Liz: Because she was too . . . overtly . . . *feminine*. There's too much . . . femininity. The sort of – I suppose the – kind of – *make-up* and the *blonde* hair, and I never – I just never liked that look. I really liked Audrey Hepburn; I liked Doris Day. Now I thought she was, again in those films, you know, I sort of went to watch all her early films, or at least, they weren't early, but the films in the fifties and sixties, and she had this sort of, *tomboy* kind of look, and image, and I liked her – she appealed to me, and *also*, the other one, that was a sort of – much more – there were two others who were more available, more accessible – one was Una Stubbs –

RM: Oh right –

Liz: – who at the time was – very . . . *boyish*, she had very, very short hair, feathery hair, and she used to, she used to be on an advert for chocolate or Cadbury's or Milk Tray, or something [laughs] and she had a really sort of, *boyish* look, and I really liked that, had my hair cut like that – so I liked her, and I also liked Petula Clark, 'cos I think she had that, she wasn't . . . over . . . *glamorous*, or overtly *feminine*, somehow. Although she was feminine, but it wasn't a kind of . . . *excessive* – there was no excess . . .

Bernie

Bernie: But going back to Audrey Hepburn, she . . . you see, you had like, Sandra Dee which was sort of, very cute.

RM: Was she? Cute?

Bernie: Oh yes –

RM: Was she blonde?

Bernie: – and 'beachy' – *yes*!

RM: 'Beachy'?

Bernie: Well, you know – sort of American 'beachy', you know.

RM: I do.

Bernie: And they were sort of . . . and they went from . . . I don't know how [laughing] – how they would have afforded this, but they would be at school one minute, then they'd all, for the summer holidays, all these kids would be together – no parents were in sight!

RM: [laughs] Yeah –

Bernie: You know – and they were all, and they were staying at these, well, they – motels – we didn't even know what a bloody motel was, but – this motel, there was always a swimming pool in the courtyard, and palm trees, and you know – whatever, and there was all that, which was like, *unreal*, then you'd go to . . . I mean then, the older one, was of course Doris Day –

RM: Of course – and she had a bit of a short but 'mumsy' hairdo, didn't she?

Bernie: That's right, and she was '*older* cute', *whatever*, but Audrey Hepburn [tone changes – signals 'distinction' in both senses] . . . she – Audrey – she was . . . I don't know . . . *classy*.

RM: Mmm.

Bernie: *Classy*.

RM: Yeah.

Bernie: *That's* it.

RM: Definitely.

Bernie: *Class* . . . but fun.

RM: Right . . . was that important then, do you think? That sort of, 'being classy'?

Bernie: At nineteen and twenty? Yes, it certainly *was*.

RM: Really? Why was that, do you think, particularly? I mean, why her over, not Sandra Dee any more? Was Sandra Dee not classy, really, do you think?

Bernie: No, *I* don't think she was. No, no I don't think she was. No, and I don't think any of her, any of her, no.

RM: That's very interesting . . .

Bernie: No . . . no, she's sort of . . . it was . . . everything she portrayed was *totally* unobtainable anyway . . .

RM: Ah, right –

Bernie: I mean, you know, I could never see me jumping into the back of – not even bothering to open the door of a car – they all just climbed all over the bodywork, [inaudible] into these fabulous big American cars – it was all totally way out of . . . it was like . . . imaginary.

RM: Right . . .

Bernie: Audrey – you'd go and see her, Audrey Hepburn, and it was
like, it was just, they *were* . . . I don't know . . . I don't know, I could
just relate to . . . [. . .] Yes – I mean Sophia Loren was gorgeous, but
she was older somehow . . . and then she had these huge boobs, and
it was a bit like, she was more . . . the men would fall over Sophia
Loren. They didn't seem to notice Audrey Hepburn. Audrey Hepburn was one of the *girls* – that's something as well, you know what
I mean? You could really relate to her.

RM: But when you say it was more obtainable . . . is that –

Bernie: The *look*.

RM: The look – is that because of, you know, *financially*, or because it
was more, more *you* –

Bernie: Well –

RM: – or both?

Bernie: *No*. [laughs] I think it was all to do with the type of films she
made as well – either they were, er . . . the much *younger* type films
were all filmed in Hollywood, on, or they were located in Los Ange-
les, or whatever, on the West Coast where it was sunny and it was all
. . . it was just so totally removed climatically –

RM: Right, right –

Bernie: – from anywhere I would *ever* holiday – or – not that I used to
holiday – but even remotely had a chance of –

RM: It was out of –

Bernie: Totally gone, yeah. She didn't do 'beachy'-type films – did she,
she did . . . she'd still go out and have a laugh, and there was parties,
and there was different things going on, but . . . it was sort of, I don't
know, you could just relate to it. More comfortable, more *possible*.

RM: What about, I mean, something that people often say about
Audrey Hepburn, is about the shape of her body. You know, the fact
that she didn't have big boobs –

Bernie: She was *very* boyish.

RM: Yeah – was that appealing?

Bernie: *Yes* – because – all the – it was sort of oh, Marilyn Monroe, and
er, Ava Gardner, and Jane Russell – all these . . . to me, and I'm sure
to – they were *ugly*! These big, forty, size forty tits banging out
everywhere! And there's *no way* we could walk around the streets
like that! You couldn't attain that!

RM: I mean, why would that be, would that be just 'cos you weren't that
size, or because it would have been . . . it wouldn't have been ri – ?

Bernie: It wouldn't have been right, would it.

RM: Well, no.

Bernie: You wouldn't walk up the high street and see somebody
dressed like that! Well you *wouldn't*!

RM: No.

Bernie: But Audrey, you could . . . *sexy*, she was *sweet*, she was smart . . . she was *everything*. And it was all within reach, if you like.

RM: But it's interesting that – its the –

Bernie: But you'll find 90 per cent of the fans of Audrey Hepburn are *female*.

RM: Exactly – that's why I'm so interested –

Bernie: Why, *why*?

RM: Well . . .

Bernie: Katherine Hepburn? *Exactly* the same thing!

RM: I know, this is why –

Bernie: *Why*?

RM: – I'm interested –

Bernie: I'll tell you why.

RM: Why?

Bernie: Because they were *strong women*.

RM: Yeah – do you think so?

Bernie: *Strong women*.

RM: Do you think so?

Bernie: Yes –

RM: At that time?

Bernie: At that time. And they – they were *new* women.

RM: Yeah –

Bernie: You know – something to be reckoned with.

RM: And they weren't – the men didn't go for them, did they?

Bernie: No – know why? Because (a) they didn't flash their titties, right . . . and show everything they'd got, so, erm, well, they didn't have to, did they, really?

RM: No.

Bernie: But now, then . . . you ask *now*, people say 'Oh . . . *class*.'

RM: Exactly.

Bernie: Like . . . Princess Diana didn't show all this that and the other, she was just classy . . . know what I mean? It was just I think, after the war, and it was 'phwoarr', you know, and all this. So all the *female* icons if you like, that were everywhere, they were all [laughs] . . . *sex*.

RM: Yeah.

Bernie: Right? Everything that you'd been told: 'You can't, you mustn't, it's not –'

RM: Oh, *right* –

Bernie: '– and if you do, they won't love you anyway.'

RM: Oh, right . . .

Bernie: Right – so everything the blokes – or, all these unobtainable . . .

which you couldn't do, and you wouldn't want to anyway – there
was this one that you *could.*

RM: In every way –

Bernie: In every way.

RM: Very interesting –

Bernie: You *could*, in *every* way. And she was, she *was* fun.

RM: Yes, she was, yes.

Bernie: And she *was* different.

RM: Definitely.

Bernie: And . . . *modern.*

RM: Is that the word that sort of stands out to you?

Bernie: Yes, she was *modern.*

RM: When you look back on what it was like –

Bernie: She was *modern* because she was *different.* There was – tell me
another!

RM: Well, you see –

Bernie: There wasn't one!

RM: I don't think there is one –

Bernie: Well there isn't, and there wasn't, and . . . there ain't!

RM: There wasn't anybody else?

Bernie: No. [in a deliberately refined voice] *Absolutely not.* Of the
same era, the women that are in the films, at the same time, if you
like, or in the books, or whatever, I'm telling you now [counting off
on her fingers] – Brigitte Bardot – forget it. Marilyn Monroe
[laughs], Jane Russell, Ava Gardner, Sophia Loren – or, coming
down, you've got Sandra Dee, Annette Funicello, or something,
[quietly] Sandra Dee, and there was another one . . . Tuesday Weld,
or something, I think her name was.

RM: Yes – that would be right.

Bernie: And they were all . . . [searching for words] . . . these sort of,
you couldn't even . . . it ain't never gonna happen!

RM: Right –

Bernie: You know – get outta there!

RM: – very interesting –

Bernie: Totally . . . impossible! You couldn't even dream about it!
Because – you couldn't dream about it, or think about it, or con –
'cos you couldn't understand their . . . how come . . . how can she
drive that car? She looks about twelve, how is she driving that car?

RM: [laughs]

Bernie: How are they letting her, how is she allowed, by law, to drive
that car, how has she got the brains to drive the car!

RM: [laughs]

Bernie: I mean, it was all impossible!

RM: Beyond the realms of –
Bernie: *Yes.*
RM: – belief.
Bernie: And *American.*
RM: Right, yeah –
Bernie: Which was *great* –
RM: But –
Bernie: *but* . . . you ain't never gonna get it. Forget it.

Filmography

Starring Audrey Hepburn

Roman Holiday (William Wyler, Paramount, USA, 1953)
Producer·and director: William Wyler
Screenplay: Ian McLellan Hunter, John Dighton
Story: Ian McLellan Hunter
Director of photography: Franz Planer, Henri Alekan
Editor: Robert Swink
Art direction: Hal Pereira, Walter Tyler
Sound: Joseph de Bretagne
Music: Georges Auric
Costumes: Edith Head
Make-up: Wally Westmore, Alberto de Rossi
Main cast: Audrey Hepburn (Princess Ann); Gregory Peck (Joe Bradley);
Eddie Albert (Irving Radovich)

Sabrina (*Sabrina Fair*, UK) (Billy Wilder, Paramount, USA, 1954)
Producer and director: Billy Wilder
Screenplay: Billy Wilder, Samuel Taylor, Ernest Lehman, from the play by
Samuel L. Taylor
Director of photography: Charles Lang Jr
Editor: Arthur Schmidt
Art direction: Hal Pereira, Walter Tyler
Sound: Harold Lewis and John Cope. Songs adapted and additional music
composed by Frederick Hollander
Costume supervision: Edith Head and Hubert de Givenchy (uncredited)
Make-up supervision: Wally Westmore
Main cast: Audrey Hepburn (Sabrina Fairchild); Humphrey Bogart (Linus
Larrabee); William Holden (David Larrabee); John William (Thomas
Fairchild); Martha Hyer (Elizabeth Tyson)

War and Peace (*Guerra e Pace*) (King Vidor, Ponti-de Laurentiis, USA/Italy, 1956)
Producer: Dino de Laurentiis
Adaptation: Bridget Boland, Robert Westerby, King Vidor, Mario Camerini, Ennio de Concini, Ivo Perilli, from the novel by Leo Tolstoy
Director of photography: Jack Cardiff
Director of photography, second unit: Aldo Tonti
Editor: Leo Catozzo
Art direction: Mario Chiari
Set decoration: Piero Gherardi
Sound: Leslie Hodgson
Costumes: Maria de Matteis
Make-up supervision: Alberto de Rossi
Music: Nino Rota
Main cast: Audrey Hepburn (Natasha); Henry Fonda (Pierre Bezukhov); Mel Ferrer (Andrei Bolkonski); Vittorio Gassman (Anatole Kuragin)

Funny Face (Stanley Donen, Paramount, USA, 1956)
Producer: Roger Edens
Screenplay: Leonard Gershe
Director of photography: Ray June
Special photographic effects: John P. Fulton
Editor: Frank Bracht
Art direction: Hal Pereira, George W. Davis
Set decoration: Sam Comer, Ray Moyer
Special visual consultant and main title backgrounds: Richard Avedon
Sound: George and Winston Leyerett
Costume: Edith Head and Hubert de Givenchy
Make-up supervision: Wally Westmore
Hairstyle supervision: Nellie Manley
Music and lyrics: George and Ira Gershwin. Music adapted and conducted by Adolph Deutsch
Choreography: Eugene Loring and Fred Astaire
Main cast: Audrey Hepburn (Jo Stockton); Fred Astaire (Dick Avery); Kay Thompson (Maggie Prescott); Michel Auclair (Emile Flostre)

The Nun's Story (Fred Zinneman, Warner Brothers/Fred Zinneman, USA, 1958)
Producer: Henry Blanke
Screenplay: Robert Anderson, from the book by Kathryn C. Hulme
Director of photography: Franz Planer
Editor: Walter Thompson
Art direction: Alexander Trauner

Costume: Marjorie Best
Sound: Oliver S. Garretson
Make-up: Alberto Rossi
Hair: Grazia de Rossi
Music: Franz Waxman
Main cast: Audrey Hepburn (Gabrielle van der Mal/Sister Luke); Peter
  Finch (Dr Fortunati); Edith Evans (Mother Emmanuel); Peggy Ashcroft
  (Mother Mathilde)

Green Mansions (Mel Ferrer, Avon Productions, USA, 1959)
Producer: Edmund Grainger
Screenplay: Dorothy Kingsley, from the novel by W. H. Hudson
Director of photography: Joseph Ruttenberg
Special effects: A. Arnold Gillespie, Lee LeBlanc, Robert R. Hoag
Editor: Ferris Webster
Art direction: Preston Ames, William A. Horning
Set decoration: Henry Grace, Jerry Wunderlich
Make-up: William Tuttle
Hair stylist: Sydney Guilaroff
Music: Bronislau Kaper, Hector Villa-Lobos
Choreography: Katherine Dunham
Main cast: Audrey Hepburn (Rima); Anthony Perkins (Abel); Lee J. Cobb
  (Nuflo)

The Unforgiven (John Huston, Hecht-Hill-Lancaster Productions/James
  Productions, USA, 1959)
Producer: James Hill
Screenplay: Ben Maddow, based on a novel by Alan Le May
Director of photography: Franz Planer
Editor: Russell Lloyd
Art direction: Stephen Grimes
Sound: Basil Fenton Smith, Leslie Hodgson
Costume: Dorothy Jeakins
Make-up: Frank McCoy, Frank LaRue
Music: Dimitri Tiomkin
Main cast: Audrey Hepburn (Rachel Zachary); Burt Lancaster (Ben
  Zachary); Lillian Gish (Mathilda Zachary); Audie Murphy (Cash Zachary)

Breakfast at Tiffany's (Blake Edwards, Jurow-Shepherd Productions/Para-
  mount Pictures Corporation, USA, 1961)
Producers: Martin Jurow, Richard Shepherd
Screenplay: George Axelrod, based on the novel by Truman Capote
Director of photography: Franz F. Planer

Special photographic effects: John P. Fulton
Editor: Howard Smith
Art direction: Hal Pereira, Roland Anderson
Sound: Hugo Grenzback, John Wilkinson
Set decoration: Sam Comer, Ray Moyer
Costume supervision: Edith Head
Miss Hepburn's wardrobe principally by Givenchy
Miss Neal's wardrobe principally by Pauline Trigere
Make-up supervision: Wally Westmore
Hairstyle supervision: Nellie Manley
Music: Henry Mancini
Main cast: Audrey Hepburn (Holly Golightly); George Peppard (Paul
   Varjak); Patricia Neal (2E); Buddy Ebsen (Doc Golightly); José Luis de
   Villalonga (José da Silva Pereira); Mickey Rooney (Mr Yunioshi)

The Children's Hour (*The Loudest Whisper*) (William Wyler, United
   Artists/Mirisch, USA, 1961)
Producer and director: William Wyler
Screenplay: John Michael Hayes, Lillian Hellman, from the play by Lillian
   Hellman
Director of photography: Franz F. Planer
Editor: Robert Swink
Sound: Don Hall Jr, Fred Law
Art direction: Fernando Carrere
Set decoration: Edward G. Boyle
Costume: Dorothy Jeakins
Make-up: Emile LaVigne, Frank McCoy
Hair stylist: Jean St Oegger
Main cast: Audrey Hepburn (Karen Wright); Shirley MacLaine (Martha
   Dobie); James Garner (Dr Joe Cardin)

Charade (Stanley Donen, Universal/Stanley Donen Productions, USA, 1963)
Producer and director: Stanley Donen
Screenplay: Peter Stone
Story: Peter Stone, Marc Behm
Director of photography: Charles Lang Jr
Editor: James Clarke
Art direction: Jean d'Eaubonne
Sound: Jacques Carrere, Bob Jones
Miss Hepburn's clothes: Givenchy
Make-up: Alberto de Rossi, John O'Gorman
Music: Henry Mancini
Title song: Johnny Mercer (lyrics)

Main cast: Audrey Hepburn (Regina Lambert); Cary Grant (Joshua); Walter
  Matthau (Hamilton Bartolomew)

My Fair Lady (George Cukor, Warner Brothers Pictures, USA, 1964)
Producer: Jack L. Warner
Based upon the musical play as produced on the stage by Herman Levin,
  book and lyrics by Alan Jay Lerner and Frederick Loewe, from a play by
  Bernard Shaw
Director of photography: Harry Stradling
Editor: William Ziegler
Art direction: Gene Allen
Sound: Francis J. Scheid, Murray Spivack
Set decoration: George James Hopkins
Costumes, scenery and production designed by Cecil Beaton
Make-up supervision: Gordon Bau
Supervising hair stylist: Jean Burt Reilly
Music: Frederick Loewe
Lyrics: Alan Jay Lerner
Choreography: Hermes Pan
Main cast: Audrey Hepburn (Eliza Doolittle); Rex Harrison (Henry Higgins);
  Wilfrid Hyde White (Colonel Pickering); Stanley Holloway (Alfred Doo-
  little); Gladys Cooper (Mrs Higgins); Jeremy Brett (Freddy Eynsford-Hill);
  Theodore Bikel (Zoltan)

Two for the Road (Stanley Donen, Stanley Donen Films/Twentieth Century
  Fox Film Corporation, GB, 1966)
Producer and director: Stanley Donen
Written by Frederick Raphael
Director of photography: Christopher Challis
Editors: Richard Marden and Madeleine Gug
Sound: Jo de Bretagne
Art direction: Willy Holt
Miss Hepburn's clothes: Ken Scott, Michèle Rosier, Paco Rabanne, Mary
  Quant, Foale and Tuffin and others
Mr Finney's clothes: Hardy Amies
Make-up: Alberto de Rossi
Hair: Grazia de Rossi
Music: Henry Mancini
Main cast: Audrey Hepburn (Joanna Wallace); Albert Finney (Mark Wallace)

Wait Until Dark (Terence Young, Warner Brothers-Seven Arts, USA, 1967)
Producer: Mel Ferrer
Screenplay: Robert Carrington and Jane-Howard Carrington, based on the
  play by Frederick Knott

Director of photography: Charles Lang Jr
Editor: Gene Milford
Sound: Everett Hughes
Art direction: George Jenkins
Make-up supervision: Gordon Bau
Hair: Jean Burt Reilly
Song 'Wait until dark': Henry Mancini (music), Jay Livingston, Ray Evans
   (lyrics)
Music: Henry Mancini
Main cast: Audrey Hepburn (Susy Hendrix); Alan Arkin (Roat); Richard
   Crenna (Mike Talman); Efrem Zimbalist Jr (Sam)

Other films cited

Now, Voyager (Irving Rapper, Warner Brothers Pictures, USA, 1942)
Main cast: Bette Davis (Charlotte Vale); Paul Heinreid (Jerry Durrance);
   Claude Rains (Dr Jackworth); Gladys Cooper (Mrs Henry Windle Vale)

Blue Jeans (*Blue Denim*) (Philip Dunne, Twentieth Century Fox Film Cor-
   poration, USA, 1959)
Main cast: Brandon de Wilde (Arthur Bartley); Carol Lynley (Janet Willard);
   MacDonald Carey (Major Bartley); Marsha Hunt (Jessie Bartley)

Some Like It Hot (Billy Wilder, Mirisch Company/Ashton Productions,
   USA, 1959)
Main cast: Marilyn Monroe (Sugar Kane); Tony Curtis (Joe/Josephine);
   Jack Lemmon (Jerry/Daphne)

A Summer Place (Delmer Daves, Warner Brothers Pictures, USA, 1959)
Main cast: Sandra Dee (Molly Jorgenson); Troy Donahue (Johnny Hunter)

Let's Make Love (George Cukor, Twentieth Century Fox Film Corporation,
   USA, 1960)
Main cast: Marilyn Monroe (Amanda); Yves Montand (Jean-Marc Clément)

The Subterraneans (Ranald MacDougall, Arthur Freed Productions/Loew's
   Inc., USA, 1960)
Main cast: Leslie Caron (Mardove Fox); George Peppard (Leo Percepeid)

West Side Story (Jerome Roberts, Robert Wise, Beta Productions/Mirisch
   Films/Seven Arts Productions/United Artists, UK/USA, 1961)
Main cast: Natalie Wood (Maria); Richard Beymer (Tony); Russ Tamblyn
   (Riff); Rita Moreno (Anita)

Georgy Girl (Silvio Narizzano, Columbia Pictures Corporation/Everglades, GB, 1966)
Main cast: James Mason (James Leamington); Alan Bates (Jos); Lynn Redgrave (Georgy); Charlotte Rampling (Meredith)

Pretty in Pink (Howard Deutch, Paramount Pictures Corporation, USA, 1986)
Main cast: Molly Ringwald (Andie Walsh); Harry Dean Stanton (Jack); Jon Cryer (Duckie); Andrew McCarthy (Blane McDonough); Annie Potts (Iona)

The Color Purple (Steven Spielberg, Amblin Entertainment/Guber-Peters Company/Warner Brothers, USA, 1985)
Main cast: Danny Glover (Albert); Whoopi Goldberg (Celie); Margaret Avery (Shug Avery); Oprah Winfrey (Sofia); Willard E. Pugh (Harpo); Akosua Busia (Nettie)

Working Girl (Mike Nichols, Twentieth Century Fox Film Corporation, USA, 1988)
Main cast: Melanie Griffith (Tess McGill); Harrison Ford (Jack Trainer); Sigourney Weaver (Katharine Parker); Joan Cusack (Cyn)

Pretty Woman (Garry Marshall, Touchstone Pictures/Silver Screen Partners IV, USA, 1990)
Main cast: Julia Roberts (Vivian Ward); Richard Gere (Edward Lewis)

Daughters of the Dust (Julie Dash, American Playhouse/Geechee Girls/ WMG Film, USA, 1991)
Main cast: Cora Lee Day (Nana Peazant); Alva Rogers (Eula Peazant); Barbara O. Jones (Yellow Mary); Trula Hoosier (Trula); Umar Abdurrahamn (Bilal Muhammed); Adisa Anderson (Eli Peazant); Kaycee Moore (Haagar Peazant); Bahni Turpin (Iona); Chery Lynn Bruce (Biola Peazant)

I Love Trouble (Charles Shyer, Caravan Pictures/Touchstone Pictures, USA, 1994)
Main cast: Nick Nolte (Peter Bracker); Julia Roberts (Sabrina Peterson)

Only You (Norman Jewison, Fried/Wood Films/Yorktown Productions, USA, 1994)
Main cast: Marisa Tomei (Faith Corvatch); Robert Downey Jr (Peter Wright); Bonnie Hunt (Kate); Joaquin de Almeida (Giovanni)

Sabrina (Sydney Pollack, Paramount Productions/Scott Rudin Entertainments/Mirage Entertainments/Sandollar Productions/Constellar Films, USA, 1995)

Main cast: Julia Ormond (Sabrina Fairchild); Harrison Ford (Linus Larrabee); Greg Kinnear (David Larrabee)

She's All That (Robert Iscove, Miramax, USA, 1999)
Main cast: Rachel Leigh (Geeky Girl); Freddie Prinze Jr. (Zach); Anna Paquin (Mackenzie)

References and further reading

Alasuutari, P. (1995) *Researching Culture: Qualitative Method and Cultural Studies*, London: Sage.

Altman, R. (ed.) (1980) *Genre: The Musical*, London: Routledge and Kegan Paul/Comedia.

Ang, I. (1985) *Watching Dallas: Soap Opera and the Melodramatic Imagination*, London: Methuen.

Ang, I. and Hermes, J. (1991) 'Gender and/in media consumption', in J. Curran and M. Gurevitch (eds) *Mass Media and Society*, pp. 325–347.

Ash, J. and Wilson, E. (eds) (1992) *Chic Thrills: A Fashion Reader*, London: Pandora.

Attfield, J. and Kirkham, P. (eds) (1989) *A View From the Interior: Feminism, Women and Design*, London: The Women's Press.

Avedon, R. (1978) *Avedon: Photographs 1947–77*, London: Thames and Hudson.

—— (1990) 'That girl with the eyes: nine Audrey Hepburn fans', *Interview* 20, 8: 94.

Barker, F. (1961) 'Review of *Breakfast at Tiffany's*', *Evening News* (19 October).

Barthes, R. (1972) 'The face of Garbo', in *Mythologies*, London: Jonathan Cape, pp. 56–57.

Baskette, K. (1954) 'Dutch treat', *Modern Screen* (April): 92.

Beaton, C. (1964) *Cecil Beaton's Fair Lady*, London: Weidenfeld and Nicolson.

—— (n.d.) 'The changing Venus', in *Face of the World: An International Scrapbook of People and Places*, London: Weidenfeld and Nicolson, pp. 165–172.

Benjamin, J. (1990) *The Bonds of Love: Psychoanalysis and the Problem of Domination*, London: Virago.

Benjamin, W. (1985) [1935] 'The work of art in the age of mechanical reproduction', repr. in G. Mast and M. Cohen (eds) *Film Theory and Criticism*, pp. 675–694.

Blackburn, D. (1998) 'And the Beats go on', *Guardian* (*Guide*) (6 December): 4–5.

Bobo, J. (1995) *Black Women as Cultural Readers*, New York: Columbia University Press.

Bourdieu, P. (1986) *Distinction: A Social Critique of the Judgement of Taste*, London: Routledge.

—— (1990) [1980] (trans. Richard Nice) *The Logic of Practice*, Cambridge: Polity Press.

Braun, E. (1981) 'The Hepburn quality revisited', *Films* 1, 9: 20–25.

Breen, J. (1961) 'Review of *Breakfast at Tiffany's*', *Sight and Sound* 31, 1: 41.

Brett, S. (1964) 'Audrey Hepburn: innocence is the strength of Hollywood's choice of a fair lady', *Films and Filming* 10, 6: 9–12.

Brittain, V. (1953) *Lady into Woman: A History of Women from Victoria to Elizabeth II*, London: Andrew Darkers.

Brooks, A. (1997) *Postfeminisms: Feminism, Cultural Theory and Cultural Forms*, London: Routledge.

Brown, M. E. (1994) *Soap Opera and Women's Talk: The Pleasure of Resistance*, Thousand Oaks, CA: Sage.

Brunsdon, C. (1997) *Screen Tastes: Soap Opera to Satellite Dishes*, London: Routledge.

Bruzzi, S. (1997) *Undressing Cinema: Clothing and Identity in the Movies*, London: Routledge.

Burgin, V., Donald, J. and Kaplan, C. (eds) (1986) *Formations of Fantasy*, London: Methuen.

Burman, B. (ed.) (1999) *The Culture of Sewing: Gender, Consumption and Home Dressmaking*, Oxford: Berg.

Bushnell, C. (1996) *Sex and the City*, London: Abacus.

Butler, J. G. (ed.) (1991) *Star Texts: Image and Performance in Film and Television*, Detroit: Wayne State University Press.

Butler, J. and Scott, J. W. (eds) (1992) *Feminists Theorise the Political*, London: Routledge.

Capote, T. (1961) [1958] *Breakfast at Tiffany's*, Harmondsworth: Penguin.

de Certeau, M. (1984) *The Practice of Everyday Life*, Berkeley: University of California Press.

Chapell, C. (1952) 'The future belongs to Audrey', *Picturegoer* (11 October).

Cinémonde (1962) 'Audrey Hepburn', no. 1468: 17–19.

Clarke, J. and Simmonds, D. (1980) *Move Over Misconceptions: Doris Day Reappraised (BFI Dossier Number 4)*, London: BFI.

Coates, J. (1986) *Women, Men and Language: A Sociolinguistic Account of Sex Differences in Language*, London: Longman.

Collins, A. F. (1995) 'When Hubert met Audrey . . .', *Vanity Fair* (December) 166–76, 180–183.

Collins, J., Radner, H. and Preacher Collins, A. (eds) (1993) *Film Theory Goes to the Movies*, New York: Routledge.

Collins, R., Curran, J., Garnham, N., Scannell, P., Schlesinger, P. and Sparks, C. (eds) (1986) *Media, Culture and Society: A Critical Reader*, London: Sage.

Conolly, M. (1954) 'What price beauty?', *Photoplay* (March): 23.

Cook, P. (1996) *Fashioning the Nation: Costume and Identity in British Cinema*, London: BFI.

Cook, P. and Dodds, P. (eds) (1993) *Women and Film: A Sight and Sound Reader*, London: Scarlet Press.

Coppock, V., Haydon, D. and Richter, I. (1995) *The Illusions of 'Post-feminism': New Women, Old Myths*, London: Taylor and Francis.

Corliss, R. (1993) 'Serene majesty', *Film Comment* 29, 2: 3–4.

Craik, J. (1994) *The Face of Fashion: Cultural Studies in Fashion*, London: Routledge.

Craik, L. (1999) 'Hip, hip Hepburn! Why we all want to look like Audrey', *Guardian* (G2) (7 May): 8–9.

Curran, J. and Gurevitch, M. (eds) (1991) *Mass Media and Society*, London: Edward Arnold.

Day, P. (1953) 'Look out Garbo – Audrey's here', *Picturegoer* (12 December): 8.

Deem, R. (1986) *All Work and No Play? A Study of Women and Leisure*, Milton Keynes: Open University Press.

Desser, D. and Jowett, G. S. (eds) (2000) *Hollywood goes Shopping*, Minneapolis: University of Minnesota Press.

Dika, V. (1987) 'A feminist fairytale', *Art in America* (April): 31–33.

Doane, M. A. (1982) 'Film and the masquerade: theorising the female spectator', *Screen* 23, 3/4: 74–87.

—— (1987) *The Desire to Desire: The Woman's Film of the 1940s*, Basingstoke: Macmillan.

—— (1989) 'The economy of desire: the commodity form in/of the cinema', *Quarterly Review of Film and Video* 11: 23–33.

Douglas, S. (1994) *Where the Girls Are: Growing Up Female with the Mass Media*, New York: Times Books.

Dubino, J. (1993) 'The Cinderella complex: romance fiction, patriarchy and capitalism', *Journal of Popular Culture* 27, 3: 103–118.

Dundes, A. (ed.) (1988) *Cinderella: A Casebook*, London: University of Wisconsin Press.

Durgnat, R. (1967) *Films and Feelings*, London: Faber and Faber.

Dyer, R. (1979) *Stars*, London: BFI.

—— (1980) 'Entertainment and utopia', in R. Altman (ed.) *Genre: The Musical*, pp. 175–189.

—— (1982) '*A Star is Born* and the construction of authenticity', in C. Gledhill (ed.) *Star Signs*, pp. 13–22.

—— (1986) *Heavenly Bodies: Film Stars and Society*, London: BFI.

—— (1991) 'Four films of Lana Turner', in J. G. Butler (ed.) *Star Texts*, pp. 214–239. [Orig. pub. in *Movie* 25 (Winter 1977–78): 30–52.]

—— (1993) 'Never too thin: Richard Dyer on the awkward perfection of Audrey Hepburn', *Sight and Sound* 3, 12: 59.

—— (1997) *White*, London: Routledge.

Elsaesser, T. (ed.) (1990) *Early Cinema: Space Frame Narrative*, London: BFI.

Evans, C. and Thornton, M. (1989) *Women and Fashion: A New Look*, London: Quartet Books.

Faludi, S. (1992) *Backlash: The Undeclared War Against Women*, London: Vintage.

Featherstone, M. (1991) *Consumer Culture and Postmodernism*, London: Sage.

Fell, A. (1985) 'Rebel with a cause', in L. Heron (ed.) *Truth, Dare or Promise*, pp. 11–25.

Fiske, J. (1992) 'The cultural economy of fandom', in L. Lewis (ed.) *The Adoring Audience*. pp. 30–49.

Foster, H. (1983) *The Anti-Aesthetic: Essays on Postmodern Culture*, Seattle: Bay Press.

Foucault, M. (1987) [1970] 'The order of discourse', in R. Young (ed.) *Untying the Text*, pp. 48–78.

—— (1988) 'Technologies of the self', in L. H. Martin *et al.* (eds) *Technologies of the Self*, pp. 16–49.

Francke, L. and Wilson, E. (1993) 'Gamine against the grain', *Sight and Sound* 3, 3: 30–32.

Frankenberg, R. (1993) *White Women, Race Matters: The Social Construction of Whiteness*, London: Routledge.

Fraser, N. and Nicholson, L. J. (1990) 'Social criticism without philosophy: an encounter between feminism and postmodernism', in L. J. Nicholson (ed.) *Feminism/Postmodernism*, pp. 19–38.

Frow, J. (1991) 'Tourism and the semiotics of nostalgia', *October* 57: 123–151.

Gaines, J. (1988) 'White privilege and looking relations: race and gender in feminist film theory', *Screen* 29, 4: 9–27.

—— (1989) 'The Queen Christina tie-ups: convergence of show window and screen', *Quarterly Review of Film and Video* 11: 35–60.

—— (1990) 'Costume and narrative: how dress tells the woman's story', in J. Gaines and C. Herzog (eds) *Fabrications*, pp. 180–211.

Gaines, J. and Herzog, C. (eds) (1990) *Fabrications: Costume and the Female Body*, New York: Routledge.

Geraghty, C. (1997) 'Women and sixties British cinema: the development of the "Darling" girl', in R. Murphy (ed.) *The British Cinema Book*, pp. 154–163.

—— (1998) 'Audiences and "Ethnography": questions of practice', in C. Geraghty and D. Lusted (eds) *The Television Studies Book*, pp. 141–157.

Geraghty, C. and Lusted, D. (eds) (1998) *The Television Studies Book*, London: Arnold.

Gillespie, M. (1995) *Television, Ethnicity and Cultural Change*, London and New York: Comedia/Routledge.

Gledhill, C. (ed.) (1987) *Home is Where the Heart is: Studies in Melodrama and the Woman's Film*, London: BFI.

—— (1988) 'Pleasurable negotiations', in E. D. Pribham (ed.) *Female Spectators*, pp. 64–89.

—— (ed.) (1991) *Stardom: Industry of Desire*, London: Routledge.

—— (ed.) (1992) *Star Signs: Papers from a Weekend Workshop*, London: BFI.

Gray, A. (1992) *Video Playtime: The Gendering of a Leisure Technology*, London: Routledge.

de Grazia, V. with Furlough, E. (eds) (1996) *The Sex of Things: Gender and Consumption in Historical Perspective*, Berkeley: University of California Press.

Grossberg, L. (1992) 'Is there a fan in the house? The affective sensibility of fandom' in L. Lewis (ed.) *The Adoring Audience*, pp. 50–65.

Gunning, T. (1990) [1986] 'The cinema of attractions: early film, its spectator and the avant-garde', in T. Elsaesser (ed.) *Early Cinema: Space Frame Narrative*, pp. 56–62.

Gustavson, R. (1982) 'The power of the screen: the influence of Edith Head's designs on the retail fashion market', *The Velvet Light Trap* 19: 8–10.

Halliwell, L. (1992) *Halliwell's Film Guide, 8th edn*, London: Grafton.

Hansen, M. (1991) *Babel and Babylon: Spectatorship in American Silent Film*, Cambridge, MA: Harvard University Press.

Haskell, M. (1987) [1973] *From Reverence to Rape: The Treatment of Women in the Movies*, 2nd edn, Chicago: University of Chicago Press.

—— (1991) 'Our fair lady', *Film Comment* 27, 2: 9–17.

Head, E. and Calistro, P. (1983) *Edith Head's Hollywood*, New York: E. P. Dutton.

Head, E. and Kesner Ardmore, J. (1959) *The Dress Doctor*, Boston: Little, Brown and Company.

Hebdige, D. (1979) *Subculture: The Meaning of Style*, London: Methuen.

—— (1988) *Hiding in the Light: On Images and Things*, London and New York: Routledge/Comedia.

Henriques, J., Hollway, W., Urwin, C., Venn, C. and Walkerdine, V. (1984) *Changing the Subject: Psychology, Social Regulation and Subjectivity*, London: Methuen.

Hermes, J. (1993) *Easily Put Down: Women's Magazines, Readers, Repertoires and Everyday Life*, Amsterdam: University of Amsterdam Press.

Heron, L. (ed.) (1985) *Truth, Dare or Promise: Girls Growing Up in the Fifties*, London: Virago.

Hollander, A. (1978) *Seeing Through Clothes*, New York: The Viking Press.

Hollows, J. (2000) *Feminism, Femininity and Popular Culture*, Manchester: Manchester University Press.

Hollway, W. (1984) 'Gender difference and the production of subjectivity', in J. Henriques *et al. Changing the Subject*, pp. 227–263.

Horowitz, T. (1975) 'From élite fashion to mass fashion', *Archives Européennes de Sociologie* 16, 2: 283–295.

Hubert de Givenchy: 40 Ans de Création (1991) (Exposition 24 octobre 1991–15 mars 1992, Musée de la Mode), Paris: Diffusion Paris–Musées.

Hulanicki, B. (1983) *From A-to-Biba*, London: Hutchinson.

Jackson, S. and Moores, S. (1995) *The Politics of Domestic Consumption: Critical Readings*, London: Prentice Hall.

Jacobs, L. (1981) '*Now, Voyager*: some problems of enunciation and sexual difference', *Camera Obscura* 7: 89–109.

Jameson, F. (1983) 'Postmodernism and consumer society', in H. Foster (ed.) *The Anti-Aesthetic*, pp. 111–125.

Jenkins, H. (1992) *Textual Poachers: TV Fans and Participatory Culture*, London: Routledge.

Jenkins, R. (1992) *Pierre Bourdieu*, London: Routledge.

Jones, A. M. (1994) 'An Audrey Hepburn for the 1990s', *Independent* (17 November): 27.

Kael, P. (1961/1962) 'Fantasies of the arthouse audience', *Sight and Sound* 31, 1: 5–9.

Kauffman, S. (1996) '*Roman Holiday*: Stanley Kauffman reassesses a favorite film', *American Film* 3, 6: 66–68.

Kelley, K. (1994) 'A modern Cinderella', *Journal of American Culture* 17, 1: 87–92.

King, B. (1991) [1985] 'Articulating stardom', in J. G. Butler (ed.) *Star Texts*, pp. 125–154.

Kirkham, P. (1995) 'Dress, dance, dreams and desire: fashion and fantasy in *Dance Hall*', *Journal of Design History* 8, 3: 195–214.

Kuhn, A. (1995) *Family Secrets: Acts of Memory and Imagination*, London: Verso.

LaPlace, M. (1987) 'Producing and consuming the woman's film: discursive struggle in *Now, Voyager*', in C. Gledhill (ed.) *Home is Where the Heart is*, pp. 138–166.

de Lauretis, T. (1987) *Technologies of Gender: Essays on Theory, Film and Fiction*, Basingstoke: Macmillan.

Lewis, L. (ed.) (1992) *The Adoring Audience: Fan Culture and Popular Media*, London: Routledge.

Leydesdorff, S., Passerini, L. and Thompson, P. (eds) (1996) *International Yearbook of Oral History and Life Stories, Volume IV: Gender and Memory*, Oxford: Oxford University Press.

Light, A. (1994) 'Masks and faces: the photography of Angus McBean', *Sight and Sound* 4, 11: 28–31.

Lowthorpe, R. (2002) 'Audrey Hepburn: fashion icon or style tyrant?', *Independent on Sunday* (13 January): 4.

Lury, C. (1996) *Consumer Culture*, Cambridge: Polity Press.

MacLaine, S. (1959) 'Shirley MacLaine's advice to women', *Picture Show and TV Mirror* (23 May): 15.

McCabe, C. and Petrie, D. (eds) (1995) *BFI Working Papers: New Scholarship from BFI Research*, London: BFI.

McGilligan, P. (1995) 'Irony: George Axelrod interviewed by Patrick McGilligan', *Film Comment* 31, 6: 10–24.

McGuigan, J. (ed.) (1997) *Cultural Methodologies*, London: Sage.

McRobbie, A. (1978) 'Working-class girls and the culture of femininity', in Women's Studies Group, *Women Take Issue: Aspects of Women's Subordination*, London: Hutchinson, pp. 96–108.

—— (1982) 'The politics of feminist research: between talk, text and action', *Feminist Review* 12: 46–57.

—— (1989) *Zoot Suits and Second Hand Dresses: An Anthology of Fashion and Music*, London: Macmillan.

Martin, L. H., Gutman, H. and Hutton, P. H. (eds) (1988) *Technologies of the Self: A Seminar with Michel Foucault*, London: Tavistock Press.

Mast, G. and Cohen, M. (1985) *Film Theory and Criticism: Introductory Readings, 3rd edn*, Oxford: Oxford University Press.

Mayne, J. (1993) *Cinema and Spectatorship*, London: Routledge.

Meij, L. (1988) *Hubert de Givenchy Haute Couture: Gedragen Door Audrey Hepburn*, Den Haag: Nederlands Kostuummuseum.

Mellencamp, P. (ed.) (1990) *Logics of Television: Essays in Cultural Criticism*, Bloomington: Indiana University Press.

Mepham, J. (1990) 'The ethics of quality in television', in G. Mulgan (ed.) *The Question of Quality*, pp. 56–72.

Moi, T. (1991) 'Appropriating Bourdieu: feminist theory and Pierre Bourdieu's sociology of culture', *New Literary History* 22: 1017–1049.

Moores, S. (1993) *Interpreting Audiences: The Ethnography of Media Consumption*, London: Sage.

Morley, D. (1986) *Family Television: Cultural Power and Domestic Leisure*, London: Comedia.

—— (1992) *Television, Audiences and Cultural Studies*, London: Routledge.

Morley, D. and Brunsdon, C. (1999) *The* Nationwide *Television Studies*, London: Routledge.

Morris, M. (1990) 'Banality in cultural studies', in P. Mellencamp (ed.) *Logics of Television*, pp. 56–72.

Mort, F. (1996) *Cultures of Consumption: Masculinities and Social Space in Late Twentieth Century Britain*, London: Routledge.

Moseley, R. (1996) '"On how to be lovely": the enduring appeal of Audrey Hepburn', unpub. MA dissertation, University of East Anglia.

—— (2000) 'Makeover takeover on British television', *Screen* 41, 3: 299–314.

—— (2001) 'Respectability sewn up: dressmaking and film star style in the fifties and sixties', *European Journal of Cultural Studies* 4: 4, 473–490.

Mulgan, G. (ed.) (1990) *The Question of Quality*, London: BFI.

Muller, R. (1954) 'Review of *Ondine*', *Picture Post* (3 April).

Mulvey, L. (1975) 'Visual pleasure and narrative cinema', *Screen* 16, 3: 6–18.

Murphy, R. (ed.) (1997) *The British Cinema Book*, London: BFI.

Muschamp, H. (1990) 'That girl with the eyes', *Interview* 20, 8: 94–101.

Nava, M. (1992) *Changing Cultures: Feminism, Youth and Consumerism*, London: Sage.

Nicholson, L. J. (ed.) (1990) *Feminism/Postmodernism*, London: Routledge.

Nightingale, V. (1996) *Studying Audiences: The Shock of the Real*, London: Routledge.

Nixon, S. (1996) *Hard Looks: Masculinities, Spectatorship and Contemporary Consumption*, London: University College London Press.

Oakley, A. (1981) 'Interviewing women: a contradiction in terms', in H. Roberts (ed.) *Doing Feminist Research*, London: Routledge, pp. 30–61.

Pacteau, F. (1994) *The Symptom of Beauty*, London: Reaktion Books.

Panttaja, E. (1993) 'Going up in the world: class in Cinderella', *Western Folklore* 52, 1: 85–104.

Paris, B. (1998) *Audrey Hepburn*, London: Orion.

Partington, A. (1992) 'Popular fashion and working class affluence', in J. Ash and E. Wilson (eds) *Chic Thrills*, pp. 145–161.

Passerini, L. (1984) *Fascism in Popular Memory: The Cultural Experience of the Turin Working Class*, Cambridge: Cambridge University Press.

—— (1989) 'Women's personal narratives: myths, experiences and emotions', in The Personal Narratives Group (ed.) *Interpreting Women's Lives: Feminist Theory and Personal Narratives*, Bloomington and Indianapolis: Indiana University Press, pp. 189–197.

Perez Prichard, S. (1981) *Film Costume: An Annotated Bibliography*, London: The Scarecrow Press.

Perrault, C. (1697) 'Cinderella, or The Little Glass Slipper', in A. Dundes (ed.) (1988) *Cinderella: A Casebook*, pp. 14–21.

The Personal Narratives Group (ed.) (1989) *Interpreting Women's Lives: Feminist Theory and Personal Narratives*, Bloomington and Indianapolis: Indiana University Press.

Petrie, D. (ed.) (1993) *Cinema and the Realms of Enchantment: Lectures, Seminars and Essays by Marina Warner and Others (BFI Working Papers)*, London: BFI.

Poovey, M. (1984) *The Proper Lady and the Woman Writer: Ideology as Style in the Works of Mary Wollstonecraft, Mary Shelley, and Jane Austen*, Chicago: University of Chicago Press.

Potter, J. and Wetherall, M. (1987) *Discourse and Social Psychology: Beyond Attitudes and Behaviour*, London: Sage

Press, A. L. (1991) *Women Watching Television: Gender, Class and Generation in the American Television Experience*, Philadelphia: University of Pennsylvania Press.

Pribram, E. D. (ed.) (1988) *Female Spectators: Looking at Film and Television*, London: Verso.

Probyn, E. (1993) *Sexing the Self: Gendered Positions in Cultural Studies*, London: Routledge.

Puttnam, E. J. (1970) [1910] *The Lady: Studies of Certain Significant Phases of her History*, Chicago: University of Chicago Press.

Radner, H. (1993) 'Pretty is as pretty does: free enterprise and the marriage plot', in J. Collins *et al.* (eds) *Film Theory Goes to the Movies*, pp. 56–76.

—— (1995) *Shopping Around: Feminine Culture and the Pursuit of Pleasure*, London: Routledge.

Radway, J. A. (1991) [1984] *Reading the Romance: Women, Patriarchy and Popular Literature*, Chapel Hill: University of North Carolina Press.

Read, J. (2000) *The New Avengers: Feminism, Femininity and the Rape–Revenge Cycle*, Manchester: Manchester University Press.

Rickey, C. (1982) 'The couture theory', *American Film* 8, 3: 57-61.

Riley, D. (1988) *Am I That Name? Feminism and the Category 'Women' in History*, London: Macmillan.

Ringgold, G. (1971) 'Audrey Hepburn: added post-Hitler realism to the movies' image of the child-woman', *Films in Review* 22, 10: 585–605.

Roach, M. E. and Eicher, J. B. (eds) (1965) *Dress, Adornment and the Social Order*, New York: John Wiley and Sons.

Roberts, H. (ed.) (1981) *Doing Feminist Research*, London: Routledge.

Roman, L. G., Christian-Smith, L. K. with Ellsworth, E. (eds) (1988) *Becoming Feminine: The Politics of Popular Culture*, Lewes: The Falmer Press.

Rosen, M. (1973) *Popcorn Venus: Women, Movies and the American Dream*, London: Peter Owen.

Schor, N. (1987) *Reading in Detail: Aesthetics and the Feminine*, New York: Methuen.

Scott, J. W. (1992) 'Experience', in J. Butler and J. W. Scott (eds) *Feminists Theorise the Political*, pp. 22–40.

Seiter, E. (1990) 'Making distinctions in TV audience research: case study of a troubling interview', *Cultural Studies* 4, 1: 61–84.

Shaw, G. B. (1947) [1916] *Pygmalion: A Romance in Five Acts*, Harmondsworth: Penguin.

Sheridan, S. (ed.) (1988) *Grafts: Feminist Cultural Criticism*, London: Verso.

Skeggs, B. (ed.) (1995) *Feminist Cultural Theory: Process and Production*, Manchester: Manchester University Press.

—— (1997) *Formations of Class and Gender: Becoming Respectable*, London: Sage.

Skov, L. and Moeran, B. (eds) (1995) *Women, Media and Consumption in Japan*, Richmond: Curzon Press.

Smith, D. E. (1988) 'Femininity as discourse' in L. G. Roman, L. K. Christian-Smith with E. Ellsworth (eds) *Becoming Feminine*, pp. 37–59.

Sparke, P. (1995) *As Long as It's Pink: The Sexual Politics of Taste*, London: Pandora.

Spigel, L. and Mann, D. (1989) 'Women and consumer culture: a selective bibliography', *Quarterly Review of Film and Video* 11: 85–105.

Stacey, J. (1994) *Star Gazing: Hollywood Cinema and Female Spectatorship*, London: Routledge.

Staiger, J. (1992) *Interpreting Films: Studies in the Historical Reception of American Cinema*, Princeton, NJ: Princeton University Press.

Stanley, L. and Wise, S. (1983) *Breaking Out: Feminist Consciousness and Feminist Research*, London: Routledge.

Starks, L. S. (1997) 'Educating Eliza: fashioning the model woman in the "Pygmalion film"', *Postscript: Essays in Film and the Humanities* (special issue: Literacy and Film) 16, 2: 44–55.

Steedman, C. (1986) *Landscape for a Good Woman*, London: Virago.

—— (1997) 'Writing the self: the end of the scholarship girl', in J. McGuigan (ed.) *Cultural Methodologies*, pp. 106–125.

Steele, V. (1988) *Paris Fashion: A Cultural History*, Oxford: Oxford University Press.

Stern, L. (1988) 'Acting out of character: the performance of femininity', in S. Sheridan (ed.) *Grafts*, pp. 25–34.

Studlar, G. (2000) '"Chi-chi Cinderella": Audrey Hepburn as couture countermodel', in D. Desser and G. S. Jowett (eds) *Hollywood goes Shopping*, pp. 159–178.

Summerfield, P. (1998) *Reconstructing Women's Wartime Lives*, Manchester: Manchester University Press.

Swann Jones, S. (1995) *The Fairy Tale: The Magic Mirror of Imagination*, New York: Twayne.

Swanson, P. (1954) 'This girl is magic', *Photoplay* (UK) (June): 12.

Tasker, Y. (1998) *Working Girls: Gender and Sexuality in Popular Cinema*, London: Routledge.

Taylor, H. (1989) *Scarlett's Women: Gone With the Wind and its Female Fans*, London: Virago.

Thompson, F. (1990) 'Audrey Hepburn: it's hard to be a critic when you fall in love', *American Film* 15, 8: 54–56.

Threlfall, A. (1997) 'Martine Go-lightly', *Enjoy* (January): 6–7.

Thumim, J. (1992) *Celluloid Sisters: Women and Popular Cinema*, New York: St. Martin's Press.

—— (1995) 'Film and female identity: questions of method in investigating representations of women in popular cinema', in C. MacCabe and D. Petrie (eds) *BFI Working Papers*, pp. 157–186.

Tobin, Y. (1991) 'Audrey Hepburn ou la politique des actrices', *Positif* 365/366: 100–105.

Tolmach Lakoff, R. and Scherr, R. L. (1984) *Face Value: The Politics of Beauty*, London: Routledge and Kegan Paul.

Tomlinson, A. (ed.) (1990) *Consumption, Identity and Style: Marketing, Meanings, and the Packaging of Pleasure*, London: Routledge.

Tulloch, C. (1999) 'There's no place like home: home dressmaking and creativity in the Jamaican community of the 1940s to the 1960s', in B. Burman (ed.) *The Culture of Sewing*, pp. 111–125.

Vargas, A. (1960) 'Une actrice victime de son personnage: Audrey Hepburn', *Cinéma* 42: 104–109.

Viotti, S. (1954) 'Britain's Hepburn', *Films and Filming* 1, 1: 7.

Walkerdine, V. (1986) 'Video replay: families, films and fantasies', in V. Burgin *et al.* (eds) *Formations of Fantasy*, pp. 167–199.

—— (1990) *Schoolgirl Fictions*, London: Verso.

—— (1997) *Daddy's Girl: Young Girls and Popular Culture*, Basingstoke: Macmillan.

Walsh, M. (1979) 'The democratization of fashion: the emergence of the women's dress pattern industry', *Journal of American History* 66, 2: 299–313.

Walters, S. D. (1995) *Material Girls: Making Sense of Feminist Cultural Theory*, Berkeley: University of California Press.

Warner, M. (1986) 'The Cinderella Story: a magical tale of incest, cruelty and domination', *The Listener* (23 January): 12–14.

Welsch, J. R. (1978) *Film Archetypes: Sisters, Mistresses, Mothers, Daughters*, New York: Arno Press.

Whelehan, I. (1995) *Modern Feminist Thought: From the Second Wave to 'Post-Feminism'*, Edinburgh: Edinburgh University Press.

Williams, R. (1977) *Marxism and Literature*, Oxford: Oxford University Press.

Williamson, J. (1986) *Consuming Passions: The Dynamics of Popular Culture*, London: Marion Boyars.

Wilson, Earl (1954) 'What she doesn't need, she doesn't have', *Modern Screen* (June): 94.

Wilson, E. (1985) *Adorned in Dreams: Fashion and Modernity*, London: Virago.

—— (1993) 'Audrey Hepburn: fashion, film and the 50s', in P. Cook and P. Dodds (eds) *Women and Film*, pp. 36–40.

Winship, J. (1981) 'Woman becomes an "individual" – femininity and consumption in women's magazines 1954–69', stencilled occasional paper, Centre for Contemporary Cultural Studies, University of Birmingham.

—— (1987) *Inside Women's Magazines*, London: Pandora.

—— (1998) 'New disciplines for women and the rise of the chain store', unp. paper, University of Sussex.

Women's Studies Group (CCCS, University of Birmingham) (1978) *Women Take Issue: Aspects of Women's Subordination*, London: Hutchinson, in association with CCCS, University of Birmingham.

Woodward, I. (1984) *Audrey Hepburn*, London: W. H. Allen.

Wright, L. (1989) 'Objectifying gender: the stiletto heel', in J. Attfield and P. Kirkham (eds) *A View from the Interior*, pp. 7–19.

Yolen, J. (1977) 'America's Cinderella', in A. Dundes (ed.) (1988) *Cinderella: A Casebook*, pp. 294–306.

Young, R. (ed.) (1987) *Untying the Text: A Post-Structuralist Reader*, London: Routledge and Kegan Paul.

Index

Note: Literary works can be found under authors' names; page numbers in italics refer to illustrations; 'n.' after a page number indicates the number of a note on that page.